QUALITATIVE AND DIGITAL RESEARCH IN TIMES OF CRISIS: METHODS, REFLEXIVITY, AND ETHICS

Edited by
Helen Kara and Su-ming Khoo

P

First published in Great Britain in 2022 by

Policy Press, an imprint of
Bristol University Press
University of Bristol
1–9 Old Park Hill
Bristol
BS2 8BB
UK
t: +44 (0)117 954 5940
e: bup-info@bristol.ac.uk

Details of international sales and distribution partners are available at
policy.bristoluniversitypress.co.uk

British Library Cataloguing in Publication Data
A catalogue record for this book is available from the British Library

ISBN 978-1-4473-6379-8 hardcover
ISBN 978-1-4473-6381-1 ePub
ISBN 978-1-4473-6382-8 ePdf

Cover design: Nicky Boroweic
Front cover image: Adobe Stock/oraziopuccio
Bristol University Press and Policy Press use environmentally
responsible print partners.
Printed and bound in Great Britain by TJ Books, Padstow

Contents

List of figures and tables

Figures

Table

Notes on contributors

Loretta Baldassar is Professor of Anthropology and Sociology and Director of Social Care and Social Ageing Living Lab at the University of Western Australia.

Anirban Basu is Honorary Research Fellow at the University of Sussex, UK, and Researcher at Hitachi, Japan.

Holly Bowen-Salter is Senior Research Officer for Military and Emergency Services Health Australia who is an advocate for Higher Degree Researchers, and their mental health and well-being.

Bibek Dahal is an MPhil Research Fellow at Kathmandu University School of Education. His research interests lie in the areas of Social Research Methods; Research Ethics and Academic Integrity in Higher Education. Highly devoted to methodological research, he has already completed many projects independently. His recent publication is 'Research ethics: A perspective of South Asian context'.

Tessa Darbyshire is Scientific Editor at Patterns, Cell Press, UK.

Natasha Dwyer is Senior Lecturer in Digital Media at Victoria University, Australia.

Bettina Evans is Lecturer and Coordinator of the Postgraduate Diploma in Arts Therapy within the School of Creative Arts Therapies, Whitecliffe College, Aotearoa/New Zealand.

Ali FitzGibbon is Head of Arts Management and Cultural Policy at Queen's University Belfast. She has over 25 years' experience as a producer and programmer in international arts, theatre, and festivals, and works regularly as a cultural policy and strategy advisor at city and regional government levels. A member of the editorial board of the *Irish Journal of Arts Management and Cultural Policy*, her research has been published in a number of academic journals and her doctoral thesis was shortlisted for the ENCATC 2020 Research Award.

Deborah Green is based at the School of Creative Arts Therapies, Whitecliffe College, Aotearoa/New Zealand where she is Programme Leader and Research Coordinator for the Master of Arts in Arts Therapy

(Clinical) and the originator of abr+a. She is a passionate advocate and published author of arts-based research.

Sarah Marie Hall is Reader in Geography at the University of Manchester, UK.

Kahryn Hughes is Associate Professor of Sociology, University of Leeds, UK. She is Director of the Timescapes Archive, Editor-in-Chief of the BSA Sociological Research Online, and Senior Fellow of the National Centre for Research Methods (NCRM). Her research funding has been from flagship ESRC methods programmes, including the Research Methods Programme and Timescapes. She is internationally recognised for innovation in qualitative longitudinal methods, and Qualitative Secondary Analysis.

Maria Grazia Imperiale is Academic Coordinator of the Culture for Sustainable and Inclusive Peace Network Plus, at the School of Education, University of Glasgow, UK, and a member of the UNESCO Chair in Refugee Integration through Languages and the Arts. She holds a PhD in Language Education from the University of Glasgow and an MA in Linguistic Sciences from the University for Foreigners of Siena, Italy.

Helen Kara has been an independent researcher since 1999 and an independent scholar since 2011. She writes on research methods and ethics, and teaches at universities around the world. Helen is an Honorary Senior Research Fellow at the University of Manchester, UK, and a Fellow of the Academy of Social Sciences. She and Su-ming Khoo co-edited three Rapid Response e-books on *Researching in the Age of COVID-19* for Policy Press, published in 2020.

Su-ming Khoo is Senior Lecturer in the School of Political Science and Sociology at the National University of Ireland, Galway. Her research interests are in development studies, human rights, public goods, higher education, and decolonial, inter- and transdisciplinary theory, research and practice. She and Helen Kara co-edited three Rapid Response e-books on *Researching in the Age of COVID-19* for Policy Press, published in 2020.

Zania Koppe is a final-year PhD candidate at the School of Sociology and Political Science at the National University of Ireland, Galway. Her research interests lie in exploring other forms of world making that exist in the cracks or the margins of what is considered possible, through ethnography and creative practice.

Lukasz Krzyzowski is Senior Lecturer and Manager of the Social Care and Social Ageing Living Lab at the University of Western Australia.

Wendy Lawson is a practising artist and registered clinical arts therapist, coordinating Clinical Placements for the Master of Arts in Arts Therapy (Clinical) within the School of Creative Arts Therapies, Whitecliffe College, Aotearoa/New Zealand.

Amanda Levey is Head of the School of Creative Arts Therapies at Whitecliffe College, Aotearoa/New Zealand. She has published on arts-based research and is a passionate advocate of this approach.

Kathrin Marks is Lecturer and Coordinator of the Postgraduate Diploma in Arts Therapy in the School of Creative Arts Therapies, Whitecliffe College, Aotearoa/New Zealand.

Steve Marsh is Associate Professor of Trust Systems at Ontario Tech University, Canada.

Richard McGrath is Lecturer and Researcher at the University of South Australia whose work focuses on sociology of health, social justice, and qualitative research.

Emma Milanese is an academic researcher at the University of South Australia. Her research interests include sport for development approaches and rural health issues, seeking to improve or make change to local communities.

Hector Miller–Bakewell is an independent Quantum Computer Science Researcher and Data Science Consultant, based in the UK.

Hien Thi Nguyen is a PhD candidate in Anthropology and Sociology in the School of Social Sciences at the University of Western Australia.

Lisa Oliver is a proud member of the Gomeroi Nation of north-western New South Wales. She previously worked in areas of natural and cultural resource management across North Australia. She is currently undertaking a PhD which explores the role that Aboriginal women's groups play in building social capital.

Phoebe Pearce is a Bachelor of Health Science graduate from the University of South Australia.

Gbenga Akinlolu Shadare completed his PhD at the University of Sheffield, UK and his MA at the University of Nottingham, UK. He researches social policy and social work in development contexts, having been involved in international development consulting for over two decades working in Asia, Africa, and the Caribbean. He is engaged in supporting development of social work practice in Nigeria through the Centre for Social Protection and Policy Studies (CSPPS), Nigeria.

Gemma Sou is Vice Chancellor's Research Fellow at the RMIT University Australia and Visiting Lecturer at the University of Manchester, UK.

Gretchen Stolte is a Nimi'ipuu (Nez Perce) woman and has degrees in art history and anthropology focusing on the material culture of First Nations peoples in North America and Australia. Based at the University of Western Australia, she is intrigued by the material culture traditions often overlooked by galleries and museums and is well published on such topics.

Anna Tarrant is Associate Professor in Sociology at the University of Lincoln, UK, and is a UKRI Future Leaders Fellow. Her research interests include men and masculinities; family life; the lifecourse; and methods of qualitative secondary analysis. Her current funded study, 'Following Young Fathers Further', is a qualitative longitudinal, participatory study of the lives and support needs of young fathers. She is also co-editor, with Dr Kahryn Hughes, *Qualitative Secondary Analysis* (Sage, 2020).

Aaron Teo is a doctoral candidate in the School of Education at the University of Queensland, Australia, and a Secondary Business teacher at a Brisbane-based independent school. Aaron is Postgraduate Representative of the Australian Critical Race and Whiteness Studies Association. He is also an Executive of the Business Educators' Association of Queensland and a General Business Endorser and Confirmer with the Queensland Curriculum and Assessment Authority. Aaron's research focuses on the subjectivities of teachers from Asian backgrounds in the Australian context. He is interested in qualitative research methods, particularly the use of critical autoethnography as a form of reflexive, emancipatory inquiry.

Aisling Walsh is currently working towards a PhD in Sociology at the National University of Ireland, Galway, where she is researching decolonial and feminist practices of healing justice in Guatemala, supported by the Andrew Grene Postgraduate Scholarship in Conflict Resolution, Irish Research Council. She is also a freelance writer and translator based between

Ireland and Guatemala, with stories, essays, and reports published in *Pank*, *Entropy Mag*, *Pendemic.ie*, *The Irish Times*, *The Sunday Business Post*, *Open Democracy*, and *The Establishment*. Her personal essay 'The centre of the universe' was selected as runner-up in the So To Speak CNF Prize for 2021.

Hoda Wassif is Principal Lecturer in Medical & Dental Education at the University of Bedfordshire, UK. Dr Wassif teaches and supervises Masters and PhD students and is interested in creative research methods. She is a Senior Fellow of the Higher Education Academy (SFHEA) and a Fellow of the Institute of Leadership and Management (FInstLM).

Raelene Wilding is Associate Professor in Sociology and Head of the Social Inquiry Department, School of Humanities and Social Sciences, La Trobe University, Australia.

Maged Zakher is Senior Lecturer in Cross-Cultural Management at the University of Northampton, UK. He teaches international business, intercultural competence, and research methods. Dr Zakher is a Fellow of the Higher Education Academy (FHEA) and a Certified Management and Business Educator (CMBE).

Introduction

Su-ming Khoo and Helen Kara

'Times of crisis' brings to mind unexpected, unprecedented circumstances that appear suddenly. Yet 'crisis' has somehow become commonplace. The word 'crisis' has two roots – one denotes 'a vitally important or decisive stage in the progress of anything; a turning-point', which in more recent use implies a sense of 'difficulty, insecurity, and suspense' (OED). The other, connected root meaning relates this sense of turning point specifically to disease, a critical point when a patient might get better or worse (OED). This dual sense is useful to think with, as this book was written during the global COVID-19 pandemic. Researchers were severely impacted by its effects, even as other diseases, economic and political crises, conflict, climate catastrophe and connected ecological crises of wildfires, water shortages, flooding, and hurricanes continued to occur. The pandemic presented an opportunity to call for engagement in a process of collective reflection and to think about how research might get better (or worse), and how we might think of methodological problems and solutions, discomfort and comfort, dis-ease or ease in the conduct of research. We edited and published three e-books rapidly, in the midst of the continuing and unfolding global public health crisis (Kara and Khoo, 2020 a,b,c). These rapid publications, and this volume, now sit alongside other collectively created responses, such as the crowd-sourced advice on doing fieldwork in pandemic conditions collected by Deborah Lupton (Lupton, 2020) and the rapid review conducted by the UK National Centre for Research Methods (Nind, Meckin, and Coverdale, 2021).

This volume takes time to reflect on qualitative and digital methods, taking 'crisis' as a turning point for reflexivity and positionality in research methods and ethics. Its 15 chapters draw on the experiences and reflections of 33 researchers doing diverse research in the context of the COVID-19 pandemic, from the UK, Ireland, Nepal, New Zealand, Australia, Puerto Rico, Gaza, Nigeria, and Guatemala. The editors' geographically diffuse interests and networks probably influenced the character and spread of the contributions in this book. Many concern different locations as ethical environments, making different types of connections and ethical and creative dialogues across researcher-researched relationships and their settings.

1

Located in the 'Global North' setting of Australia, the chapter by Stolte and Oliver connects First Nations and Indigenous creators from the Pacific Northwest and Australia; those by Teo and Nguyen et al concern minority Asian experiences in Australia and 'digital kinning'; while the chapter by Dahal addresses phenomenology centred on Nepali researchers as the point of departure. The chapter by Imperiale connects UK-based researchers and teachers in the Gaza Strip. The chapter by Koppe concerns ethnography accompanying a community including people with cognitive disability in Ireland, while Walsh (also based in Ireland) reflexively researches with a transformative learning organisation and community in Guatemala. The transnational dimension of this book forms an appropriate backdrop for the rich and complex discussions of methods and ethics in its chapters.

Reviewing two decades of social science research on disasters, Alexander (2002) found too much reliance on 'pet' intra-disciplinary discourses and too little discussion integrating and interlinking insights. This book's collection of diverse responses and reflections on crisis presents some important integrative and interlinked threads connecting researcher reflexivity and ethical and relational concerns to the ways research can be done. We believe this is not happenstance, but reflective of a wider moment of acknowledgement that deeper thinking and self-reflection about methods and ethics are needed in this time of ongoing, intersecting, recurring, and protracted crises.

Crises make it necessary to consider researchers' and research participants' capacities for safety and resilience, and their needs for care. Arguing over definitions of 'crisis' can itself become a means to justify the denial of care, delaying action until crisis is definitively declared, for example in the case of famines (Howe and Devereaux, 2007), or genocide (Petrie, 2018), compared with cases when crises are promptly declared and authoritative (and authoritarian) policies enacted (Ghosh, 2020). We take 'crisis' not as a definitional game but in the spirit of a turning point for methods and ethics. Crisis response can make research more flexible and lead researchers to innovate, as well as to try out more thoughtful and creative practices. As research practices have pivoted towards the digital realm, we can learn from the researchers and communities who regularly use these methods. Their experiences raise deeper questions about researcher identity and connection, place more emphasis on affiliations and commitments, and foreground subjectivity and relational ethics in the research process.

In times of crisis, researchers may turn to qualitative and digital methods for practical reasons, since large-scale in-person data collection may be disrupted, difficult, or impossible. For researchers who specialise in disasters, crises, and emergencies, doing research often requires direct engagement with affected people, while also having to consider their own safety and well-being. In a pandemic, everyone is vulnerable so researcher and research participant safety and well-being are both important, while trying to not overburden potential participants who are already beset with significant risks and hardships. The COVID-19 pandemic presented a novel opportunity for every researcher to be both subject and object in the research process, and to question their own methods and ethics. 'A disaster exposes what is already there, and our methods are not exempt' (Van Brown, 2020: 1051).

Disaster researchers comment that there are insufficient resources in place to answer serious ethical and methodological challenges in the field (Browne and Peek, 2014; Gaillard and Peek, 2019; Van Brown, 2020: 1054). They have both practical and ethical concerns around accessing research sites, vulnerability and expectations of affected communities, and questions around reciprocity and giving back (Browne and Peek, 2014; Kendra and Gregory, 2019). They notice that ethics guidelines and toolkits tend to be developed after the fact (Browne and Peek, 2014). Emergencies, crises, and disasters undoubtedly result in high levels of vulnerability for both affected people and researchers (Råheim et al, 2016). Researchers are likely to be under pressure to collect time-sensitive, 'perishable' data as crises are unfolding, while their participants are experiencing sometimes extreme trauma, dislocation, and hardship. There is heightened demand for urgent information and analysis, yet everyone involved is also very exposed. In repeated and protracted crisis settings, people may already be over-researched and research fatigued. Yet, researchers working in crisis settings observe that research ethics often come late in the research process (Reed, 2002), or are retrospectively introduced. Humanitarian ethics remains an arena of considerable political and moral ambiguity and struggle (Slim, 2015), while crisis researchers may try to evade requirements to comply with the ethical codes and institutional ethics review procedures in place by classifying information-gathering as something other than research (Reed, 2002).

The continuation, recurrence, and protractedness of crises have spurred more investments in developing frameworks and methods, including advanced data integration, prediction, and simulation. One example is the work done in the new transdisciplinary Research Institute for Disaster Science, established in Sendai, Japan, in the wake of the 2011 combined earthquake, tsunami, and nuclear disaster (Aguirre and El-Tawil, 2020). There have been notable recent quantitative innovations such as computational and data mining methods (Nind, Meckin, and Coverdale, 2021: 6), promising major advances in prediction and modelling. However, ethical considerations have not always been well integrated with methodological advances, since quantitative approaches tend to focus on efficiency, not ethics. The uncertainties, challenge, and incompleteness brought by critical and ethical reflection tend to be seen as inefficient (Aguirre and El-Tawil, 2020: 1164). Qualitative digital methods may be seen as 'aggravating' from a positivist naturalistic perspective, creating methodological qualms and 'disarray' (Aguirre and El-Tawil, 2020: 1170). Approaches that rely on technical treatment of data may overlook the fact that the 'data' concern people whose exposure, vulnerability, and coping capacity should be paramount. Quantitative and datafied approaches are not particularly good at asking fundamental questions about a researcher's right to be present and to conduct research (Van Brown, 2020: 1058).

In mid-2020, a special issue of *American Behavioral Scientist* highlighted how the COVID-19 pandemic was intensifying questions about research practice, methods, and ethics (Van Brown, 2020). Ethical principles have been in place to protect human research participants since the late 1970s, when the Belmont Report responded to issues of abuses experienced by research participants (Friesen et al, 2017). The main principles of research ethics it set out, widely accepted since, are: respect for persons, beneficence, and justice. However, these principles have been consistently questioned in reality, for example 'parachute projects' that fail to properly involve and benefit affected people (O'Mathúna, 2010, 2018). A recent review finds the Belmont principles to be insufficient today; suggests reconsidering the line between research and practice; acknowledges that harms occur to communities and not just individuals; advocates for greater transparency; and extends the duty of researchers to protect participants towards more contemporary concerns for participation and inclusion. It argues that the Belmont Report's deductive attribution of single ethical principles to applications ought to be transcended (Friesen et al, 2017).

Although existing Human Subject Research protocols offer some ethical protection, it seems that they do not go far enough. Most institutional research ethics review bodies have not programmatically addressed the ethics of researching in a crisis. Furthermore, we should consider the narrowing of ethical scope in the crisis response sector in the 1990s, following a spate of incidents where international aid offices were targeted and attacked. Donors responded by narrowing humanitarian assistance to focus on effectiveness and 'minimum targeted lifesaving activities' and researchers' frames of reference followed suit. Thus, the scope for applying the ethical principles of respect, informed consent, beneficence and justice, and fair distribution of risks and benefits dramatically contracted (Reed, 2002; Khoo, 2019), just as research ethicists were beginning to find the ethical principles to be insufficient and in need of expansion (Friesen et al, 2017).

Van Brown's rallying byline was 'methods matter' (2020), calling for a 'paradigm shift' towards a unified code of conduct to give ethical concerns equal standing, even primacy over research methods. Van Brown calls this paradigm shift 'methics', a call to expand the ethical frame of concern in research to include taking a broader justice approach (Van Brown, 2020; Louis-Charles et al, 2020). As the COVID-19 pandemic continues, other crises, disasters, and emergencies continue and intersect, producing a disturbing pattern of manifest injustice (Sen, 2009). Research is still needed and must continue on, amid ongoing crises, emergencies, and disasters. The extended duration of the pandemic forced researchers to think again about routine and sedimented research norms and practices and how they find, select, and reach research participants and gather data.

Varda (2017) points out that disruption is not a static element, but a point from which we can see dynamics playing out. The dynamic nature of crises requires research designs to be aware, flexible, and capable of dealing with emergent and transitory qualities. These are not easy to study, nor can they be solely apprehended through introspection. Nevertheless, the pause for introspection can be a valuable opportunity for innovation, creativity, care, and transformative change. Disruptions may introduce a welcome opening in the research process, 'a crack, a crack in everything. That's how the light gets in', as the song goes (Cohen, 1992). This 'crack' is a turning point in the research imaginary (Brydon, 2010), affording a moment for reflection, flexibility, and creativity in thinking about research, and a valuable opportunity to question underlying givens and taken-for-granted assumptions. As such, a 'crisis' is not only an opportunity to review how-to, technical questions about practicalities of doing research, but also it is an invitation to return to more perennial problems and considerations. For us, 'methods' encompasses much more than a focus on techniques and procedures for getting research done, though these are certainly important.

'Methods' also includes new approaches to knowledge creation and considerations of epistemic injustice and decoloniality. These include co-creation and co-production, ways of working with and through (rather than working over or above) communities and their knowledge traditions. This questions the division between academics as the knowledge producers, the 'knowers' and community members as data objects, 'the known' (Connell, 2007). 'Good' research involves not only technical considerations of validity or reliability but also ethical responsibilities and reciprocity towards people involved in the research process who might be considered as co-producers and co-owners. Co-production works on the premise that all communities are capable of producing valid and relevant knowledge, yet academic research has a historical record of exploitative and extractive treatment of communities and of broken relationships, which are largely academic researchers' responsibilities to mend (Shilliam, 2016). Shilliam (2013) suggests that there is a great difference between 'producing' knowledge as a process of accumulation and imperial extension and 'cultivating' knowledge, which requires an intellectual turning-over and oxygenation of the past, and 'habitation' that enfolds the enquirer in communal matter, creatively releasing knowledge in the process.

Despite much uncertainty, there is some convergence on what the main challenges are: how to deal with communities and not just individuals; navigating cultural differences; and practicalities, dilemmas, and ethical limitations surrounding consent. There are fundamental questions concerning the ethical warrant to conduct research at all, and (if so) how much and what types of research. There are also questions about what happens after the research and accompanying practical interventions are concluded. Is it simply enough to do no harms, or should we be trying actively to do good through our research in general, and ensure direct benefit for participants in particular (Kara, 2018)? Enduring ethical considerations include avoiding coercion, ensuring safety and confidentiality for participants, and the problem of secondary or vicarious trauma that may harm both participant and researcher. Issues of researcher safety, self-care, and well-being must also be addressed (Boynton, 2020).

Disasters and emergencies have a way of taking over and overshadowing the broader subject matter of scope and action. In doing so, they may narrow the scope for thinking about the ethics of research and action. This narrowing has led some to argue that 'resilience' has become a problematic framing (Hilhorst, 2018), though we see it as potentially helpful if asymmetry and lack of reciprocity are addressed and researcher–participant relationships are foregrounded (Kara and Khoo, 2020b). 'Crisis' and 'emergency' are concepts steeped in histories of coloniality, dispossession, and oppression. Many unethical and harmful interventions and *necropolitics*, of making live by letting die (Mbembe, 2003), have resulted from the invocation of crisis, from the colonial annexation of territories to the forced removal of children from their families.

In *Against Crisis Epistemology*, Kyle White (2020) writes against the presumptions of unprecedentedness and urgency that accompany 'crisis'. To counter this epistemology of crisis, White draws on Indigenous intellectual traditions to emphasise an alternative *epistemology of coordination* that speaks to an ethics of responsibility and connection, moral bond, or kinship relationships that generate responsible capacities to respond to challenge and change. 'Coordination' expects to respond to drastic changes, but avoids validating structures of harm or violence. We see this reflected clearly in our contributors' work.

Looking across the contributions to this book, we discern four emergent themes and have organised the chapters accordingly:

- Reflexivity and ethics
- Arts–based approaches
- Digital methods
- Recurring and longer–term crises

Reflexivity and ethics are always necessary, but can go by the board if we do not make enough time and space. They are especially needed in times of crisis and may yield important and surprising insights. The arts, and connections to nature and others, provide solace and comfort in times of crisis, and can also help us endure, learn, create, and even flourish in challenging times. The contributions on digital methods helpfully expand what there is to learn from the pivot to digital methods, taking insights from the technical and practical realm towards considerations of ethics and relationality. Research in conflict/post-conflict zones presents particular challenges, but 'fast' crises also echo recurrent and 'slower' crises. Seeing these together offers the possibility of avoiding the trap of crisis epistemology, and help us to survive and learn from, and not merely document, crises.

We hope that by sharing experiences of researching in crises, research practice may become more open-ended, multi-dimensional, inclusive, and potentially transformative. There is huge potential for research across different disciplines and practices to become more ethical and transformative, with methodology acting as an open-ended, inviting space for discussing and confronting critical and challenging questions connecting knowledge creation and ethics (Khoo et al, 2019: 183).

Part I: Reflexivity and ethics

Part I pivots on the crisis moment, turning towards reflexivity and ethics. Ali FitzGibbon takes us through a process of reflection, to ask whether or not to conduct research in a time of crisis. The COVID-19 pandemic surfaces immediate demands and ethical desires to act or help. Instead of proceeding immediately, she asks when and how it is desirable to step into an active research mode. Felt responsibility and demands to make research 'useful' may align with self-interest in ways that could easily tip into opportunist academic parasitism. FitzGibbon pauses to understand what drives academic research responses, sifting through ideas of usefulness and conflicting needs or demands which might be more about the neoliberal search for academic impact than crisis mitigation.

Zania Koppe confronts twin crises of her research community's existence and the onset of COVID-19. She reconsiders methodology, ethnography, and ethics in the cracks opened by a crisis for the community that her research accompanies, exploring how methodology and ethics are challenged and changed as crises unfold. Initially, ethical considerations focused on the vulnerable status of intellectually disabled community members and requirements connected to formal ethics approval. As the research progressed, an existential crisis for the research location required difficult considerations about 'usefulness', doing research and what research can do. Koppe asks how flexible ethnography might be and whether it can be a sensitive and flexible enough tool to enable the comprehension of complex micro-contexts in times of crisis.

Bibek Dahal takes us into hermeneutic phenomenology, asking how a researcher can capture the myriad dynamism of lived experiences and interactions of researchers and research ethics. Dahal outlines a hermeneutic arc of description, interpretation, and critical questioning, using protocol writing with his research participants who are themselves researchers. The 'hermeneutic arc' develops a sense of researchers' processes, experiences, and understanding, even though the restrictions occasioned by the COVID-19 pandemic changed the normal conduct of phenomenological research. This new situation added another layer of reflection about different horizons of identity, meaning, and ethics.

Part II: Arts-based approaches

Part II opens with a contribution by a group of New Zealand-based arts therapists: Deborah Green, Amanda Levey, Bettina Evans, Wendy Lawson, and Kathrin Marks, offering a deep dive into methods that transgress divisions between researchers, research methods, and research participants. Combining arts-based research, therapeutic arts practice, and collaborative autoethnography, they reject rigid and reductive research designs. Their performative autoethnographic research approach, which they term *abr+a* (arts-based research through autoethnography) engages creative activities like videography, painting, stitching, and collage as methods for self-expression, teaching, therapy, and research, to striking effect. Restricted by the COVID-19 pandemic, they have repurposed arts therapeutic methods into performative research methods. This turn helps the authors, and potentially also a wider research, practice, and educational community, to express, explore, and endure the uncertainties brought on by the COVID-19 pandemic. Responding to situations of disaster and distress, *abr+a* enabled this researcher and therapist group to engage poietic creativity and to interact with art and nature in generative and hopeful ways.

Gretchen Stolte and Lisa Oliver discuss a turn to creative making as a practice-based museum research method, in response to enforced lockdown. Unable to access collections, museum researchers innovatively turned to learning basket-weaving as a new way to understand the objects in their museum collections. Learning from contemporary Indigenous makers and artists enables museums to learn about Indigenous creative methods and make their record more inclusive – by documenting Indigenous methods, acknowledging and representing Indigenous technologies and knowledges. Online weaving courses offered by an Indigenous artist provided a way for First Nations women to connect and recover connections to land and traditions, making survivorship, healing, emotional connection, and flourishing possible.

Gemma Sou and Sarah Hall's chapter exemplifies how comics can be used as a method for communicating and translating research results. This extends the discussion of 'research methods' to take in often-neglected dimensions of research translation and dissemination and to consider critical questions about representational politics and pedagogy. Sou's research concerns how low-income households recover from 'natural' disasters, in this case Hurricane Maria which hit Puerto Rico in 2017. Her research comic *After Maria: Everyday Recovery from Disasters* became an invaluable tool for creatively communicating research on crises. Sou and Hall argue that comics make research more accessible to participants as well as the wider public, enabling a more participatory process whereby participants can shape how their story is told. Comics challenge reductive, dehumanising, and apolitical narratives that circulate in mainstream media in the wake of crises, by highlighting everyday experiences that are often overlooked.

Part III: Digital methods

Part III situates digital research methods in the pivot of both research practice and ordinary life towards the digital sphere, due to the COVID-19 pandemic and associated public health restrictions. Richard McGrath, Holly Bowen-Salter, Emma Milanese, and Phoebe Pearce share experiences of online writing support groups that arose to support research writing during the COVID-19 emergency. Their Collaborative AutoNetnography methodology combines more documented forms of collaborative autoethnography and netnography to explore the impact and benefits of a regular, online writing support group, using Zoom. While this combined approach is relatively novel, we expect collaborative approaches that treat researcher and researched as a continuum, and emphasise the lenses of community, to gain greater importance in research methods and ethics.

Natasha Dwyer, Hector Miller-Bakewell, Tessa Darbyshire, Anirban Basu, and Steve Marsh examine how digital technologies afford researchers opportunities to access people's most personal thoughts. They outline the ethical risks and implications involved when taking advantage of these new technologies. Debates are emerging around how digital data collection and surveillance are used and regulated as such technologies become ubiquitous. Using chatbot transcripts, Dwyer et al interrogate the potential of explainable artificial intelligence to explicate the internal system logic to users, and work towards designing trust-enabling systems that allow users to make informed decisions and determine their own level of trust or comfort.

Maged Zakher and Hoda Wassif take the opportunity to reflect on the practice of enhanced online interviewing, a method that aims for a flowing conversation to produce rich and varied data. There are various ways to enhance interviews, using photographs or focusing on a making activity such as Lego or collage, or an artefact (Kara, 2020: 107–9). Zakher and Wassif invited their research participants to bring an object of their choice to enhance their interview. This made the interviews more interviewee-centred and created a dialogue that was both more empowering and more interviewee-relevant.

Anna Tarrant and Kahryn Hughes suggest that qualitative data re-use is a valuable, but under-utilised, method. Studying the longitudinal dynamics of poverty and inequality in family contexts over several decades enabled socio-historical insight into how crises and shocks (for example, the 2008 global recession) and subsequent political austerity rendered low-income families and households vulnerable. Accessing archival data resources and 'data histories' enables researchers to ask important sociological questions about the extent of continuity and change engendered by new crises like the COVID-19 pandemic.

Hien Thi Nguyen, Loretta Baldassar, Raelene Wilding, and Lukasz Krzyzowski examine how technology use enables 'digital kinning': 'the processes of engagement with new technologies for the purpose of maintaining support networks to sustain social support and connections, maintain cultural identity, and protect social identity, which are all particularly at risk during the ageing process' (Baldassar and Wilding, 2020: 319). Adapting their 'Ageing and New Media' project on older Vietnam-born parent migrants/ visitors' experiences of ageing in Australia, the pivot towards digital research has further extended understandings of digital kinning.

Part IV: Recurring and longer-term crises

Part IV acknowledges that not all crises are immediate. Yu Ming Aaron Teo, an Asian-Australian migrant researcher and teacher, offers reflections using critical autoethnography. This research method connects the autobiographical and personal to the cultural, social, and political. Teo's research on Asian migrant teachers points to a double crisis – the immediate and 'fast' crisis of COVID-19 and its intensifying effects on a pre-existing 'slow' crisis of anti-Asian racism. This double crisis underlines the urgency of telling stories to expose, analyse, and challenge majoritarian racial privilege. Using the self-as-event, Teo's narrative draws on private details and emotions to enable different audiences to empathise and co-create meanings, while considering different standpoints.

Maria Grazia Imperiale discusses participatory methodologies in her online study researching critical English language education in a context of protracted crisis, in the Gaza Strip (Palestine). The Gaza Strip has been under blockade since 2007, and military operations have severely hindered everyday life, placing two million inhabitants in protracted conditions of forced immobility. Imperiale focused on co-constructing and developing critical and creative language teaching pedagogies, suitable for use in this context of protracted crisis. The researcher and her English teacher participants held critical participatory action research workshops entirely online, using digital interactions to analyse, develop, trial, and evaluate teaching materials and lesson plans.

Gbenga Shadare discusses his journey in understanding and managing ethical tensions arising from conducting research on conditional cash transfers in fragile and conflict-affected contexts in Nigeria. This multi-method qualitative study involved semi-structured in-depth interviews, elite interviews, focus groups, and participant observation. Shadare argues that it is impossible to follow a pre-determined ethics protocol in fragile contexts because of the extreme levels of uncertainty and the need to be accountable to participants, while also being mindful of both cultural relevance and researcher safety.

Aisling Walsh offers reflections from researching sexualised violence in conflict-affected Guatemala. She is concerned with ethical problems surrounding research extractivism and research fatigue in an over-researched setting. Her autoethnographic reflection explores her motivation and efforts to move beyond extractivism, taking on the coloniality of how locations and people get used as resources, in an exploitative, even monstrously 'vampiric' manner. Walsh critically reflects on the unsatisfactory nature of researching in a donor-driven context that repeatedly references human rights and justice. She starts again – with a more equitable and collaborative research design that also fits better with a feminist sensibility and values. Conflicts, crises, disasters, and emergencies create 'victims', and the ethics of victimhood are particularly troubling when victimhood itself becomes a commodity.

As we were compiling this book, we were challenged to justify the idea of new times, as well as any claim to be opening up new insights. We do not make either of these claims. As the contributions in this volume each show in their own way, pre-existing problems, concerns about relationships, identities, care, resilience, creativity, and the importance of considering avoidable harm are perennial ethical considerations that come with doing research. What we do argue is that these considerations merit more, not less, attention in times of crisis. Each of the four clusters of contributions from researchers reflects potential challenges of, and practical responses to, crisis epistemology. We hope these accounts will help researchers critically question, and inspire and support, current or future research in ways that gesture towards possibilities for an epistemology of coordination (White, 2020). Such an epistemology responds to the necessities occasioned by drastic change, yet orients itself towards research ethics that avoid enacting, reproducing, or validating harm to researchers and participants alike.

References

Aguirre, B. and El-Tawil, S. (2020) 'Emergence of transdisciplinary research and disaster science', *American Behavioral Scientist*, 64(8): 1162–78.

Alexander, D. (2002) 'The study of natural disasters, 1977–97: some reflections on a changing field of knowledge', *Disasters*, 21(4): 238–304.

Baldassar, L. and Wilding, R. (2020) 'Migration, aging, and digital kinning: the role of distant care support networks in experiences of aging well', *The Gerontologist*, 60(2): 313–21.

Boynton, P. (2020) 'Do the best that you can', in H. Kara and S. Khoo (eds) *Researching in the Age of COVID-19 Volume 2: Care and Resilience*, Bristol: Bristol University Press.

Browne, K. and Peek, L. (2014) 'Beyond the IRB: an ethical toolkit for disaster research', *International Journal of Mass Emergencies and Disasters*, 32(10): 82–120.

Brydon, D. (2010) 'Cracking imaginaries: studying the global from Canadian space', in J. Wilson, C. Sandru, and S. Welsh (eds) *Rerouting the Postcolonial: New Directions for the New Millennium*, Abingdon: Routledge, 105–17.

Cohen, L. (1992) 'Anthem', *The Future*, New York: Columbia.

Connell, R. (2007) *Southern Theory*, Cambridge: Polity.

Friesen, P., Kearns, L., Redman, B., and Caplan, A. (2017) 'Rethinking the Belmont Report?', *The American Journal of Bioethics*, 17(7): 15–21.

Gaillard, J. and Peek, L. (2019) 'Disaster-zone research needs a code of conduct', *Nature*, 575(7783): 440–2.

Ghosh, J. (2020) 'The "shock doctrine" in India's response to COVID-19', *The Hindu* podcast, 15 June 2020, available from: https://www.thehindu.com/podcast/comment-the-shock-doctrine-in-indias-response-to-covid-19/article31831402.ece

Hilhorst, D. (2018) 'Classical humanitarianism and resilience humanitarianism: making sense of two brands of humanitarian action', *Journal of International Humanitarian Action*, 3(15).

Howe, P. and Devereaux, S. (2007) 'Famine scales: towards an instrumental definition of famine', in S. Devereaux (ed) *The New Famines*, Abingdon: Routledge, 27–49.

Kara, H. (2018) *Research Ethics in the Real World: Euro-Western and Indigenous Perspectives*, Bristol: Policy Press.

Kara, H. (2020) *Creative Research Methods: A Practical Guide* (2nd edn), Bristol: Policy Press.

Kara, H. and Khoo, S. (eds) (2020a) *Researching in the Age of COVID-19 Volume 1: Response and Reassessment*, Bristol: Bristol University Press.

Kara, H. and Khoo, S. (eds) (2020b) *Researching in the Age of COVID-19 Volume 2: Care and Resilience*, Bristol: Bristol University Press.

Kara, H. and Khoo, S. (eds) (2020c) *Researching in the Age of COVID-19 Volume 3: Creativity and Ethics*, Bristol: Bristol University Press.

Kendra, J. and Gregory, S. (2019) 'Ethics in disaster research: a new declaration', in J. Kendra, S. Knowles, and T. Wachtendorf (eds) *Disaster Research and the Second Environmental Crisis*, Springer, 319–41.

Khoo, S., Haapakoski, J., Hellstèn, M., and Malone, J. (2019) 'Moving from interdisciplinary research to transdisciplinary educational ethics', *European Educational Research Journal*, 18(2): 181–99.

Khoo, S. (2019) 'Ethical dilemmas in the development–security nexus: a human development and capabilities approach', *Policy and Practice: A Development Education Review*, 28(Spring): 14–37.

Louis-Charles, H. et al (2020) 'Ethical considerations for postdisaster fieldwork and data collection in Caribbean', *American Behavioral Scientist*, 64(8): 1129–44.

Lupton, D. (ed) (2020) 'Doing fieldwork in a pandemic' [crowd-sourced document]. Available at: https://docs.google.com/document/d/1clGjGABB2h2qbduTgfqribHmog9B6P0NvMgVuiHZCl8/edit?ts=5e88ae0a#

Mbembé, J. (2003) trs L. Meintjes, 'Necropolitics', *Public Culture*, 15(1): 11–40.

Nind, M., Meckin, R., and Coverdale, A. (2021) *Changing Research Practices: Undertaking Social Research in the Context of Covid-19*, Southampton: National Centre for Research Methods.

O'Mathúna, D. (2010) 'Conducting research in the aftermath of disasters: ethical considerations', *Journal of Evidence-Based Medicine*, 3(2): 65–75.

O'Mathúna, D. (2018) *Disasters: Core Concepts and Ethical Theories*, Dordrecht: Springer.

Petrie, C. (2018) 'Debating the definition of genocide will not save the Rohingya', *The Guardian*, 4 September 2018, available from: https://www.theguardian.com/commentisfree/2018/sep/04/genocide-rohingya-international-community-myanmar-rwanda

Råheim, M., Magnussen, L., Sekse, R., Lunde, Å., Jacobsen T., and Blystad, A. (2016) 'Researcher-researched relationship in qualitative research: shifts in positions and researcher vulnerability', *International Journal of Qualitative Studies in Health and Well-being*, 11(30996). doi: 10.3402/qhw.v11.30996.Reed, H. (2002) *Research Ethics in Complex Humanitarian Emergencies: Summary of a Workshop*, National Academies Press.

Sen, A. (2009) *The Idea of Justice*, New York: Allen Lane.

Shilliam, R. (2013) 'Living knowledge traditions and the priestly caste of the Western Academy', *The Disorder of Things*, 1 December 2013, available from: https://thedisorderofthings.com/2013/12/01/living-knowledge-traditions-and-the-priestly-caste-of-the-western-academy/

Shilliam, R. (2016) 'Discovering knowledge traditions through co-creation – learning from and with communities', 27 October 2016, available from: https://www.qmul.ac.uk/publicengagement/blog/2016/items/discovering-knowledge-traditions-through-co-creation-learning-from-and-with-communities.html#

Slim, H. (2015) *Humanitarian Ethics: A Guide to the Morality of Aid in War and Disaster*, Oxford: Oxford University Press.

Van Brown, B. (2020) 'Disaster research "methics": ethical and methodological considerations of researching disaster-affected populations', *American Behavioral Scientist*, 64(8): 1050–65.

Varda, D. (2017) 'Social network analysis of disaster response, recovery, and adaptation', in E. Jones, and A. Faas (eds) *Strategies for Researching Social Networks in Disaster Response, Recovery, and Mitigation*, Butterworth-Heinemann, 41–56.

White, K. (2020) 'Against crisis epistemology', in B. Hokowhitu et al (eds) *Handbook of Critical Indigenous Studies*, Abingdon: Routledge.

PART I

Reflexivity and ethics

Just because you can, doesn't mean you should

Ali FitzGibbon

Introduction

This chapter concerns how we navigate the decision-making process in research: how do we decide to do research or not in a time of, or in response to, an external crisis? It is a questioning process, drawing from reflexive approaches in different disciplines. Concerned principally with research of contemporary practices, it challenges the researcher to consider whether action is better than inaction; speed better than contemplation; and to what end and for whose purpose she pursues research.

In the 1990s, working as a young theatre producer, I attended a workshop on time and task management which proposed a mantra to 'do less, better'. In 2020, at a loss for how to proceed, I tried to consider what such 'doing' would be, what constituted 'better', who might gain or lose by doing 'less'. I formulated a reflexive questioning strategy built around time, purpose, and legitimacy for my research decision-making, offered here. This enabled me to sift through perceived usefulness, conflicting needs and demands, actual beneficiary impact or the notional 'impact' pursued by the neoliberal academy (Belfiore, 2015).

To start. All research is an act of decision-making

To choose to give *this* time at *this* particular time to *this* topic in *this* way is both multiple decisions and one. How we disseminate research – to publish, to collaborate, to protest – is a decision of how and with whom we 'share knowledge' (Smith, 2012). Our decisions are shaped by a range of influences: our social position, political motivations, our relationship to the field we research (Berger, 2015). As I write, I reflect on intersections between our personal and working selves in our research motivations. Which bit of my self is 'doing' research? I wonder which bit of my research decision-making is pulled by, and pushing back at, the institutional drivers to 'perform' our research in the 'right' way at the 'right' time in the carelessness and silo-ed branding of academia (Lynch, 2010; Tähtinen et al, 2016; Blackmore, 2020).

All research is decision-making in which the researcher makes implicit and explicit choices informed by pre-articulated values and processes

We form toolkits for thinking which we adapt as our research life advances. I deliberately avoid the term 'career'. Having had multiple 'careers', I no longer believe my working life is in any way as linear as the term suggests. My choice now but maybe not forever is to embrace a 'solo transdisciplinarity', my own toolkit fashioned from arts management and cultural policy studies, leadership and management studies, and cultural labour research. My toolkit helps me to work at the intersection of these fields, focusing on precarity, ethics, and decision-making in cultural production. My toolkit is an assemblage of multiple concepts and experiences, selected for their value to my research. Beneath these, lie the perceived norms and processes of our discipline(s), evolved through progressions and infractions, imbued with bureaucracy and ghosts of earlier academic histories. Some combination of these forms what can be termed 'academic rigour'.

I start again. All research is decision-making and its approach is disrupted in times of crisis

Whether personal, local, or global, crisis disrupts our understanding of how to respond. Our tools no longer fit the task. Our research may not fit either. New urgencies distort and undo earlier purpose and influences. We find just moments after assessing a situation that we must reassess. And then reassess again. How then should we proceed? Which influences should we accept or resist? Which tools are no longer 'fit for purpose' and for how long should we set them aside?

Context

To situate this exploration, I draw out my research context. My research to date has focused on the role of freelance artists and creative workers in leadership, management, and policymaking systems of the performing arts. This interest derives from my background as a performing arts and multi-artform producer, consultant, and festival programmer for over 25 years. My research has touched on the emotional pulls or assumptions this insider position imbues, and the privileged knowledge it affords.

The outbreak of COVID-19 prompted most of the arts and cultural industries to shut down worldwide in Spring 2020. As they closed, many populations in lockdown turned to creativity to aid their well-being and make sense of this strange world, accompanied by a surge in artists and cultural organisations providing their work digitally for free. In the UK (the focus of my research), these industries were under-served by state aid while creative freelancers were almost entirely excluded. This immediate human crisis was amplified by pre-existing precarity of these freelancers (Tsioulakis and FitzGibbon, 2020). As 2020 advanced, the widening uncertainty of when, if, how, and where any parts of these industries could reopen posed deeper existential crises for its entire workforce. The future of cultural consumption/production was radically altered and re-imagination rather than recovery was needed, not least to address the fractured and inequitable system that pre-dated COVID-19 (Banks, 2020; Eikhof, 2020; Murphy, 2020). Many of these calls for radical change chimed with the re-ignited #BlackLivesMatter movement. Wider discourses of a reimagined creative 'ecosystem' or 'ecology' had a common sustainable development agenda with the Green New Deal and post-growth economic theory (Banks and O'Connor, 2020). While governments, academics, 'industry leaders' debated these long-term ideas, the voice of freelancers was often absent while their immediate survival was ignored.

These competing urgencies prompted calls for rapid research. Campaigners sought advocacy research to evidence the problems of organisations and individuals left with inadequate support to survive let alone re-imagine. Policy and labour research scrambled to examine COVID-19's amplification of persistent and growing inequalities and what systemic change might look like. Alongside these, researchers responded to the need to document creative making and lived experiences under lockdown as part of the human response to the virus (Arvanitis, 2020; Bakhshi et al, 2020). Those of us teaching in any cultural field asked ourselves what knowledge would still be relevant for our students. In moments of snatched reflection, we also asked what of our pre-existing research would have meaning in this new and altered world.

Approach

These urgencies were placed at my door as opportunities to comment and advocate, a frenzy of rapid research bidding, a desire to capture such moments. In Spring 2020, I found myself negotiating the pandemic (like all humankind), caring for family and negotiating my first child leaving home. These happened alongside a cranked-up workload of heightened student pastoral care, escalating academic administration, 'pivots' to online teaching, staffing gaps. Although advanced in my working life, I was still defined by my time in academia as an 'early career' researcher. My research plans fell apart as the world I studied was utterly changed. Yet I was also shielded by salary and reasonably secure employment. I felt an urge to be 'helpful'. I began to receive emails, messages, posts on social media, from freelancers and cultural organisations telling me what was happening and asking what I might do. These came from both acquaintances and strangers. I received repeated requests from my university to do activities, talks, policy contributions that might be 'career-enhancing' but felt morally contradictory to the demands from those affected, those whose lives I researched. My research, long driven by passion, began to affect my health.

This convergence of competing pressures prompted my questioning if, when, and how to step into active research mode. While this chapter is prompted by the COVID-19 outbreak, as Leah Hamilton (2019) proposes, we can learn from one crisis how we might respond to another. Since 2000, there have been many crises: the Twin Towers attacks; the 2008 banking crash; SARS and Ebola virus outbreaks; the wildfires of Australia, Brazil, and California; the Icelandic ash cloud; countless outbreaks of violence and political warfare. Smaller-scale crises ripple towards me: intermittent violence and political tension in the 'post-conflict' society of Northern Ireland where I live and work; policy changes triggering crisis in my research fields.

This chapter offers an approach to sift such competing demands and our own positionality to consider not what we *can* do but what we *should* do when researching in and about a crisis. In this, it posits that there are legitimate reasons not to do research at all.

Time

We are schooled to understand what 'timely research' means, the serendipity of our investigation (often years long) arriving at an intersection with a public moment or need for knowledge. This is, however, often more a situation of fortuitous 'timing' than 'timeliness'. Crisis is temporal in nature, with urgencies changing while it lasts, pushing us to respond faster than we are used to. It is relevant then to consider how time plays different roles in 'doing', and making decisions about, research.

Is the timing of my intervention useful or valuable in this moment?

When I moved from artistic management to research, I struggled with the different construct of academic time: the enforced pauses and time-lags to review, revise, and await publication. I wonder now about this chapter's relevance in ten years. As I consider my response to the present crisis, I am caught between two rhythms: the urgencies described (to deliver urgent research, posit an informed view) and the concern that the rush for a 'hot take' undermines real sustainable change (Banet-Weiser, 2018). This runs deeper than concerns about inaction (closing the door of the 'ivory tower') or producing 'bad' research. It is the complicity of a rapid response in perpetuating systems and discourses we ordinarily resist, both within and beyond academia.

Researchers giving their time to a concern can produce useful responses or add weight to particular issues. Scholars have successfully campaigned for social justice and human rights, informing change by dint of their speed or long-term commitment (Brook et al, 2018; De Londras and Enright, 2018; Scraton, 2019). Arvanitis (2020) emphasises that gathering spontaneous responses to lived and rapidly changing experiences is both important and urgent in crisis. Our usefulness may be then in gathering knowledge for later, not rushing to produce it. In crisis, it is the speed at which we must decide to commit that changes; to do or not do. This is about 'pace' and 'speed' as much as it is about 'timing'.

Is there enough time to do this research in the way it needs to be done?

De Beukelaer (2020) suggests we may achieve more if we resist the accelerated 'publish or perish' pace of the neoliberal academy. His argument to read/ observe more and write less may offer 'better' research. 'Slow' scholarship may be seen as a privilege of salaried academics (Meyerhoff and Noterman, 2019) but it may be a privilege denied by neoliberalising academic performance metrics. Separately, crisis may demand we do more and faster. Rather than think solely about publishing, might our time be better spent another way? Claims on our available time to pursue research are greater than we can absorb. Therefore, we should consider how much of our time is needed to do the work well and whether we have that time to give. We should also ask if we can give it *right now*.

Researching creative precarity from a salaried but demanding position, my time to research is often extremely scarce. But time behaves differently for different people and carries different meaning (Banks, 2019). We construct meaning through temporality (Phelan, 2014). I can make distinctions between my (paid) time and how my research decisions make (unpaid) claims on the time of others. The freelancers I study are thrown into indefinite waiting but are also busy working to survive. My attention may not be a good use of *their* time. Feminist and inclusive practices in research and practice can offer us rebalancing approaches (Sandoval, 2016; Nind et al, 2017). Nevertheless, our research decisions must consider the implications and claims on others' time. This leads to a final question about how we understand time in research decision-making.

What if now is not a good time for you?

Peggy Phelan (2014), in her essay 'On the Difference between Time and History', reflects on her response to losing her writing; once years earlier as pages flying out a car window, later as her hand shuts down a laptop before saving her work. She notes that in her different response between early and later career she had become 'alert to the force of individual history' (Phelan, 2014: 115). That is, she relates her personal understanding and place in time (as age, changing circumstance, and in the moment of doing/writing) as intrinsic to her interpretation of her research. Not only must we understand the different behaviours and meanings of time in those lives we research, a reflexive researcher must understand that their response at a given time is conditioned by their own temporality. As a white cis working woman and parent, my research is informed by my past and present time. A global pandemic arrives while other crises are happening. This may mean it is the 'right' time to do research but not for you, or not in this way.

Care of self and personal circumstances is equally a consideration of time, timing, and timeliness. Such consideration is not capitulation but a response to institutional carelessness (Lynch, 2010; Blackmore, 2020). As Chatzidakis et al (2020) argue, care should be part of our wider resistance to capitalist norms and discourses that commodify our labour (time) and economic value over wider social and moral values.

Purpose

Considering competing demands and the nature of time in my research decisions prompts consideration of its underlying research purpose. In many research disciplines and artistic practices, there exists this underlying question: why? It appears as purpose or 'intention' or 'mission': the core rationale that, once established, informs all plans and choices (informing 'major and minor decisions' and 'shaping direction' as per Drucker, 1995; Bryson, 2004). Approaches to artistic performance evaluation ask that before you talk about aesthetics or ability or the necessity of the experience, you ask: why? What was the intention behind this artistic work (Langsted et al, 2003; Danish Association of Theatre for Children, 2004)? As noted before, crisis can make decisions more difficult and, pressed for time, we rush to decide. This could (or *should*) bring our attention to *why* we research and what influences shape our purpose.

Why am I doing this?

I turn this question 'why?' reflexively on myself. We are schooled to find research purpose in investigating other literature but our research response to crisis often starts before there is sufficient wider knowledge (we may be its gatherers). Reflexivity draws our attention to the underlying assumptions and positionality in our research decision-making, our personal legitimising of what we see as necessary or salient. It can bring clearer insight to how our interpretation of purpose is influenced (consciously and unconsciously) by other interests.

I may be mobilised in my purpose to be 'helpful'. I may see my purpose as offering expert knowledge to a difficult situation. This may be the ideal moment (for my 'timely' contribution). And yet, we must as scholars, be open to our research purpose being influenced by other things. Might my purpose be influenced by my own professional ambition, self-interest, or insecurity? Am I pursuing an end result to satisfy someone or something else? Am I trying to resolve competing demands by telling myself the story of one purpose when in truth I am pursuing another? Have I asked myself why or have I just dived in? Revealing what influences our purpose to ourselves may help us in making 'better' decisions.

Who or what is it for?

It is likely we will always be negotiating the varied agendas of different stakeholders. We can theorise from different literatures the question of 'for whom do we research': to whom are we accountable in deciding research purpose? From who or what do we form our researcher identity? What needs of our own research and lives are informing our decisions? In balancing academic and practice/policy demands, we should recognise how some may dominate other weaker and more vulnerable interests.

Cultural policy research and stakeholder literature reveal the implicit and dominant influences on decision-making and how we are mobilised to shape our research to particular ends (Belfiore, 2016; Bridoux and Vishwanathan, 2018). Particularly when research seeks to inform policy, we can find ourselves annexed into 'research as advocacy' (Belfiore, 2009). By contrast we may also shape our approach to reveal unheard or invisible voices (Comunian and England, 2020).

Returning to how interrogation of purpose has developed in artistic practice, Liz Lerman's Critical Response Process (Lerman and Borstel, 2003), developed to interrogate dance performance, proposes we invite others to shape our purpose. It starts with participants responding to a performance of unfinished work with 'statements of meaning'. That is, at a crucial stage of developing something new, it invites a critical audience in to say what *they* have understood to be its purpose and meaning. This process may expose us to possible failure, error, misdirection but equally may reveal new directions or unseen assumptions. As crisis is an unfolding process, such iterative pauses and preparedness for review may mean we stop our work, realising it lacks relevance. By contrast, adopting openness to review, inviting others into the construction of our research can also produce richer meaning and clearer purpose.

Whose purpose will not be met: who wins and who loses?

When we make research decisions around the time we can give and demand, and whose purpose(s) the research satisfies, we eventually arrive at points of exclusion. If we are mobilised by phronesis or 'the capacity to act with regard to human goods' (Aristotle, 1998 in Grint, 2007: 236), we must act with moral knowledge that our limitations as individual researchers will inevitably fail to satisfy all needs. Grint (2007: 237–8) drawing from Flyvberg (2001) proposes to mobilise phronesis as leadership learning through four elemental questions:

'Where are we going?
Is this desirable?
What should be done?
Who gains and who loses?'

I can mobilise these questions to interpret and clarify my research purpose. Dwelling on the last question introduces what we exclude by our decisions. Loss, in this sense in a global pandemic or other crisis, may be the exclusion of particular individuals or perspectives from our research focus. We may fail to support worthwhile advocacy campaigns or neglect to offer meaningful recommendations. We may disappoint families and colleagues through our inattention or we may need to mobilise collaboration. Our decisions of what to do may equally be a decision *not* to do.

Legitimacy

The demands and interpretations of time and questioning of purpose lead to concerns of legitimacy, either of our involvement or of the research itself. 'Legitimacy' is conceptualised in multiple ways by different fields but it can be articulated as a desirable or acceptable position or action within a given set of norms or beliefs (Mitchell, Agle, and Wood, 1997). In research decision-making, it raises questions about whether we as scholars have the right to claim the platforms for dissemination or the research space of the phenomenon we are exploring.

If me, then why? If not me, then who else?

Our individual decisions are bound up in wider concerns in theoretical inquiry of representation, status, and the (de)legitimisation of different voices and platforms of shared knowledge (hooks, 1991). We may ask whether the turbulence and change of a crisis opens up opportunities for better allyship and equity (reflecting on Meyerhoff and Noterman, 2019). Our

24

presence in new and unfolding discourses may be produced by privilege, by collaboration and supporting of others, or through the emotional labour of representing and the important knowledge we carry. In 'doing less better', we may recognise that our voice *is* or *is not* the one that needs to be heard in *this* time and in *this* way.

Contemporary practice research draws from and seeks to amplify voices beyond the academy, attempting to bring theory and practice together. In crisis (and at other times), we should consider how much we should be silent and give space to those voices, shifting platforms for sharing knowledge to more meaningful realms for those we intend to help. Responding to crisis in contemporary policy and practice research, we are motivated to use our academic standing to highlight problems. While this is ennobling, it risks practising a form of 'felt' responsibility (Ebrahim, 2003), positioning ourselves as the problem-solvers having already decided what the problem is and how it should be fixed. Leadership and accountability literatures discuss awareness of self-interest and attention to downward accountabilities as key in providing transparent decision-making (Doh and Quigley, 2014; Wellens and Jegers, 2014). We should consider what checks exist on our 'helpfulness' and what selectivity we apply to it, mitigated by our own self-interest.

This is an uncomfortable chair to sit on. We are conditioned to amplify our own original contributions and research voice. Equally, self-interest can be legitimised and is not wholly negative (for example, self-care). In response to crisis, we face even greater need to tailor our ethical self-questioning and invite scrutiny. From such 'negotiated ethics' (Lehner-Mear, 2019), we can create different ways to form allyship in engaged and collaborative research, sharing decision-making. Through this, we better understand our own role and that of our contributors/beneficiaries, resisting what disability studies has termed 'academic parasitism' (Stone and Priestley, 1996). Such interrogation may result in stepping back, stepping away, rescinding control, passing to others. Perhaps most significantly, such reflexive examination recognises that our partners and beneficiaries must be able to refuse as well as dictate the terms of our 'help'.

Conclusion

Opportunities to reflect such as writing this chapter are valuable. I write, not from a position of success or failure, but of mixed outcomes and ongoing review. Through my repeated questioning, I have reconciled my responses to need; to question my purpose and attempt 'better'. While many pressures still exist, making doing less a challenge, how I understand or interpret these pressures is clearer. I have held up my hand in refusal as often as saying yes. I have had my help refused. I have switched off my messages and replied to emails saying 'I am sorry I cannot do X but I could do Y'. I have tried to say 'Z would be a better person to do, speak, …'. I have tried to distinguish whose purpose(s) I adopt. I do not always succeed. People around me gain and lose my time, my attention, and my labour. I strike (I hope) a better balance than at the start of this crisis.

Reflection and reflexivity are more important to my toolkit than before. External crisis prompts an iterative and adaptive approach in which research may not be conclusive. Decision-making is not a single action but multiple decisions and decisions revisited. To treat it otherwise is to attempt to hammer a nail into a river. This is not a failure of indecisiveness or completion but openness to the fluidity of context and changing knowledge. We must respond with humility that we cannot know or control the outcomes of what we embark upon.

Throughout 2020, I started research projects and not others, contributed to policy and public debate. These decisions and exchanges found clearer purpose through the questioning strategy here. It helped me engage with participants as collaborators and controllers of our shared work. I distinguished between administrative funding-driven boundaries which dictate a project end and my collaborators' more open-ended commitments to changing their lives and wider communities. I supported discussions that others led and were not really research but 'helpful'. I set aside prior research until I could consider its revised value. I re-appraised future research plans. Through these exercises, I formulated new ideas and saw how stepping back can be meaningful. I recognised that my voice, my help, could only be offered if I could give it and articulate its usefulness. Approaching these experiences in this way helped me sift thoughts about future research and pedagogies in my field(s) and opened up new collaborations.

So I offer this strategy to other researchers. Even if you *can* do research it does not mean that you *should*. Before you embark on a response or rush to research an urgent crisis (or anything else), reflect on why you are doing this. What and whose purpose will it accomplish? How will time be treated in your decisions? Should you do this or should someone else?

References

Arvanitis, K. (2020) 'What collecting spontaneous memorials can tell us about collecting COVID-19: Part 1', *Cultural Practice: The Magazine of the Institute for Cultural Practices* [online] 24 April, available from: https://culturalpractice.org/collecting-covid-19-part1/ [accessed 5 June 2020].

Bakhshi, H., Humphries, D., and Haq, S. (2020) *Digital Culture: Consumer Tracking Study. Wave 8 (September 2020)*, London: NESTA; Intellectual Property Office; AudienceNet.

Banet-Weiser, S. (2018) 'Popular feminism: feminist flashpoints', *Los Angeles Review of Books* [online] 5 October, available from: https://lareviewofbooks.org/article/popular-feminism-feminist-flashpoints/ [accessed 27 September 2020].

Banks, M. (2019) 'Precarity, biography, and event: work and time in the cultural industries', *Sociological Research Online*, DOI: 136078041984452.

Banks, M. (2020) 'The work of culture and C-19', *European Journal of Cultural Studies*, 23(4): 648–54.

Banks, M. and O'Connor, J. (2020) '"A Plague upon Your Howling": art and culture in the viral emergency', *Cultural Trends*, DOI: 10.1080/ 09548963.2020.1827931.

Belfiore, E. (2009) 'On bullshit in cultural policy practice and research: notes from the British case', *International Journal of Cultural Policy*, 15(3): 343–59.

Belfiore, E. (2015) '"Impact", "value" and "bad economics": making sense of the problem of value in the arts and humanities', *Arts and Humanities in Higher Education*, 14(1): 95–110.

Belfiore, E. (2016) 'Cultural policy research in the real world: curating "impact", facilitating "enlightenment"', *Cultural Trends*, 25(3): 205–16.

Berger, R. (2015) 'Now I see it, now I don't: researcher's position and reflexivity in qualitative research', *Qualitative Research*, 15(2): 219–34.

Blackmore, J. (2020) 'The carelessness of entrepreneurial universities in a world risk society: a feminist reflection on the impact of Covid-19 in Australia', *Higher Education Research & Development*, DOI: 10.1080/ 07294360.2020.1825348.

Bridoux, F. and Vishwanathan, P. (2018) 'When do powerful stakeholders give managers the latitude to balance all stakeholders' interests?', *Business & Society*, 59(2): 232–62.

Brook, O., O'Brien, D., and Taylor, M. (2018) *Panic! It's An Arts Emergency*, London: Create London/ArtsEmergency.

Bryson, J. (2004) *Strategic Planning for Public and Nonprofit Organizations: A Guide to Strengthening and Sustaining Organizational Achievement*, New York: John Wiley & Sons.

Chatzidakis, A., Hakim, J., Littler, J., Rottenberg, C., and Segal, L. (2020) 'From carewashing to radical care: the discursive explosions of care during Covid-19', *Feminist Media Studies*, 20(6): 889–95.

Comunian, R. and England, L. (2020) 'Creative and cultural work without filters: Covid-19 and exposed precarity in the creative economy', *Cultural Trends*, DOI: 10.1080/09548963.2020.1770577.

Danish Association of Theatre for Children (2004) *Keynotes of the Seven Criteria for Quality* (unpublished summary from Imaginate Festival, Edinburgh, 2004).

De Beukelaer, C. (2020) 'An argument for reading more and writing less', *Times Higher Education*, 31 January, available from: https:// www.timeshighereducation.com/blog/argument-reading-more-and-writing-less [accessed 26 October 2020].

De Londras, F. and Enright, M. (2018) *Repealing the Eighth: Reforming Irish Abortion Law*, Bristol: Policy Press.

Doh, J. and Quigley, N. (2014) 'Responsible leadership and stakeholder management: influence pathways and organizational outcomes', *Academy of Management Perspectives*, 28(3): 255–74.

Drucker, P. (1995) *Managing the Non-Profit Organization*, Cambridge: Routledge.

Ebrahim, A. (2003) 'Making sense of accountability: conceptual perspectives for northern and southern nonprofits', *Nonprofit Management and Leadership*, 14(2): 191–212.

Eikhof, D. (2020) 'COVID-19, inclusion and workforce diversity in the cultural economy: what now, what next?', *Cultural Trends*, DOI: 10.1080/09548963.2020.1802202.

Flyvbjerg, B. (2001) *Making Social Science Matter: Why Social Inquiry Fails and How it Can Succeed Again*, Cambridge: Cambridge University Press.

Grint, K. (2007) 'Learning to lead: can Aristotle help us find the road to wisdom?', *Leadership*, 3(2): 231–46.

Hamilton, L. (2019) 'Embracing crises as normal: a new approach for arts managers', *Arts Management Quarterly*, 131: 43–8.

hooks, b. (1991) 'Theory as liberatory practice', *Yale Journal of Law & Feminism*, 4(1).

Langsted, J., Hannah, K., and Rørdam Larsen, C. (2003) 'Ønskekvist-modellen. Kunstnerisk kvalitet i performativ kunst [The IAN-Model. Artistic Quality in the Performing Arts]', available from: https://yamspace.org/toolkit/ian-model [accessed 21 October 2020].

Lehner-Mear, R. (2019) 'Negotiating the ethics of Netnography: developing an ethical approach to an online study of mother perspectives', *International Journal of Social Research Methodology*, DOI: 10.1080/13645579.2019.1634879.

Lerman, L. and Borstel, J. (2003) *Critical Response Process*, Takoma Park: Dance Exchange.

Lynch, K. (2010) 'Carelessness: a hidden doxa of higher education', *Arts and Humanities in Higher Education*, 9: 54–67.

Meyerhoff, E. and Noterman, E. (2019) 'Revolutionary scholarship by any speed necessary: slow or fast but for the end of this world', *ACME: An International E-Journal for Critical Geographies*, 18(1): 217–45.

Mitchell, R., Agle, B., and Wood, D. (1997) 'Toward a theory of stakeholder indentification and salience: defining the principle of who and what really counts', *Academy of Management Review*, 22: 853–86.

Murphy, Y. (2020) 'Dear Phil George, the world has changed & so should we' [online], *Omidaze Productions* [online], 3 June, available from: https://omidaze.wordpress.com/2020/06/03/dear-phil-george-the-world-has-changed-so-should-we/ [accessed 5 June 2020].

Nind, M., Armstrong, A., Cansdale, M., Collis, A., Hooper, C., Parsons, S., and Power, A. (2017) 'TimeBanking: towards a co-produced solution for power and money issues in inclusive research', *International Journal of Social Research Methodology*, 20(4): 387–400.

Phelan, P. (2014) 'On the difference between time and history', *Performance Research*, 19(3): 114–19.

Sandoval, M. (2016) 'Fighting precarity with co-operation? Worker co-operatives in the cultural sector', *New Formations*, 88(2016): 51–68.

Scraton, P. (2019) *The Hillsborough Independent Panel and the UK State: An Alternative Route to 'Truth', 'Apology' and 'Justice'*, London/New York: Routledge.

Smith, L.T. (2012) *Decolonizing Methodologies: Research and Indigenous Peoples* (2nd edn), Dunedin, NZ: Zed Books.

Stone, E. and Priestley, M. (1996) 'Parasites, pawns and partners: disability research and the role of non-disabled researchers', *The British Journal of Sociology*, 47(4): 699–716.

Tähtinen, J., Ryan, A., and Holmlund, M. (2016) 'How to develop theory and keep our jobs? The role of academic "gatherings" in our theory development practice', *Marketing Theory*, 16(2): 250–6.

Tsioulakis, I. and FitzGibbon, A. (2020) 'Performing artists in the age of COVID-19: a moment of urgent action and potential change', 9 April, available from: http://qpol.qub.ac.uk/performing-artists-in-the-age-of-covid-19/ [accessed 9 April 2020].

Wellens, L. and Jegers, M. (2014) 'Beneficiary participation as an instrument of downward accountability: a multiple case study', *European Management Journal*, 32(6): 938–49.

2

Ethnography in crisis: methodology in the cracks

Zania Koppe

While the all-encompassing nature of large-scale crises dominates the news, small-scale, localised, and less newsworthy forms of crisis occur continually, altering people's lives and creating unexpected change. The OED defines crisis as a 'decisive stage in the progress of anything' (OED, 2021). I see crisis here as a point of change, or a series of events, that disrupt the social world, introducing a period of uncertainty.

This chapter is based on the ethnographic part of my doctoral research in 2018–21[1] exploring the potential of a collaborative co-housing project to disrupt the social and spatial boundaries of inclusion/exclusion of intellectually disabled people. Designers, artists, and architects collaborated with members of a supported housing provider to co-create interdependent and supportive neighbourhoods together with people with additional needs. Invested in ideas of 'housing the social' (Nimble Spaces, nd) and civic engagement, the project developed as a pilot project to explore housing for residents with diverse abilities in Callan, Ireland. National housing shortages were exacerbated by the 2008 financial crisis and policy austerity impacted social housing. There was therefore a need to build alternative options for people with support needs beyond large, congregated residential facilities (HSE, 2011; ILMI, 2019).

However, during my fieldwork, a series of unexpected crises stalled the project and impacted on my research. The emerging stories changed from focusing solely on building new homes towards the experience of negotiating and adapting to the changes and transitions occurring. The situated and deductive research practices of ethnography facilitate shifting directions in research as a response to changes in the field (ASA, 2020). As a result, my research aims and objectives turned from focusing on the project alone towards a consideration of the ideas and values that informed it. Opening up the research questions in a changing environment allowed me to consider what was, is, and might be. In this chapter, I am interested in the potential of ethnography as a reflexive and flexible research method and to explore its potential to facilitate my negotiated response.

Co-production and collaboration

Nimble Spaces began as a collaboration between Camphill Callan, Workhouse Union (formerly known as Commonage), and their neighbours. Camphill Callan is an intentional life-sharing community providing homes for intellectually disabled residents in supported settings. Workhouse Union, an arts organisation working with artists, architects, and community groups, 'engages people with the spaces and places we live' (Workhouse Union, nd) through collaborative methods and design. Together with a diverse group of arts practitioners, Nimble Spaces developed a participatory design process that encouraged active citizenship for all. During a series of workshops in 2013–15 (Nimble Spaces, nd), they worked together with people of all abilities to explore how art could facilitate decision-making through an exploration of individual relationships with space, others, and the self (LiD Architecture, nd). The ideas that emerged from these workshops translated into architectural plans, as well as funding and planning permission for 25 houses to be built on four sites in the town (Nimble Spaces, nd). These imagined 'neighbourhoods' (Nimble Spaces, nd) retained collective, social space while making provision for private space and 'my own home' (Nimble Spaces, nd). Nimble Spaces is both a process of design and a housing project, as well as a set of ideas for thinking about support, interdependence, and the co-production of collective social worlds.

Crisis as interruption

Shortly after I began my research, a series of crises affected the national governing body of Camphill Callan. Camphill Communities of Ireland (henceforth referred to as CCoI) is a registered charity that receives funding from the Irish Health Service Executive (HSE) (CCoI, 2016: 10). However, CCoI and individual communities are responsible for the governance and daily running of the communities themselves. In 2017, one neighbouring Camphill Community had its registration revoked by the Health Inspection and Quality Authority. Subsequently, it came under the direct control of the HSE (Cullen, 2017). Initially, this closure of one community had a peripheral impact on the project and my research. However, as I entered the field in September 2018, this one closure triggered a series of crises that changed the governance structures of CCoI before transforming the way in which Camphills in Ireland can operate. As the crisis developed, one participant expressed concern that the consequences of the changes at the national level of CCoI, would have a 'contagious' effect that would transform Camphill's scope of practice. This proved true and during the time I accompanied Nimble Spaces, Camphill Communities in Ireland have been re-thought in ways that some participants see as no longer 'in the spirit of Camphill' (Snellgrove, 2013: 16). While the revocation of registration of one community did not directly affect Nimble Spaces and Camphill Callan, the subsequent changes to CCoI impacted the people and places involved in Nimble Spaces and, by extension, my research.

Shared lives

Relational support and shared lives have been at the centre of Camphill Community care in Ireland since 1972. Developed in Scotland in 1940 Camphill pioneered a form of extended home-based care in intentional communities that prioritised inclusive and respectful care-giving, alongside community and cultural inclusion (Christie 1989; Cushing, 2015). Founded by Dr Karl König (König, 2018) and inspired by the philosophy of Rudolf Steiner they formed something of 'an experiment in radical inclusion' (McKanan, 2020: 5). However, as Maria Lyons points out (2015), Camphills are also countercultural and therefore operating outside the 'norm'. This makes them potentially 'at odds with the ideal of inclusion' (Lyons, 2015: 6), and they can be seen instead as a slightly 'peculiar form of the institution' (Lyons, 2015: 3).

Traditionally in Camphills in Ireland and internationally, people with and without support needs have lived and worked together without financial remuneration. This came from the belief that to work without wages invites you to meet the other person as a whole person. 'To *live* with' (Roth in Pietzner, 1991: 65; emphasis in original), rather than to care for, challenges the idea of care as a service provision. In meeting the needs of the other while the collective meets your own needs, there is a shift in the quality of the relationship beyond the transactional (Weihs and Tallo, 1988; Pietzner, 1991; König, 2018). Focusing on the individual person, rather than on their level of ability (Salman, 2020: 11), Camphill pioneered ways of living collectively 'that are less disabling for others' (McKanan, 2020: 3). Camphill Callan brought these values to the Nimble Spaces process, offering the possibility for insights into a model of support that could contribute to alternative ideas for interdependent living that prioritises 'the constructive neighbour' and mutual support (Nimble Spaces, nd).

Ethnography as accompaniment and response

I developed the initial research design as an accompaniment to the project as they explored material outcomes and conceptions of home and worked towards building new neighbourhoods. The fieldwork was designed as a cyclical entering and exiting of the field (Tsing, 2015) as the housing clusters were built. To create a coherent vision of ethnography that could produce something 'useful', I looked to feminist ethnographers

(Scheper-Hughes, 1993; Tsing, 1993; Cushing and Lewis, 2002; Davids, 2014) and their commitment to self-reflexivity, as well as to Community Based Research Practices (CBR) (Reid and Brief, 2009) to inform being of use. Accompaniment was a framework through which to think about how knowledge and understanding are generated through relational processes of 'scholarship and citizenship' (Tomlinson and Lipsitz, 2013 in Bucholz and Casillas, 2016: 27) while acknowledging that 'all participants contribute different forms of expertise and understanding' (Bucholz and Casillas, 2016: 27). Initially, what seemed most useful was a record and analysis of the Nimble Spaces process as they built collective housing, and moved into new homes. However, as realities shifted in response to crisis, the focus of my research necessarily shifted alongside.

The dialogical nature of ethnography created both a space to adapt to the change in focus emerging from the field and contributed to long periods of uncertainty about how the research would develop. As I focused on the outcomes of the planned new neighbourhoods, my preconceived ideas of how the fieldwork *should* progress concentrated on the material completion of new homes. Being in the field forced a confrontation with this illusion of my ability to control the direction of the research. Ethnography, as a method adapted to unknown worlds and scenarios, helped me to process these changes as the very engagement with ethnographic research practices and ways of thinking insists on a flexible approach (ASA, 2020).

The ideas that informed the project as well as values of kindness, support, and the importance of friendship emphasised by participants, became more important as the crisis unfolded. However, my commitment to contribute something of use, in a context where what was useful changed continually, also raised ethical questions of 'response-ability' (Haraway, 2016: 34), and my ability to respond adequately. Questions of usefulness became linked to my ideas about method, ethics, and response, and while the framework remained intact, the evolving changes continually tested the question of what was, in fact, 'useful' (Ahmed, 2019). At times, the conflicting responsibilities to participants, funders, institutional backers, and myself as a researcher tested my capacity to respond.

Negotiations of consent

The changes impacting the field called for a revaluation of different aspects of the research and the changing context caused me to question aspects of the initial design. The process of gaining institutional ethical approval focused my attention on the potential ethical pitfalls of including people in research 'with different ways of thinking and learning' (McKanan, 2020: 5). Assumptions of vulnerability linked to a diagnosis, particularly in relation to intellectual disability within institutional ethics guidelines, often discourage the inclusion of participants considered vulnerable (Snipstad, 2020: 1). However, from a moral and human rights perspective (CRPD, 2014; NDA, 2009), persons with support needs have the same rights to self-determination as non-disabled citizens.

As my research questions were interested in the possibilities for inclusive processes to disrupt social boundaries, the inclusion of participants with diverse abilities was important. Joanne Watson's (2016) challenge to societal perceptions of profound disability in light of the UN Convention on the Rights of Persons with Disabilities offered a model for including people in research irrespective of ability. Simultaneously, the Assisted Decision-Making Act 2015 provided an Irish framework through which to negotiate the capacity to consent. Meanwhile, ethnographic practices provided a flexible, non-intrusive framing for the inclusion of participants with additional needs. However, in practice my aspirations came up against the complexity of including people with profound and complex disabilities including challenges with verbal communication. As the tension between my commitment and what was possible became clearer, I initially placed the emphasis on myself as a researcher to solve the difficulties of enabling consent by adapting the consent process to individual needs over time, paying attention to will and preference (Watson, 2016).

However, to be comfortable that potential participants wanted to participate and full and informed consent was possible, I would have needed to engage in long-term, sustained work alongside each potential participant where this was unclear (Watson, 2016; Mietola et al, 2017: 268). Together with gatekeepers and staff I considered a third-party approach to consent in cases where capacity was unclear requiring families and responsible others to give initial consent (Mietola et al, 2017: 265). However, this approach raises complex questions of *who decides*. In light of time limitations in PhD research, my concerns and those raised by staff, I made the decision to exclude possible participants with profound disabilities and difficulties with verbal communication. The exclusion of some people in a research project considering questions related to social boundaries of inclusion/exclusion seemed to contradict my initial theoretical commitment to a rights-based approach to inclusion (Watson, 2016). However, while considering my discomfort with this tension during the fieldwork, I also came to question my assumptions that full inclusion in research would reduce disabling boundaries in meaningful ways.

While I was negotiating this process, the use of co-creation and collaborative arts-based methods seemed to offer a partial solution to the dilemma of inclusion. Visual methods such as drawings or photovoice (Harper, 2012) initially offered a way to strengthen CBR and collaborative methods that might provide alternative ways of communicating. Due to the creative practices in the project and surroundings, many disabled and non-disabled participants also worked in the arts or were familiar with creative engagement. However, together with gatekeepers and participants, I had decided early in the research design to name Nimble Spaces in line with CBR. This was necessary for the findings to be 'of use' to participants in a meaningful way. As such, my ethical commitment to protect individual identities as much as possible came into conflict with participants' experiences as professionals in their field.

While including aspects of visual ethnography initially appeared to provide a way of making space for participant voices, these imagined images could not then be attributed to the artist. A tension became explicit between the ethical imperative to protect research participant identity and the ethical imperative to attribute creative authorship. Negotiating these sticky points that emerged in the initial negotiations of consent, raised questions about the possibilities and limits of inclusive processes that accompanied me as the field became unsteady.

The complicated ideas that I began with, in order to create space in the research for participants' voices, faded as the crisis unfolded. For some participants simply saying yes or no to being included directly in the research became a way in which to exercise agency when individual agency was being curtailed. While encouraging people to say yes was important to the success of the research, as the crisis unfolded, the act of saying no became about more than just research.

I became conscious of the importance of the research as a possible space in which to exercise the right to choose. When discussing the process of consent with people with and without support needs, it became clear that for some, filling in an 'official' form felt empowering to them, while for others, the form was another unwelcome barrier. Saying no to being included in the research, while saying yes to tea and conversations that would not be taken down in notes, became an act of agency and the 'no' became a new dimension to explore in my research.

Reflection

My initial focus on questions of vulnerability concentrated on consent processes for including people with intellectual and complex disabilities in research (Snipstad, 2020). In crisis and transition wider questions of who is vulnerable gained in importance. Taking my commitment to ethnography seriously, as a method of engagement and with an ethical commitment to social justice (Scheper-Hughes, 1993; Mietola et al, 2017: 272), required an awareness of these particular and changing vulnerabilities.

The changes to the governance structures and scope of practice within CCoI resulted in people losing their homes, sometimes with little warning (Cullen, 2017). During this critical phase in the crisis I stepped back, in order not to further complicate the research or participants' lives. My research practice during this time consisted of evaluating and revaluating processes of consent, shifting power dynamics and my position on an almost continual basis. This process was not always seamless; at times, it was messy. However, engaging in reflexive re-evaluation during a crisis made visible the importance of being clear about layered and competing positions. As the social context is transformed through the decisions of absent 'others' power and vulnerability slip and mutate, and methods need to be malleable to take these changes into account.

The break with the 'old model' of CCoI created a void in which what would come next was unclear. As CCoI shifted from what was described by one participant as a diverse 'ecosystem', towards a focus on residential care, the conception of what was *useful* for people's lives narrowed. At the same time there was a growing awareness of what might be lost at the community level. Traditionally Communities contained: an organic farm and garden, workshops that included weaving and baking, a hall or cultural space in which celebrations, concerts, and musical events took place, perhaps a café if the Community was town-based, or an arts centre or school. These places and projects' importance became more apparent as the life-sharing aspects of intentional community living reduced.

As the surrounding structures of cultural, communal, and artistic life were in danger of becoming separate from care, people began to re-focus their commitment to strengthening these places and projects. While they are no longer included within a single organisational space, or 'ecosystem', there is currently a tentative emergence of diverse places and structures that exist alongside each other, funded and operating separately, yet working interdependently (SPI and Doris, 2020). These emerging projects have continued to develop and become visible even as the consequences of the COVID-19 crisis have impacted further on possibilities for extended relational communities of support.

The participant self

It was important to me to have a robust ethical framework that was flexible and contingent on the field and fundamental to my ability to navigate sticky aspects of the research process. Research ethics and methods are connected, and they also link to feminist ideas of positionality within the research design that provided a framework through which to understand the affects of my own position as insider/outsider in the field. Born into a Camphill Community in Ireland, I spent part of my childhood and teenage years in various communities.

This loss of a space that was my childhood home for a time, and the evolving crises affecting CCoI, affected my capacity to respond. My emotional response to the loss of a previous home and my nostalgia for a particular way of life became closely entangled with my understanding of the field. As participants' focus shifted from the active creation of something new to an experience of loss for something that was gone, my clarity decreased and my attachment to place, people, and memory gained in importance.

The insider/outsider position I inhabited, will I believe, offer rich insights into alternative world-building possibilities once the analysis is complete. However, during the time in which the outcome of the crisis was still unclear, this position was ambivalent. Jodie Taylor's conception of 'the intimate insider' (Taylor, 2011), where the privileging of friendship over the extraction of data may protect both parties from possible harm, provided a partial way to evaluate my changing position. This idea of the intimate insider also centred the ethical difficulties of conducting research in spaces where there is intimate knowledge (Taylor, 2011) and provided something of a filtration system with which to separate conversations as 'data' from those with participant friends.

While I am no longer an 'insider', my position as a researcher negotiating return in a context of crisis and loss cast a layer of nostalgia over my experience of the field. Crisis made things sticky, messy, and emotional and for a time created a crack between my initial ideas of the self, and the research. While 'shared experiences [may] cultivate ... degrees of intimacy between people' (Taylor, 2011: 10) that have the potential to increase the capacity for insight, there remains the potential for my affective experience to intrude on the field in unhelpful ways. I experience this, as a series of misunderstandings in the translation and writing of partially inhabited worlds as my own loss threatens to colour my perceptions of participant responses.

Shobana Shankar (2020) highlights the importance of acknowledging difficult emotions within research processes. Drawing attention to the way in which emotion is often absent from descriptions of the research (Shankar, 2020), she also hints at the discomfort writing about emotion in academic contexts can cause. However, while it is uncomfortable, the process of being in the field during crisis and change impacted my emotional response. In turn, these feelings of discomfort continue to influence my writing and interpretation of events. The previously unimaginable consequences also contributed to my sense of responsibility as people lost their homes. Questions of what is 'useful' lost their clarity (Ahmed, 2019) as changes happened at speed and my role as a researcher could contribute little to the material needs of participants. Acknowledging how difficult emotional experiences can alter the meanings I ascribe to the impacts of the crisis is necessary when describing processes of engagement.

During this time I was grateful for the cyclical design of my fieldwork. Entering and exiting the field, and the long train journeys in between the field and my home provided empty times for reflection. Anna Tsing's reflection on processes of engagement and thought 'do, think, observe and do again' (Tsing, 2015: 264) were a reminder, to sit with, observe, adapt, and return. Though I was unprepared for the crises that enveloped CCoI, and still less prepared for the emotional toll this period would have on me as a researcher and friend, the flexibility and reflexive nature of ethnography provided space in which to process these affects. The long-term engagement with the field that ethnography demands also provided time during which I was present as a visible and known observer, rather than seeking active engagement (ASA, 2020). The possibility of being present in accompaniment of the project without the pressure to extract 'data' was particularly important during times when research questions were inappropriate. Likewise, the inclusion of feminist ideals of solidarity, reflexive positioning, and a commitment to collective methods within the initial research design also helped to provide frameworks and thinking strategies in processing and acknowledging the affects of crisis on both participant and the self. Taking note of the impact of these events on both the field as a space, and on the individual lives of participant friends, encouraged open discussions on the changing direction of the research.

At the same time, it encouraged me to step back from my feelings to view emotions and events as multiple aspects of the research experience. Communicating these ideas with participants also provided space for people to articulate where they felt conversations – or parts of conversations – fell into the realm of friendship. In line with CBR, I developed the initial research questions and methodologies with input from gatekeepers. While this was not a co-authored study, the practice of open discussion throughout translated into a pattern of communication that encouraged an easy sharing of information.

No matter how carefully I managed the methodological and ethical frameworks, the experience of witnessing crisis is uncomfortable and this discomfort challenged many of the assumptions and theoretical ideas I began with. For some time, the question of what to do with these changes caused me to question the merits of the research itself. However, ethnography is still useful (Scheper-Hughes, 1993: 28), even when my expectations of being 'of use' (Ahmed, 2019) came into question. Ethnography provides space and flexibility through which to continually re-articulate the modes of doing research, while also insisting on a careful consideration of the partial, situated nature of the emerging stories (ASA, 2020). As I attempted to rescue the initial research project, I realised that whether or not the housing clusters were built within my PhD's time limitations, the ideas that informed the project and the collaborative and social processes of co-creating are ideas worth documenting. The research practice, the doing of it, provided insights into both the initial research objectives and an exploration of research methods negotiating change in a micro-context. These insights become findings in my analysis that relate in turn to my initial questions about the possibilities for the disruption of social boundaries.

Conclusion

I came to understand the usefulness of ethnography as a process of engagement, and a method of analysis and reflection. This enabled me to engage with the stories that were emerging. The embedded and contingent nature of ethnography offered ways to be present in multiple circumstances, without demanding specific answers to specific questions.

As I begin analysing the findings of this research, I am becoming cognisant of the ways in which the process of a cyclical reflexive questioning continues and allows the data space to expand. While the housing clusters that I hoped would be the outcome of the project have not yet materialised, the importance of the Nimble Spaces process as a set of ideas about collective and supportive lives has reappeared. The way in which crisis was negotiated, adapted to, and absorbed into the ethos of collective agency, has meant that the possibility for new neighbourhoods to come about still exists. At the same time, I am aware that the physical buildings alone do not create neighbourhoods of support. Rather it is the *commitment* to build future possibilities based on social connection and mutual support that enables the creation of inclusive and mutually supportive communities. These possibilities reflect the architectural concept of the 'pragmatic Utopia' (Kasperzyk, 1991), modes of living and acting in the world for better future outcomes.

As we now negotiate the individual impacts of collective crisis during a global pandemic, the future consequences remain unclear. The threat of the disease has both an immediate and unequal effect on people's lives, while 'social distancing' and efforts to contain COVID-19 change how we relate to one another. Creating individual and collective responses for mutual support 'when certainty is shaken' (Shankar, 2020: 4–5) is complicated, yet the current crisis makes the importance of them all the more visible.

Note

[1]   This chapter is based on PhD research carried out between 2017 and 2021 at the National University of Ireland, Galway, under the supervision of Dr Kathy Powell and Dr Kevin Ryan. Funded by a Galway Doctoral Scholarship (2017–18) and an Irish Research Council Scholarship (2018–21).

References

Ahmed, S. (2019) *What's the Use?*, London: Duke University Press.

ASA 'Ethics guidelines for good research practice' [online], *Association of Social Anthropologists of the UK and the Commonwealth*, available from: https://www.theasa.org/downloads/ASA%20ethics%20guidelines%202011.pdf

Assisted Decision-Making (Capacity) Act 2015 (Commencement of Certain Provisions) (No 2) Order 2016, available from: http://www.irishstatutebook.ie/eli/2016/si/517/made/en/print.

Bucholz, M. and Casillas, D. (2016) 'Beyond empowerment: accompaniment and sociolinguistic justice in a youth research program', Santa Barbara, available from: https://escholarship.org/content/qt6033d7jj/qt6033d7jj.pdf.

Camphill Communities of Ireland (2016) *Annual Report 2016*, available at: https://www.camphill.ie/userfiles/files/Annual%20Report%202016.pdf.

Christie, N. (1989) *Beyond Loneliness and Institutions: Communes for Extraordinary People*, Oxford: Oxford University Press.

'crisis, n.' (2021) [OED online], *Oxford University Press*, available from: https://www-oed-com.libgate.library.nuigalway.ie/view/Entry/44539?redirectedFrom=crisis&.

Cullen, P. (2017) 'End to social experiment angers families and staff of care centre', *The Irish Times*, 23 October 2017, available from: https://www.irishtimes.com/news/health/end-to-social-experiment-angers-families-and-staff-of-care-centre-1.3265010.

Cushing, P. (2015) 'What counts as a community? Alternative approaches to inclusion and developmental disability', *International Journal of Developmental Disabilities*, 61(2): 83–92.

Cushing, P. and Lewis, T. (2002) 'Negotiating mutuality and agency in care-giving relationships with women with intellectual disabilities', *Hypatia*, 17(3): 173–93.

Davids, T. (2014) 'Trying to be a vulnerable observer: matters of agency, solidarity and hospitality in feminist ethnography', *Women's Studies International Forum*, 43: 50–8.

Haraway, D. (2016) *Staying with the Trouble: Making Kin in the Chthulucene*, London: Duke University Press.

Harper, D. (2012) *Visual Sociology*, Oxford: Routledge.

Health Service Executive (HSE) (2011) 'Time to move on from congregated settings: a strategy for community inclusion', *Health Service Executive*, June 2011, available from: http://www.hse.ie/eng/services/list/4/disability/congregatedsettings/congregatedsettingsreportfinal.pdf.

Independent Living Movement, Ireland (ILMI) (2019) 'Independent Living Movement Ireland submission to the Oireachtas Committee on Housing, Planning and Local Government', *Independent Living Movement, Ireland*, available from: https://ilmi.ie/wp-content/uploads/2019/07/ILMI-Submission-to-the-Joint-Oireachtas-Commitee-on-Housing-June-2019.pdf.

Kasperzyk, D. (1991) 'Pragmatic utopias: planning with nature', *Context Institute*, available from: https://www.context.org/iclib/ic29/kasprzyk/.

König, K. (2018) *The Sprit of Camphill: Birth of a Movement*, Edinburgh: Floris Books.

LiD Architecture (nd) 'Nimble Spaces: Housing Research and Design Tools', *LiD Architecture*, available from: https://www.lid-architecture.net/NimbleSpaces.

Lyons, M. (2015) 'Re-thinking community care: the Camphill village model: a critical appraisal, a discussion paper in association with the Camphill Research Network', *The Centre for Welfare Reform*, November 2015, available from: http://www.camphillresearch.com/content-stuff/uploads/2015/11/Re-Thinking-Community-Care.pdf.

McKanan, D. (2020) *Camphill and the Future: Spirituality and Disability in an Evolving Communal Movement*, California: California University Press.

Mietola, R. et al (2017) 'Voiceless subjects? Research ethics and persons with profound intellectual disabilities', *International Journal of Social Research Methodology*, 20(3): 263–74.

National Disability Authority (NDA) (2009) 'Ethical guidance for research with people with disabilities', *National Disability Authority*, available from: http://nda.ie/Policy-and-research/Research/Research-Ethics/Ethical-Guidance-for-Research-with-People-with-Disabilities.html.

Nimble Spaces (nd) [online], *Nimble Spaces*, available at: https://nimblespaces.ie/.

Pietzner, C. (ed) (1991) *A Candle on the Hill: Images of Camphill Life*, Edinburgh: Floris Books.

Reid, C. and Brief, E. (2009) 'Confronting condescending ethics: how community-based research challenges traditional approaches to consent, confidentiality and capacity', *Journal of Academic Ethics*, 7: 75–85.

Salman, S. (ed) (2020) *Made Possible*, London: Unbound.

Scheper-Hughes, N. (1993) *Death Without Weeping: The Violence of Everyday Life in Brazil*, London: University of California Press.

Shankar, S. (2020) 'Emotions as the new ethical turn in social research', *Social Science Research Council*, available from: https://items.ssrc.org/covid-19-and-the-social-sciences/social-research-and-insecurity/emotions-as-the-new-ethical-turn-in-social-research/.

Snellgrove, M. (2013) *The House Camphill Built*, University of Edinburgh, PhD in Sociology, available from: https://research.camphill.edu/wp-content/uploads/2019/12/The-House-Camphill-Built-M-Snellgrove.pdf.

Snipstad, Ø. (2020) 'Concerns regarding the use of the vulnerability concept in research on people with intellectually disability', *British Journal of Learning Disabilities*, December.

Sustainable Projects Ireland (SPI) and Doris, M. (2020) *Creating the Future We Want: Analysis and Development Project*, Callan: Trasna Productions.

Taylor, J. (2011) 'The intimate insider: negotiating the ethics of friendship when doing insider research', *Qualitative Research*, 11(1): 3–22.

Tomlinson, B., and Lipsitz, G. (2013) 'American studies as accompaniment', *American Quarterly*,. 65(1): 1–30.

Tsing, A. (1993) *In the Realm of the Diamond Queen: Marginality in an Out-of-the-way Place*, Princetown: Princetown University Press.

Tsing, A. (2015) *The Mushroom at the End of the World: On the Possibility of Life in Capitalist Ruins*, Woodstock: Princeton University Press.

(CRPD) UN General Assembly, *Status of the Convention on the Rights of Persons with Disabilities and the Optional Protocol thereto*, 7 August 2014, A/69/284, available from: https://www.refworld.org/docid/541c19fa4.html.

Watson, J. (2016) 'Assumptions of decision-making capacity: the role supporter attitudes play in the realisation of Article 12 for people with severe or profound intellectual disability', *Laws*, 5(6).

Weihs, A. and Tallo, J. (eds) (1988) *Camphill Villages*, Camphill Press.

Workhouse Union (nd), [online], *Workhouse Union*, available at: https://workhouseunion.com/about/.

3

Phenomenology of lived experience: multilayered approach and positionality

Bibek Dahal

Introduction

This chapter explores my experience of researching lived experience during a global pandemic. I used hermeneutic phenomenology with a careful approach to methods and ethics. The chapter discusses my lived experience of research, the difficulties I faced in the COVID-19 pandemic, and how these were resolved through methodological and ethical reflexivity.

Hermeneutic phenomenology research is the study of lived experiences – a study of humanness within humanistic parameters (van Manen, 1990). Humans, due to their dynamic nature, experience time and space differently. Birth, life, and death are common to all humans; however, time and space define their lived experiences subjectively with vividness. The study of human experiences within contextual phenomena, defined by time and space including body and mind, is called 'human science research'.

My interest in human experience motivates me as a human science researcher. I am exploring research ethics from the perspective of how social scientists experience *being* ethical, as researchers. In the first week of December 2019, I planned to commence my research. Coincidentally, COVID-19 started to hamper daily life of people in China (Wang et al, 2020) and soon after the global pandemic emerged. The ensuing lockdowns rendered me unable to continue the proposed research as planned using face-to-face interviews and field notes. So, I started to explore alternatives.

In this chapter, I reflect on my own experiences as a hermeneutic phenomenological inquirer during a period of global crisis. Broadly, it is framed in two sections: the first discusses researching the lived experiences of others, and the second considers the consequences of my positionality when interpreting texts.

Researching lived experience

I always wonder, how can I investigate the experience of others as I live it? How can I transcribe all lived experiences and interactions in a textual form? But, to hermeneutic phenomenologists, lived experience consists of four dimensions: time, space, body, and mind. Researching lived experience means asking how social/human science researchers make meaning of their contextual existence (Frechette et al, 2020). For me, it was an opportunity to understand the knowledge-constituted world of my participants, who are researchers embedded within their own research. Assessing my participants' lived experience was a way of understanding their world. It was also an approach to learning from their experiences. As Gadamer (2004) states, life is not only experienced; experiences give lasting importance to the existence of conscious mind and body in time and space. Learning, for me, is a social process where I can learn from the myriad dynamism of my own and the participants' experiences.

For me, researching lived experience was a process of being connected with the world and the people around my 'community' because the study was directed towards understanding and interpretation of all those phenomena that related to me as a researcher. The other primary intention was to explore the nature of being ethical in research. 'Ethics in practice' (Guillemin and Gillam, 2004) is relevant to researchers' subjectivity and research context. Thus, my exploration of lived experience valued the subjectivity and inter-subjectivity of my participants, which was associated with their personal and social constructions of experiences.

Methods for exploring lived experience depend upon the research topic and context. Due to the COVID-19 pandemic, researchers are unable to meet research participants. However, new and justifiable research approaches have emerged. Multilayered interviews and protocol writing are apt approaches to gather my participants' lived experiences without physical proximity (van Manen, 1990). Thus, I adopted online interviews for personal life stories, and protocol writings for thick descriptions of lived experience. These methods helped me to obtain texts of my participants' lived experience.

Researching lived experience comprises two dimensions: descriptive and interpretive. The focus of the descriptive dimension is to discover and describe the 'lived world' whereas the interpretive dimension leans heavily towards the interpretation of lived experience. Doing human science research in a pandemic introduced me to the task of interpreting texts of lived experience. These texts are interpreted by using subjective narration with a 'creation of hybrid text' through metaphorical analogy (Kafle, 2011: 190), explored later in the 'texts interpretation' section. The hybrid text has dual purposes; first, to integrate narrative, and second, to construct more explorative informational texts (Bintz and Ciecierski, 2017). This reflects the lived world of the audience while entering into subjective narration and the creation of hybrid text mediates a projection of the world. Such texts must restrain the power to interpret time, space, body, and mind. However, researching lived experience means potentially deepening our understanding of particular issues and phenomena from others' experiences (Farrell, 2020). Learning about other people's experiences also means opening ourselves up to becoming experienced.

Multilayered interviews

I used the online portal Google Meet for multilayered interviews to gather personal life stories. All interviews were recorded and transcribed. However, there is a viable difference between a gathering of lived experience and reflecting on lived experience (van Manen, 1990). Recorded interviews means gathering lived experience whereas transcribing them means creating an arena to reflect on lived experience. It is essential to transcribe each discourse because that prepares me for another layer of discourse.

Multilayered in-depth interviews rely on participants to revisit their experiences. To examine lived experience, Seidman (1998) suggested three serial in-depth interviews: first, assess the phenomenon of interest; second, assess current experience; and third, combine information from the previous two interviews to describe lived experience. Taking a different approach, Lauterbach (2018) used three different stages while examining lived experience of her research participants: think-aloud, stimulated recall, and semi-structured interview. She argues that these stages helped her research participants to reflect their lived experience. Seidman combines phenomenon and subjective interest whereas Lauterbach uses narrative structure in a process of exploring lived experience. Both the notion of subjective interest and narrative structure were used in my research while designing and conducting multilayered interviews; descriptive, interpretive, and critical. However, the research issue and research context may vary in the process of individual in-depth interviewing because each discourse is individualised. I have used three-layered in-depth interviews to answer questions like: what does it mean to be an ethical researcher? How does a social science researcher experience being an ethical researcher?

The first interview (descriptive layer) explores the time and space facets of research conducted by my participants. It primarily focuses on getting the answers to *what, where, when, who* questions. The second interview (interpretive layer) comprehensively focuses on my participants' experience throughout the research to dig out the answer to *how* questions based on the first layer interview (see Figure 3.1). The third interview (critical layer), based on the previous two, explores my participants' conscious embeddedness in their research. This layer critically seeks answers to *why* questions regarding

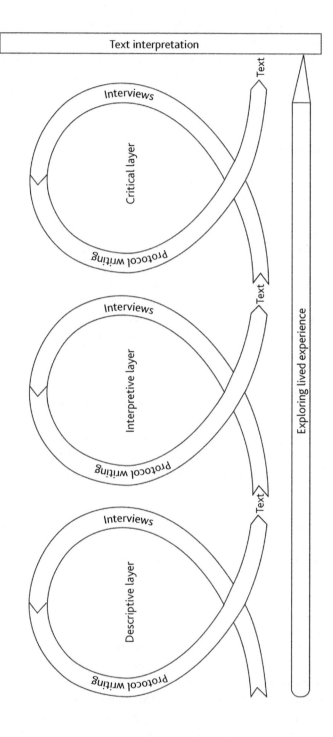

Figure 3.1: Interviews and protocol writing

my participants' overall experience of the research. The three-layered interviews, including several exploratory interactions between myself and my participants under each layer, generated lived experience texts interpretively rather than reductively (Vandermause and Fleming, 2011). The generated experiential narratives served as resources for a deeper understanding of social science research ethics and my participants' lived worlds.

Protocol writing

The COVID-19 pandemic physically separated me from my research participants. However, it did not stop me exploring their lived experience, as the multilayered interviews enabled the option of protocol writing. Protocol writing is another way to gather an individual's lived experience. As a complementary approach to individual in-depth interviews, it is an excellent tool for 'gathering original texts on which the researcher can work' (van Manen, 1990: 63). This is because some people, including myself, find it easier to write than talk about personal experiences (while it is the opposite for others).

Protocol writers (that is, research participants) are asked to address eight considerations including a focus on the particular phenomenon, avoid fancy phrases and flowery terminologies, and describe the experience from the inside, as it happened; almost like a state-of-mind account (van Manen, 1990: 64–5). It is an integral responsibility of human science researchers to make participants aware of these elements before proposing protocol writing. The protocol writing approach may not be applicable in all research contexts; for example, where participants may have low levels of literacy. However, by addressing the considerations suggested by van Manen (1990), I used protocol writing as an approach to explore my participants' lived experiences of being ethical in research. The protocol writings serve as reflective writings to explore rich, compelling, and thought-provoking descriptions of lived experience during the period of multilayered interviews (Finlay, 2012). The texts gathered from protocol writing allowed me to deepen understanding from my participants' accounts.

I used separate folders in Google Drive for descriptive, interpretive, and critical protocols. In each protocol, my participants were asked open-ended questions where they could narrate their experience of being ethical in research by focusing on a specific phenomenon. Thus, each of my participants has written three protocols throughout my research. My participants were given 15 days for each protocol to complete writing at their convenience. During this period, I transcribed the respective layer's interviews and created a 'world of text' for further processing of textual interpretations. The original texts gathered from protocol writing allowed me to gain a deeper understanding of each participant's account of being ethical in research in different contexts. Further, they provided forms and structures to reflect on my own experience as well as delve deeper on specific facets of particular phenomena of social science research (Estrada, 2018).

Here is an example of a protocol writing (that is, lived-experience description), provided by a social science researcher in the interpretive protocol, regarding his/her experience of starting to engage with research participants to conduct research ethically:

> As I started meeting my participants, it was a bit different though. I was interviewing students with some form of disability in a classroom. My consent for interviewing these early teenage kids was provided by the principal of the school. I did not know if the kids had any choice in that. For the first few sessions, the participants thought I was some kind of teacher; not that I did not try to explain what I was doing. I asked them many times if it was ok for me to question them about their classroom, teachers and family and not a single student denied my request. They were ok with every kind of question about them, their disability, their classroom, friends and family. Well, something to ponder at the moment was: were they willing? Or, were they agreeing to my request just because their principal had asked them to sit for an interview with me. If they had shown any sign of discomfiture I would have known, but I didn't notice any. And, even though I had explained I was researching; did it even make any sense to what they were doing?

Text interpretation

Texts of lived experience can be interpreted through different approaches such as a 'holistic or sententious approach; selective or highlighting approach; detailed or close-read approach' (van Manen, 1990: 92–5). To deepen the understanding of my participants' experiences, the detailed or close-read approach was appropriate for me. For both texts from multilayered interviews and protocol writings, I applied the close-read approach to construct relevant themes for further interpretation of my participants' lived experience.

Interpretation of lived experience is seen as a critical process to understand a phenomenon in the lifeworlds of others. The fundamental connections proposed by Ricoeur (1981) are distanciation, appropriation, explanation, and interpretation. The notion of distanciation I used, is to stand separate from the texts. I used the notion of appropriation to examine the ultimate horizon of my participants' lived experience by exploring the revelatory power of texts. The explanation of a certain phenomenon and its interpretation through texts is predominantly allied with interpretation of data.

I used the concepts diagrammatically while interpreting texts, which is also called *hermeneutic arc* (Ricoeur, 1981; Tan at el, 2009). I used this as a roadmap for deeper analysis. The interviews and protocols form a discourse between me and my participants regarding their lived experience. This discourse stage of the hermeneutic arc has followed the three layers; descriptive, interpretive, and critical. The three layers are used for rich description of my participants' lived experience. Then, I distanciate from the world of discourse to the world of text where everything is in written form. The world of texts has two forms; texts from multilayered interviews and texts from protocol writings. While coding the texts by following the close-read approach to construct relevant themes, I used another three layers to get the actual essence of the texts; explanation, naïve understanding, and in-depth understanding (Tan at el, 2009).

In the first layer, I examined the texts to get answers of *what, where, when, who* questions, which helped me to understand from a descriptive perspective. This has been precisely supported by the descriptive layer of interview and protocol. Similarly, in the naïve understanding, I reflectively analysed texts, which helped me to examine the texts through my embeddedness and reflexivity. This layer raised my awareness of my position as a researcher of lived experience. It helped me to answer *how* questions by using an interpretive layer of interview and protocol, which helped me to separate myself from the unfamiliar phenomenon too. In the third layer, in-depth understanding, I examined the texts from a critical perspective to get answers to *why* questions as I had used in the critical layer of interview and protocol. In this layer of in-depth understanding, I explored the internal nature of the texts (Ricoeur, 1981) such as why the texts say what they say.

In the internal world of texts I used critical reflexivity to explore different codes and enter the world of interpreter (that is, my world in my research). In the world of the interpreter, I developed relevant themes for in-depth interpretation of my participants' lived experiences by finding the meanings of time, space, body, and mind in a particular phenomenon. Along with my critical reflexivity, these processes of text interpretation supported me in constructing the new meaning of the world of discourse (Tan at el, 2009), where initially I engaged with multilayered interviews and protocol writings. I used the hermeneutic arc (the new meaning of the world of discourse) to examine the ultimate horizon of my participants' lived experience where I reviewed relevant literature and reflectively examined my experience by aligning into the descriptive, interpretive, and critical layer of interviews and protocol writing.

The stages and processes I followed while interpreting texts in my research, constructed my new world (that is, the new world of interpreter) where I could interpret the lived experience through metaphorical analogy by using hybrid texts. Throughout the text interpretation, I deploy metaphorical and creative writing (see example to follow later). The use of metaphorical language in text interpretation can take us towards the original region where language speaks through silence (van Manen, 1990: 49). A researcher as ethical researcher is tacitly compared with many other notions to create a metaphorical analogy. I used the metaphorical language to creatively describe the phenomenon of my participants' lived experience.

The account of lived experience is incomplete if it contains only descriptive text; it must contain interpretive dimensions too to explore the essence of a person's lived experience (Frechette et al, 2020). To meet the rigorous analytical standards of textual interpretation and extract meaning from those texts, I considered the notions of organisation, strength, richness, depth, analytical rigour, persuasive account, and participants' feedback (van Manen, 1990; Langdridge, 2007).

Here is an example of the metaphorical analogy by creating a hybrid text of the statement – 'Being a Tamang ethnic, I was motivated to research on Tamang people's experience on learning Nepali language' – said by one of my participants in critical layer's interview:

Sita Tamang is looking outside and observing the environment and thinking that it is really cold. After a few seconds, she turns her consciousness to the dimly lit room, where she is sitting in a chair in front of her laptop. Nearby the heater is warming up the air inside the room. Suddenly, she reaches out to her laptop and starts viewing Facebook. She scrolls down quickly and stops when she sees posts of 'people you may know'. She clicks to open the profile page of a person named Ram Tamang because she loves to view profiles of those who belong to her ethnicity. While looking at Ram's profile, she found that he, too, is inside a dimly lit room just like herself. She starts to think of her life inside the room and wonders about his experience of living in a room similar to her. After looking at his profile, she starts to think that there might be many more people who belong to her ethnicity and is living in dimly lit rooms and they might have different experiences from her while living in dimly lit rooms. She further thinks to explore others' experiences through empirical research.

Dual positionality: nature of text

The results of human science research may vary due to the researcher's position. In the research process, the researcher's relation to the issue being studied has decisive power to produce varying results. The human science researcher has a dual insider and outsider positionality from the perspective of his/her status within and across cultures (Merriam et al, 2001). In qualitative research, the researcher's dual positionalities may appear as per the research issue and context. It can appear in any stage of the research process, depending on how a researcher differs in his/her perspective based on his/her relationship with the research issue. The process of knowledge generation through qualitative research is increasingly influenced by the researcher's 'insider' or 'outsider' identity (Keikelame, 2018). An insider in their own research process, the researcher can reflect and draw parallels to his/her identity, experiential learning and meaning while the participants get space to narrate their own experiences. Multilayered interviews carry the practical notion of reflexivity where a researcher gets embedded into the lived world of her/his participants. However, in my research dual positionalities are formed in the lived experience materials based on the methods: multilayered interviews and protocol writing.

In my research, the texts from multilayered interviews have consisted of my reflexive engagement along with my participants throughout the process, whereas the texts from protocol writings have not. While generating the texts from multilayered interviews I asked probing questions of my participants, constructed through my own experience and reflective knowledge. Thus, on one hand I consciously engaged with my participants to generate the texts of their lived experience. On the other hand, the process of protocol writing is different from the multilayered interviews, where the participants individually and independently narrated their experience without any probing questions from me. Furthermore, they have freedom to ask and reflect themselves in protocol writing more than in interviews. Thus, both methodologically and epistemologically, generating text through multilayered interviews is a communal process whereas gathering text through protocol writings is individual. Thus, it has produced two types of texts for me: being and belonging. 'Being' relates to the communal process of generating text through multilayered interviews, while 'belonging' relates to the individual process of gathering text through protocol writing. Besides, knowingly and unknowingly I have introduced my position during the process of the multilayered interview which could be reflected in transcribed texts, but in the case of protocol writing, I got space to create my position after reading the entire protocol by following a close-reading approach. This allows me to understand the internal nature of texts through critical reflection and experience.

I found the dual nature of texts in my research challenging up to the stage of the internal world of text while following the hermeneutic arc. Positionality, being a researcher, was quite easy to accommodate in the stages that concern my internal world, but the next parts of the hermeneutic arc require more effort because of dual positionality in texts. However, it has not been a problem while entering into the world of interpreter (that is, my world) because, in this stage, I reflected critically on my experience, coded the texts through the close-reading approach, then constructed relevant themes for further interpretation. Throughout my research, I followed the hermeneutic arc constructively, which I found an insightful roadmap to interpret texts for hermeneutic phenomenological research. Further, it has supported me to overcome the dual positionality created by the texts from multilayered interviews and protocol writings. The close-read approach and then coding the texts together to construct relevant themes made it possible to overcome this challenge. As stated by Dwyer and Buckle (2009), I, being a human science researcher, appreciated the 'fluidity and multilayered complexity of human experience' (p 60) during my research. The dialectical approach of analysing human experience (Fay, 1996) reasonably interprets texts to construct the new world of interpreters.

Being ethical in research

A human science researcher should be able to analyse the research context and apply strategies for ethical research. Interpreting others' lived experience with connecting own critical reflexivity is crucial to mitigate ethical challenges throughout the research. In close consideration, the research method and ethical issues are separate but a researcher cannot deny their overlapping nature (Kara, 2018). In researching lived experience, being ethical means being responsible in exploring others' lived worlds interpretively without imposing any decisive roles. Generally, in phenomenological research, the researchers do not present a 'conclusive argument or with a determinant set of ideas, essences and insights through the research' (van Menan, 1990: 238). By paying close attention to the research methods, research context, participants' worlds, and researcher's world (that is, my world) and keeping them together, I have considered ethical competencies as suggested by James and Busher (2006), Kara (2018), Ess and Hard af Segerstad (2019), and Dahal (2020) throughout the research. However, ethics in research is a 'set of personal principles for interpersonal action and interpersonal conduct' (Saldaña, 2015: 80) and each of my participants has different experiences of being ethical in their research.

From the very beginning of my research, I have explored ideas for continuing to research in the period of social distancing. Thus, it is unethical for me to claim that there were no ethical issues in my research. Every step that I followed in my research, challenged me from an ethical point of view. Due to COVID-19 pandemic and lockdown, initially, I considered whether to use the pre-planned methodology or move to another methodology. It was also challenging for me to shift the interviews from face-to-face to online because I did not have experience of online research and its ethical concerns and considerations. I managed such dilemmas by reviewing the current practices of the online interview as well as online research and its ethical strategies (for example, Lobe et al, 2020). Ethically, the world of discourse has not been problematic for me but while being in the world of texts, it appeared as dual positionality. However, it has gradually resolved by following the three-layered approaches to understanding the texts: exploration, naïve understanding, and in-depth understanding. A layered approach also supported me in exploring the internal world of the texts and moving towards the world of interpreter (that is, my world) by creating reflective space.

Most repeatedly, I have faced ethical challenges to enter into the world of the interpreter. My participants were from a different culture and most of them have done their research within the same culture; for example, their process of knowledge construction and social transformation. Thus, their research is culturally more embodied and sensitive. Myself being an interpretive researcher, some of the phenomena were unfamiliar and unknown for me even though my research was more aligned to the methodological exploration. This created an enduring tension between emic and etic understandings in research while interpreting texts of my participants' lived experience. The ethical inconsistencies across layers of interpretation raise the question of cultural limitations. I have tried to mitigate that by giving special consideration to cultural sensitivity and context specific ethical challenges (Dahal, 2020) as an ethical consideration. Thus, cultural sensitivity has been considered throughout my research by taking cultural account of each research participant. Further, as suggested by Hammersley and Goldsmiths (2012), I have considered some basic principles of research ethics throughout my research such as: avoid social and emotional harm by making all participants aware about the issue and purpose of the research; respect their autonomy; protect all matters related to privacy; offer reciprocity because the participants do realise the importance of such explorations being a researcher; treat people equitably throughout the research especially while interpreting texts; explore the intrinsic notion of texts by applying the close-reading-based approach and hermeneutic arc, and thereby try to do justice to the voices of participants.

References

Bintz, W. and Ciecierski, L. (2017) 'Hybrid text: an engaging genre to teach content area material across the curriculum', *The Reading Teacher*, 71(1): 61–9.

Dahal, B. (2020) 'Research ethics: a perspective of South Asian context', *Edukacja*, 152(1): 9–20. doi: 10.24131/3724.200101

Dwyer, S. and Buckle, J. (2009) 'The space between: on being an insider-outsider in qualitative research', *International Journal of Qualitative Methods*, 8(1): 54–63.

Ess, C. and Hard af Segerstad, Y. (2019) 'Everything old is new again: the ethics of digital inquiry and its design', in A. Makitalo, T. Nicewonger, and M. Elam (eds) *Designs for Experimentation and Inquiry: Approaching Learning and Knowing in Digital Transformation*, New York: Routledge, pp 179–96.

Estrada, C. (2018) 'Be-ing with dying: a researcher's use of phenomenological writing protocols', *The End of Life Experience: Dying, Death, and Culture in the 21st Century* (1st Global Conference), Lisbon.

Farrell, E. (2020) 'Researching lived experience in education: misunderstood or missed opportunity?', *International Journal of Qualitative Methods*, 19:1–8.

Fay, B. (1996) *Contemporary Philosophy of Social Science: A Multicultural Approach*, Cambridge: Blackwell.

Finlay, L. (2012) '"Writing the pain": engaging first-person phenomenological accounts', *Indo-Pacific Journal of Phenomenology*, 12: 1–9.

Frechette, J., Bitzas, V., Aubry, M., Kilpatrick, K., and Tremblay, M. (2020) 'Capturing lived experience: methodological considerations for interpretive phenomenological inquiry', *International Journal of Qualitative Methods*, 19: 1–12.

Gadamer, H. (2004) *Truth and Method*, London: Continuum.

Guillemin, M. and Gillam, L. (2004) 'Ethics, reflexivity, and "ethically important moments" in research', *Qualitative Inquiry*, 10(2): 261–80.

Hammersley, M. and Goldsmiths, A. (2012) *Ethics and Educational Research*, London: British Educational Research Association.

James, N. and Busher, H. (2006) 'Credibility, authenticity and voice: dilemmas in online interviewing', *Qualitative Research*, 6(3): 403–20.

Kafle, N. (2011) 'Hermeneutic phenomenological research method simplified', *Bodhi: An Interdisciplinary Journal*, 5: 181–200.

Kara, H. (2018) *Research Ethics in the Real World*, Bristol: Policy Press.

Keikelame, M. (2018) 'The tortoise under the couch: an African woman's reflections on negotiating insider–outsider positionalities and issues of serendipity on conducting a qualitative research project in Cape Town, South Africa', *International Journal of Social Research Methodology*, 21(2): 219–30.

Langdridge, D. (2007) *Phenomenological Psychology: Theory, Research and Methods*, Harlow: Pearson.

Lauterbach, A. (2018) 'Hermeneutic phenomenological interviewing: going beyond semi-structured formats to help participants revisit experience', *The Qualitative Report*, 23(11): 2883–98.

Lobe, B., Morgan, D., and Hoffman, K. (2020) 'Qualitative data collection in an era of social distancing', *International Journal of Qualitative Methods*, 19: 1–8.

Merriam, S., Bailey, J., Lee, M., Kee, Y., Ntseane, G., and Muhamad, M. (2001) 'Power and positionality: negotiating insider/outsider status within and across cultures', *International Journal of Lifelong Education*, 20(5): 405–10.

Ricoeur, P. (1981) *Hermeneutics and the Human Sciences*, New York: Cambridge University Press.

Saldaña, J. (2015) *Thinking Qualitatively: Methods of Mind*, London: Sage.

Seidman, I. (1998) *Interviewing as Qualitative Research: A Guide for Researchers in Education and the Social Sciences*, NY: Teachers College Press.

Tan, H., Wilson, A., and Oliver, I. (2009) 'Ricoeur's theory of interpretation: an instrument for data interpretation in hermeneutic phenomenology', *International Journal of Qualitative Methods*, 8(4):1–15.

Vandermause, R. and Fleming, S. (2011) 'Philosophical hermeneutic interviewing', *International Journal of Qualitative Methods*, 10(4): 367–77.

van Manen, M. (1990) *Researching Lived Experience: Human Science for an Action Sensitive Pedagogy*, London: State University of New York Press.

Wang, C., Horby, P., Hayden, F., and Gao, G. (2020) 'A novel coronavirus outbreak of global health concern', *The Lancet*, 395(10223): 470–3, available from: https://doi.org/10.1016/s0140-6736(20)30185-9

PART II

Arts-based approaches

4

The arts of making-sense in uncertain times: arts-based research and autoethnography

Deborah Green, Amanda Levey, Bettina Evans,
Wendy Lawson, and Kathrin Marks

The creative arts therapies offer experiences of psychotherapy that are poly-sensory, paradoxical, performative, and provocative. This variegated practice is, however, often researched using rigid and reductive processes – causing we arts therapists-researcher-educators at Whitecliffe College (Aotearoa New Zealand) to itch for less dissonance between *what* we research and *how* we research it, and greater congruence between skill-sets practised in both research and therapy. We thus embarked upon diverse adventures with self-as-subject and creative research, which we now entangle under the investigational umbrella-term *abr+a* (arts-based research through autoethnography) (Green et al, 2018). Fuelled by belief that arts therapists enhance both self and profession using these performative research approaches, *abr+a* now influences research taught and practised by faculty and students in the Whitecliffe School of Creative Arts Therapies.

McNiff's (1998: 170) exhortation to arts therapists that 'the process of research should correspond as closely as possible to the experience of therapy' informs this choice to blend arts-based research (ABR) and autoethnography (Holman Jones, Adams, and Ellis, 2015; Leavy, 2018). Simultaneously a practice, process, and product, ABR is an 'aesthetic way of knowing' (Greenwood, 2012): the researcher investigates a research question through artistic creating during data gathering/generation and/or analysis/translation and/or presentation. Autoethnography studies 'the culture of self' (Ricci, 2003) or others through self, encouraging 'researchers to start with their own lived experiences as a way of uncovering new ways of knowing and understanding wider cultural beliefs' (Gray, 2011: 67).

When COVID-19 began affecting our personal, professional, and educational worlds, we turned to *abr+a* to help us express, explore, and endure these uncertainties. In this chapter, we demonstrate how in April 2020, during our first major lockdown in Aotearoa, we used *abr+a* to craft and share metaphors for the pandemic. During this initial iteration, we lecturers gifted our nascent metaphors for the pandemic to our Master of Arts in Arts Therapy (MAAT) students. This cohort in turn used *abr+a* to birth, explore, and share their own generative metaphors. The indirect functioning of metaphors makes them particularly useful during crises – and here they allowed us to retain our necessary psychological defences while affording us the opportunity to engage curiously, and often playfully, with the difficult arrival of this pandemic in our world.

How to video myself? I set up the iPad on a tripod facing into a mirror, the layered effects of seeing myself mirrored and reflected deepened the experience. I played the recorded spoken script and improvised the movement of the dybbuk/virus.

When a stranger comes to town: Amanda Levey

October 2020: I've just re-viewed the video I made when invited to find a metaphor in response to the first impacts of COVID-19 in Aotearoa and the wider world. When the invitation arrived, I knew this was an opportunity to use the *abr+a* research process to make sense of my multitude of feelings and non-feelings about this novel situation in our lifetime. Like many, I was spending a lot of time 'doomscrolling' – giving over to fascination about the virus and its effects. The invitation to research prompted me to save the most pertinent quotes that caught my attention online and these came to form the bulk of the 'voice-over' script for the two-minute video I made. The voice-over tapped into my knowing that, when immersed in movement, I often find it difficult to connect with the part of me that can speak. I've therefore started experimenting with recording my voice, and playing this while moving. The script expressed a metaphor that had leapt immediately to mind: the myth of 'the stranger comes to town'. My scripted voice intones:

> All great literature is one of two stories; a man goes on a journey or a stranger comes to town ... I've always been interested that arts therapy paid a great deal of attention to the first story – the hero's journey, but not to the stranger who comes to town. Traditionally it begins when the wanderer's shadow first darkens the doorway.

As a teenager I became fascinated by the *dybbuk*, a Jewish mythological being. The name comes from a Hebrew word meaning to adhere or cling, and the dybbuk is thought of as a malicious possessing spirit. The idea formed that I needed to embody the virus as this scary strange spirit invading our reality.

As online work-demands pulled my attention, I was short of time and this needed to be done with little planning or preparation. I costumed myself in black with everything covered, just face, toes, and fingers poking out. I donned an old black cloak and made a headdress from dried poppy-seeds from the garden, forming a corona-like crown. I also found myself clutching bunches of these pods in my fists … they made a satisfying rattle when shaken.

It's little more than a packet of genetic material surrounded by a spiky protein shell one-thousandth the width of an eyelash and leads such a zombie-like existence (Kaplan, Wan, and Achenbach, 2020).

Figure 4.1: Levey, A. (2020) Dybbuk/virus [video-photograph]

Viruses today are thought of as being in a grey area between living and nonliving: they cannot replicate on their own but can do so in living cells and can also affect the behaviour of their hosts profoundly (Villarreal, 2008).

The most surprising thing happened – my body in motion discovered the dybbuk/virus was indeed sneaky and malicious, but also cheeky and playful.

There's a certain evil genius to how this coronavirus pathogen works: it finds easy purchase in humans without them knowing. Before its first host even develops symptoms, it's already spreading its replicas everywhere, moving on to its next victim. It's powerfully deadly in some, but mild enough in others to escape containment. Thus, it's sneaky enough to wreak worldwide havoc (Kaplan, Wan, and Achenbach, 2020).

I had huge fun filming myself, and a profound sense that the work couldn't be improved. When I viewed the footage, it was exactly right, even though this was the first take. This was a true experience of 'flow' (Csikszentmihalyi, 1990) and viewing the piece gave me immense satisfaction. I recognised the many layers of my history of making video as artwork and research: iterations of character, costuming, movement patterns, video techniques, and interaction with my multiplicity of selfhood. The research process reconnected me with the richness of my movement therapy training, my research relationships with dear colleagues, this powerful tool of creativity and arts-based knowing, that could help me to respond to a crisis with playfulness and humour, and to make a creative product I was fully satisfied with and by. By befriending the virus, I could see it in a new light ... not as something to be feared, but a part of the fabric of living beings.

The fabric of *abr+a*

Our COVID-metaphors use a 'show and tell' approach to 'surround' rather than 'solve' this focal area (Sullivan, 2006; Vaughan, 2009). By curating our explorations, we enhance and challenge each other's meanings, acknowledging that – akin to crises – these research approaches do not yield definite single answers but, through assemblages of ideas and images, may suggest possibilities for further engagement. In this way *abr+a* embraces creative knowing, championing notions that human experience of the world, particularly in tumultuous times, cannot and should not be reduced to words and numbers alone (O'Connor and Anderson, 2015). Rather, both *abr+a* and arts therapy embrace poietic creativity. Both involve considered use of visual, performing, and/or literary artistic practices to generate, analyse, and communicate knowing/knowledge. Both stimulate 'flow-state', an optimal engagement that activates explicit and implicit/tacit information systems to process and integrate stimuli (Csikszentmihalyi, 1990). Both arts therapy and autoethnography invite intimate self-reflexivity allowing clients, clinicians, and researchers to know themselves in more meaningful ways (Gray, 2011).

In addition, *abr+a* encourages the repurposing of arts therapeutic processes into research methods (McNiff, 2013). This might equip researchers to explore distressing material in ways that may be safer, more ethical, and less triggering/traumatic than more traditional approaches. *Abr+a* thereby potentially gifts new creative research approaches to the broader research world.

The broader world

Crises (and it truly feels that our current epoch is characterised by crises – political, humanitarian, climactic, viral ...) remove us from the known, opening transitional-liminal spaces. We are called to make-it-up-as-we-go, to engage in living inquiry, in practice-led cycles of innovative action–reflexion–action. This is reflected in the emergence of a new paradigm called the 'third methodological distinction' by Haseman (2006) and the 'performative turn' by Lincoln and Denzin (2003). Riding this 'performative paradigm' (Haseman, 2006), *abr+a* disrupts what has 'become monolithic and stifling' (Adams St. Pierre, 2014: 3) within the binary of the 'approved' quantitative and qualitative paradigms. Using creative means, *abr+a* researchers reflexively explore self/other/world through postmodern/metamodern (Vermeulen and van den Akker, 2010) lenses that view truth and reality as local, shifting/oscillating, and co-constructed. New artistic forms are created to implement experiential practice-led research, ultimately understood 'in terms of the performative force of art … its capacity to effect "movement" in thought, word and deed in the individual and social sensorium' (Bolt, 2016: 130). Performative research recognises research acts are generative – they do not simply dis/un/cover what is already there, they create and/or transform both the researcher and researched (Green, 2018).

The flux of generative knowing

As *abr+a* lives within an epistemology somewhat foreign to more established research paradigms, therapist-researchers must reimagine how 'knowing' is construed and performed. This feels particularly pertinent to research enacted within the murky mutability of crises. When we live into our creative knowing, *abr+a*'s performative epistemology alchemises what is researchable, how we may research this, and what intentions and outcomes we evoke. *Abr+a* embraces knowing as an active, dynamic, and ongoing practice best expressed/explored via the multiplicity of metaphor that facilitates encounters with the 'ever-open edge' (Gendlin, 1997) of the human psyche embroiled in tumultuous times. Each researcher is thus

---

Enduring liminality: Deborah Green

I momentarily escape lockdown and the breathless seclusion of my studio, the flat pixellated cyclops-eye of my computer screen, the anxious weight of waiting. I stand on the hill above my home with my arms flung wide to the wind. The autumn sun is hot and heavy. The Bay below surges. I cast my imagination into the sky. An imaginal kite is born. The kite calls forth a story …

It's all about the string, she cries, as I, unravelling the kite, lift a spit-dampened finger to the wind. The wind comes and goes, it changes direction, it dances and dies, she says, and beneath us the ocean roils, unfathomable and unpredictable, under wild skies. But between them, between us rocking in this flimsy coracle and the kite high in the sky, is the string!

Figure 4.2: Green, D. (2020) Enduring liminality [digital collage]

The string, she says again, with a catch in her voice. It links the two. A small thin thread, a small thin vital thread. Hold it gently but firmly, for it's in your hands, she says.

But my hands sweat, I say.

You have two hands, says my dead mother, I gave you two hands so you can dry one while you hold on with the other.

As we humans ride the feckless waves of climate change and bonkers politicians and the pandemic, I revisit my guiding kite-string metaphor of 'enduring liminality' that helped me navigate living and practising therapy throughout the Christchurch earthquakes (2010–12). Anthropologist Turner (1969), studying African tribal ceremonies, identified three stages that constitute ritual. The *separation phase* removes initiates from everyday society. The *liminal phase* involves mystical processes to facilitate transformation. In the *reintegration phase* the transformed initiates rejoin society. The middle betwixt-and-between/liminal stage is a fertile metaphor for crises. Liminality dismantles social structures and hierarchies, boundaries between worlds and individuals become porous – all becomes mutable. Viewing crises through the lens of liminality illuminates core experiences of precarious suspension-in-limbo between a previous normal and something yet to emerge – all paradoxically juxtaposed with heightened feelings of community and tingling frissons of new possibilities. In such contexts, my focus as arts therapist-researcher-educator moves from working towards re/integration – (when will there be a new-normal where we may dock?) – towards creating flexibility/knowing that helps myself/clients/students keep afloat and navigate this liminal uncertainty.

> And so, perched on my wind-swept hill, I imagine softening my knees to ride the wild liminal flux, guided aloft by my dead mother's soft voice and a dancing kite. My heart lifts, my hands sweat a little less as I hold fast to the delicate kite-string and tilt my face to the kiss of the sun.

---

encouraged to purposefully dialogue with their own epistemology again and again as they plan/propose, implement/enact, and distil/interpret/curate their research endeavours.

Such 'ever-openness' to ongoing dialogue troubles epistemologies hinged upon the notion that 'truth' is out there to be found and knowledge is an outcome, a commodity to be mastered. While knowledge in this form may play a role, arts therapy – and crises – call for hospitality to not-knowing rather than imposition of facts. Knowing within *abr+a* thus privileges ambiguity and multiplicity. This isn't, however, a simple rejection of knowledge. *Abr+a* holds open curiosity about truths that seem absolute and essential. Attentive to uniquely individualised knowing as well as normative knowledge, it oscillates between obscurity/messiness/entanglement and clarity/crispness/certainty. This feature feels particularly pertinent in the face of a global pandemic. The capacity to respond appropriately to such challenges requires that we embrace a contiguous relationship between qualitative and performative research knowings – that seek to understand the contingent fluidity of human emotion – with scientific factual knowledge necessary to reduce transmission and treat the ill. This relationality takes many forms. Levey's interlacing of factual statements about the virus with her embodiment of the stranger/dybbuk/virus offers an example of how such a juxtaposition may begin the process of deepening understandings and responsivity while Evans' account demonstrates her need to pull away from obsessive fact-checking and immerse herself in nature.

Metaphor and complexity

Wrangles with such oscillating multiplicity are best served by metaphors and symbols, prominent features within creative arts therapy and arts–based research. Humans' symbol-making propensity suggests projection of the unconscious into created arts–objects and 'we can gain insight by studying the symbolic and metaphoric messages. Our art speaks back to us if we take the time to listen to those images' (Rogers, 1999: 115). Metaphors may convey and link basic elements of our nature; allow us to entertain new possibilities; enable exploration of the unconscious; give jumbled thoughts form and direction; create a mask for feelings too frightening or painful to acknowledge; offer intimate communication; bridge internal and external worlds; and extend into past and future (Gorelick, 1996 cited in Ellis, 2001). Metaphor-making helps bring understanding about one situation into the domain of another, allowing imaginative intelligence to travel between realms of experience, thereby generating personal understanding through non–confrontational means (Moon, 2007). As metaphors function indirectly, they are especially useful during crises, allowing participants to keep as–is

---

Be(ad)ing in nature: Bettina Evans

I spent the days leading up to the virus-related lockdown checking my phone obsessively for information about COVID-19, even though I became more agitated with every click. I remember vividly the physical reluctance when leaving my phone to go for a walk. I lay down on the overgrown hillside, where the swaying grasses, humming bees, and scudding clouds assured me that all but human life was continuing as usual – I was reminded, like many times before, that I'm not the centre of the universe.

I accepted this invitation to stay connected to all that thrived regardless of COVID. These daily walks inspired glass beadworks, which became my way of giving thanks to the life-giving natural environment around me. At night on the sofa I remembered the shimmering turquoise of the harbour water or the sun-bleached gold of the grasses, looking through my beads to find ones to complement or accompany nature's expressions. When I'd finished a piece I returned to the place that inspired it, carrying my offering as an invitation for a conversation. I experienced this as a mutual partnership – nature offered me sensual and sensory pleasures and impressions, I responded with colour and shape and a deepened appreciation of its wonders.

I'd never used beads for stringing and stitching before, but exploring an art material I was unfamiliar with matched the strangeness of this unprecedented time. The repetitive process of sorting and sewing beads was calming and helped me stay anchored. The virus-laden world was too overwhelming for me to deal with, but the individual bead-pixels were a safe and containing material to work with.

I stitched beads on a lemon and apricot leaf in my garden, I arranged rainbow-hued beads in an empty brown sunflower seed-husk, I draped bead-strings over oak branches, tree stumps, and grasses.

It was very satisfying to control the creation of my beadwork at home, but once outside I had to become more flexible and lean into poietic surrender. I'd imagined my bead-strings fringing a small sea-cave entrance, but high tide made this impossible, so I let the waves

Figure 4.3: Evans, B. (2020) Beaded-leaf [beads and leaf]

swish the beads through the beach sand instead. I was looking forward to seeing my bead-strings attached to floating seaweed, but the seaweed sank as soon as I tied the beads onto its swim bladder. I stood knee-deep in water, waves lapping at my shorts, gripping my camera with one hand while trying to untangle the sunken beads with the other. Wading back to the beach I felt alive and completely immersed in the moment. I walked home smiling, with dripping clothes and bead-encrusted seaweed in my pockets. These playful interactions in the natural world were highlights during my lockdown days, the glass beads' simplicity providing a metaphorical balance to the complex world around me.

---

defences in place without affecting their capacity for other psychological and/or research work to be done in the here-and-now.

Lai, Howerton, and D'esai (2019) propose that, within crises, intellectual definitions do not engender a felt connection with what is expressed. Such definitions lack the power of metaphor which, according to Rogers (1999: 126), plunges 'us into the mythical ... and kinaesthetic aspects of the unknown'. As crises tend to crack open an uncertain future, exposing us to emotionally laden transitionality, metaphors can help us make holistic sense of these unusual experiences. If we allow images to animatedly walk about on their own legs (Hillman, 1983) and avoid reducing them into simplistic this-means-that rationalisations, the multiplicit and multivocal meanings evoked by metaphors within arts-based therapy/research help us explore/express complex living experiences. Many therapists advocate listening deeply to the images we create: Jung's (1981) term 'shimmering symbol' suggests metaphoric images are living and dynamic; Levine (2009: 32) quotes Heraclitus' idea that 'being loves to hide' to express how artworks may never be completely understood as something 'will always remain hidden and will demand continued uncovering'; Simon (1997) believes the essence of art as therapy resides in how symbols carry a sense of 'and-and-and', discouraging us from reducing symbols to fixed signs. This prismatic layering encourages a playful touch and wide-open understanding (Burt, 2012) to avoid cramping the images' animation.

Helicopter-up/helicopter-down: Wendy Lawson

Metaphor is the sleeve of my favourite coat, it's the reflection of a mountain that folds into a lake, it's the deluge that travels up from the ground to form the tears on my cheek. When working with metaphor, I'm able to detach myself – with all my slippery goo – to be witness, inquirer. I become the curious one. I explore creases and crevices, I perch,

I crane my neck, I become small or big, I'm beside and inside, it is me but not me, I am it, it is thing, and things are important – in the moment or moments. Metaphor nods in agreement with me, it allows me to stomp on its face, to give birth to its monster, and to cradle it in my arms. Metaphor is the language in which I am most fluent.

Figure 4.4: Lawson, W. (2020) Helicopter-up/helicopter-down [iMovie-stills]

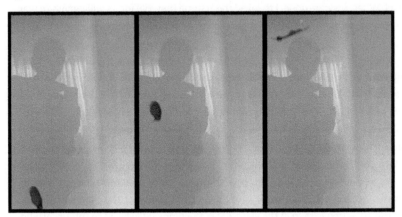

Before it was so-called helicopter, it was object. I held the object, and the object held me; a single winged sycamore seed located on the bend of a Lyttleton stairway, circa March 2019. The seed found its way into my pocket and travelled home with me to Auckland to reside in my box of precious things. This box, and the seed within the box, journeyed with me into communities near and far, where the people 'oooh-ed' and 'ah-ed' at its extraordinary shape, its paper-thin wing with weighted end, its skeleton surface with thumbprint impression, and most of all they swooned over its ability to fly! In their hands nostalgic stories were revealed, childhood antics shared, pursuits and pleasures cascaded from the fingertips of each weary yet courageous pilot. As we played with this object, we too were flying.

In early April 2020, during New Zealand's COVID-19 Alert Level 4 lockdown, I was invited to share a metaphor for this time of crisis. In a moment of searching, the sycamore seed with its avian qualities, imbued with love from its many handlings and playful encounters, became a wilful actor in my metaphor story. I think it was hope that called to me from the depths of the box of precious things that willed this sluggish human-body into action, to become the foster-tree to release this seed into the air; to float, soar, spin, to manifest a sense of aliveness within this thick, thick air.

To document this animation, I took on dual roles. I was witness; capturing the seed's spiralling descent on my camera phone, which required of me a physical state of stillness, presence, and focus. And I was activator of the seed. While recording the footage; there was pause and poise as my hand became a crane manoeuvring this precious cargo. There was blood flow in the effort of throwing the seed into the air, causing circulation in my body. Alongside, there was also anxious-waiting as I willed the seed to fly. Sometimes it would spin. Other times it would simply drop as it did when my hand gripped too tightly. This mirrored my anxiety and physical tension in the face of COVID-19. With time and repetition, I learned to relax my body to ignite the flight, combining movement with breath-work, the action of lifting with inhaling; letting go with exhaling; release leading to relief. When we were done, I thanked this natural material for its willingness to play and improvise with me and placed it back in the box of precious things.

Later, I brought the captured moments from my camera phone together via iMovie. Manipulating the raw footage, I slowed the frames down to amplify my warped association with time and space. This sense of slowing-down also acknowledged my feeling of anticipation, of watching and waiting for information, instruction on what to do next. As if ensnared in a technological whirlwind, I made the sycamore seed go down and up, disappear, re-emerge, in a continuous erratic way. It was like navigating a remote-control helicopter in the hands of a child. And when I'd finally fallen in synch with this new-dizzy, I sent the helicopter slowly upwards. It didn't come down again. I provided no audible soundtrack. There's only the sound of the beholder. All the while, my reflection is seen in the glass-door; an unmoving witness to this unsettling, unpredictable pattern of awkwardly tumbling knowns and unknowns.

At a time when the world was saying 'stay in!', this project enabled me to connect with nature and my body, to engage in playfulness, and to allow a feeling of composure to emerge in response to the threat of contagion. Through this lens-based medium I was able to create my own story and then share it with the outside world. As I knew no end, just a beginning and perhaps a middle, I was done. I walked away while the helicopter was – up.

Animated imagery

This being-that-hides within the symbology of images hosts sensations and notions that spill beyond words. Current trauma theory proposes extreme experiences, such as provoked during crises, lodge within us in ways that may only be accessed and expressed via embodied, sensory, and symbolic processes (Kass and Trantham, 2014; van der Kolk, 2014). Arts therapy and *abr+a* use such processes to deeply indwell with imagery – alive in the belief that creative expression speaks from different/deeper places than can be reached through cognitive processes alone (Hillman, 1983).

The Stag: Kathrin Marks

I'm sitting here, in this safe-haven that Aotearoa New Zealand has become as the COVID-19 pandemic rages globally. This year rattled my tertiary-teacher-self deeply and as the lockdown invited us to shelter in place, I found myself thrown into a flurry of emails and Zoom sessions, adapting part of the arts therapy curriculum to online delivery alongside my colleagues. My Stag metaphor arrived in the midst of this turmoil as I engaged with arts-making, yearning for some sort of sense (of order).

I find myself looking at him, the Stag, fatally wounded by a gunshot.

He is dying slowly, the blood trickling out from him, his life-source seeping into the ground.

Over the next couple weeks, I found myself following the Stag. Sense (of order) didn't arrive. The Stag's death felt ever-present in my creative space, permeating the air I breathed, infiltrating my thoughts. I felt unfocused, fragile, anxious. And still ...

... I stay with the Stag, cradle and soothe him with my hot tears.

He tells me he is ready. He embraces his life and his death, surrendering into the cycle.

Eventually, it is time to leave the Stag.

I gently stroke his now-stiff body, kiss his soft fur, try to find words of good-bye, but none come.

There are no words. None that matter anyway.

Bracing myself against/for the weeks and months to come ...

... I feel the weight of responsibility pushing down on me.

I have work to do.

I can't let my students down. Can't let my team down.

I can't feel. Not now.

It is then that the Stag finds me again.

His soft fur, playfully cheekily covering my pants, my jacket.

He stays with me as I stayed with him, inviting me to breathe into the turmoil.

Into my grief.

Amid the holding of both my responsibilities and my grief, I continued my art-making, following the Stag and being with the process as it unfolded. The Stag watched as I created. I made ...

... a mess. So much paint on my hands.

'Wash your hands.' 'Be careful.'

'Don't spread it anywhere.' 'Wash your hands.'

Sponge and brush. Squash and spread.

A game of luck. A game of strategy.

Tic-Tac-Toe. Noughts and crosses. Tic-Tac-Toe.

You will live, and you will die.

The arrival of COVID-19 had turned the/my world upside down, shaking it to the core. It shook me into realising that the pandemic was merely highlighting that uncertainty and unpredictability have always been the fabric that weaves our life. What I needed was art, was a metaphor to hold. And in this autoethnographic arts-based process ...

... I journeyed with the Stag. His arrival confused me and yet, I found myself feeling strangely comforted-haunted by his presence.

And I gently hold the gift he brought me:

To sit. To sit with him. To sit with anxiety and uncertainty and grief. To just sit. The Stag reminded me of the gift it is to bear witness to suffering.

Figure 4.5: Marks, K. (2020) Tic-Tac-Toe Stag [natural materials and thread]

Abr+a – a gift in times of uncertainty and grief

Therapists, therapist-researchers, and educators–of–therapists practising while embroiled in crises appear to face two competing research obligations. We are striving to understand/enhance our own and our students' capacity as clinicians while simultaneously growing new knowing useful to our profession. We believe *abr+a* may provide processes that enable the deep journeying of capacity-cultivating research while also facilitating outcome/ efficacy/evidence-based research contributing to the body of knowledge informing arts therapy.

'Deep journeying' supports our desire for research to provoke less dissonance and breed more reciprocity between skill-sets cultivated through research and therapy. Whitecliffe students and staff applying *abr+a* voice that, by engaging with a plethora of arts therapy-informed/congruent research approaches, they simultaneously produce new knowledge while developing aptitudes that markedly enhance their clinical practice. In drawing upon poietic creativity, both *abr+a* and arts therapy nurture capacity to stay with/ in the uncertainty, not-knowing, complexity, chaos – loosed by times of crisis – without premature closure. This helps meet emergent challenges by cultivating imaginative practitioners and innovative solutions. In stimulating 'flow' (Csikszentmihalyi, 1990), *abr+a* and arts therapy both facilitate optimal engagement that is intrinsically restorative and activates explicit and implicit/tacit information systems to process and integrate stimuli. The intimate self-examination of therapy and autoethnography invites clients and clinicians to deeply know themselves and their unique contexts, cultivating empathy and compassion for self and other. Engaging *abr+a* thus forms part of the practitioner's learning triangle, combining personal experience and academic research to inform future practice and enhance the development of therapist identity (Skovholt, 2012). In addition, *abr+a* encourages repurposing of arts therapy processes into research methods (McNiff, 2013) potentially gifting new creative approaches to the research world and its inhabitants and visitors. Applying such therapeutic activities as research may help hold the stress experienced while implementing research during crises. Plus, to 'overlook the beauty of the soul's speech by turning exclusively to empirical analysis ... is to expel the soul from art therapy' (McConeghey, 2017: 19).

The second 'legitimising' responsibility of our research requires *abr+a* researchers ascend from the purely personal and harvest insights useful to the therapeutic professions. While creative-self-as-subject forms of research such as *abr+a* still jostle for appreciation, recognition is mounting for research that works from insider knowing. Such research disrupts and makes visible taken-for-granted constructs, fosters engagement, and creates intersubjective response. It offers expression to silenced voices and topics, employs the generativity of metaphor to open multiple ways to address emergent problems, and recognises and embraces complexity. Performative research hereby endeavours to render academic knowledge more accessible to non-academics by turning social science inquiry into a non-alienating practice (Bochner, 2015; Holman Jones, Adams, and Ellis, 2015).

To conclude

To conclude, deepen, and legitimise,

I fossick through the creative metaphoric vignettes,

teasing out and synthesising suggestions that,

in tumultuous times,

abr+a offers:

... the gift of bearing witness to suffering,

... the ability to respond with playfulness and humour,

... simplicity to balance the complex world around us, and

... no end, just a beginning and perhaps a middle.

And so, our hands sweat a little less as we hold the delicate kite-string and tilt our faces to the kiss of the sun.

References

Adams St. Pierre, E. (2014) 'A brief and personal history of post qualitative research: toward "post inquiry"', *Journal of Curriculum Theorizing*, 30(2): 2–19.

Bochner, A. (2015) 'Autoethnography's existential calling', in S. Holman Jones, T. Adams, and C. Ellis (eds) *Handbook of Autoethnography*, Walnut Creek: Left Coast Press, pp 50–6.

Bolt, B. (2016) 'Artistic research: a performative paradigm', *Parse Journal*, 3: 129–42.

Burt, H. (2012) 'Multiple perspectives: art therapy, postmodernism and feminism', in H. Burt (ed) *Art Therapy and Postmodernism: Creative Healing through a Prism*, London: Jessica Kingsley, pp 17–31.

Csikszentmihalyi, M. (1990) *Flow: The Psychology of Optimal Experience*, New York: Harper and Row.

Ellis, R. (2001) 'Movement metaphor as mediator: a model for the dance/movement therapy process', *The Arts in Psychotherapy*, 28: 181–90.

Gendlin, E. (1997) *Experiencing and the Creation of Meaning*, Evanston, IL: Northwestern University Press.

Gray, B. (2011) 'Autoethnography and arts therapy: the arts meet healing', *Australia and New Zealand Journal of Arts Therapy*, 6(1): 67–80.

Green, D. (2018) 'Making-sense of poietic presense in arts therapy and education', *Creative Arts in Education and Therapy*, 4(2): 139–48.

Green, D. et al (2018) 'The arts of making sens/e', *Australia and New Zealand Journal of Arts Therapy*, 12(1): 112–30.

Greenwood, J. (2012) 'Arts-based research: weaving magic and meaning', *International Journal of Education & the Arts*, 13(1), available from: http://www.ijea.org/v13i1/

Haseman, B. (2006) 'A manifesto for performative research', *Media International Australia incorporating Culture and Policy, theme issue 'Practice-led Research'*, (118): 98–106.

Hillman, J. (1983) *InterViews: Conversations with Laura Pozzo on Psychology, Biography, Love, Soul, the Gods, Animals, Dreams, Imagination, Work, Cities, and the State of the Culture,* Woodstock, CT: Spring Publications.

Holman Jones, S., Adams, T., and Ellis, C. (2015) *Handbook of Autoethnography*, Walnut Creek: Left Coast Press.

Jung, C. (1981) 'The archetypes and the collective unconscious', in G. Adler and R. Hull (eds) *The Collected Works of C.G. Jung: Volume 9* (2nd edn), Princeton, NJ: Princeton University Press.

Kaplan, S., Wan, W., and Achenbach, J. (2020) 'Coronavirus isn't alive that's why it's so hard to kill', *Washington Post*, [online], available from: https://www.washingtonpost.com/health/2020/03/23/coronavirus-isnt-alive-thats-why-its-so-hard-kill/ ...

Kass, J. and Trantham, S. (2014) 'Perspectives from clinical neuroscience: mindfulness and the therapeutic use of the arts', in L. Rappaport (ed) *Mindfulness and the Arts Therapies: Theory and Practice*, London: Jessica Kingsley, pp 288–315.

Lai, V., Howerton, O., and D'esai, R. (2019) 'How the brain finds meaning in metaphor', *Neuroscience News*, [online], available from: https://neurosciencenews.com/metaphor-meaning-eeg-10979/?fbclid=IwAR0B5XWFvrvQWswPb5ij-0-WsGONjup6HIdmcSJ2P4rdfTordj3ongW_4CE

Leavy, P. (2018) *Handbook of Arts-Based Research*, New York: The Guildford Press.

Levine, S. (2009) *Trauma, Tragedy, Therapy*, London: Jessica Kingsley.

Lincoln, Y. and Denzin, K. (2003) *Turning Points in Qualitative Research: Tying Knots in a Handkerchief*, Walnut Creek: Altamira Press.

McConeghey, H. (2017) *Art and Soul* (2nd edn), Lexington, KY: Spring Publications.

McNiff, S. (1998) *Art Based Research*, Boston, MA: Shambhala Publications.

McNiff, S. (2013) *Art as Research: Opportunities and Challenges*, Chicago, IL: Intellect Publishers.

Moon, B. (2007) *The Role of Metaphor in Art Therapy: Theory, Method, and Experience,* Springfield, IL: Charles C. Thomas.

O'Connor, P. and Anderson, M. (2015) *Applied Theatre: Research: Radical Departures*, Sydney: Bloomsbury.

Ricci, R. (2003) 'Autoethnographic verse: Nicky's boy: a life in two worlds', *The Qualitative Report*, 8(4): 591–6.

Rogers, N. (1999) 'The creative connection: a holistic expressive arts process', in S. Levine and E. Levine (eds) *Foundations of Expressive Arts Therapy Theoretical and Clinical Perspectives*, London: Jessica Kingsley, pp 113–31.

Simon, R. (1997) *Symbolic Images in Art as Therapy*, London: Routledge.

Skovholt, T. (2012) *Becoming a Therapist: On the Road to Mastery*, New Jersey: John Wiley & Sons.

Sullivan, G. (2006) 'Research acts in art practice', *Studies in Art Education*, 48(1): 19–35.

Turner, V. (1969) *The Ritual Process: Structure and Antistructure*, Chicago, IL: Aldine.

van der Kolk, B. (2014) *The Body Keeps the Score: Brain, Mind, and Body in the Healing of Trauma*, New York: Penguin.

Vaughan, K. (2009) 'A home in the arts: from research/creation to practice or the story of a dissertation in the making, in action – so far!', *International Journal of Education & the Arts*, 10(13), available from: http://www.ijea.org/v10n13/

Vermeulen, T. and van den Akker, R. (2010) 'Notes on metamodernism', *Journal of Aesthetics & Culture*, 2, available from: http://aestheticsandculture.net/index.php/jac/article/viewArticle/5677

Villarreal, L. (2008) 'Are viruses alive?', *Scientific American*, [online], available from: https://www.scientificamerican.com/article/are-viruses-alive-2004/

5

Practice-based research in times of crisis: weaving community together during lockdown

Gretchen Stolte and Lisa Oliver

Introduction

The COVID-19 pandemic marked 2020 with a range of challenges for researchers and any projects they had going. For example, material culture research is inherently location-based with many objects accessible via museums and collecting institutions like libraries and galleries or among the creators in communities and studios. With cultural institutions having to close in order to protect staff and the public and community borders shut to protect vulnerable populations, it would be reasonable to think that it would be no longer possible to conduct material culture and collections research. However, by shifting the examination of objects away from museums and towards a more practice-based exploration, material culture research can continue in new and innovative ways. This chapter explores the method of practice-based research in material culture studies during a time of crisis and all the benefits as well as ethical considerations that need to go into its execution. Practice-based research can be an effective method of exploring and learning as long as one understands the necessary cultural and ethical considerations.

For researchers engaging in material culture projects, practice-based research is the act of physically creating works in order to become informed about and educate themselves about the techniques of construction. Crucially, it is not the re-creation of museum objects, nor is it a lens into understanding people's motivations or desires. It is not a wholly phenomenological approach where understanding of an artist's subjective processes is attempted. Instead, practice-based research develops a greater sense of how to appreciate the works found in museums collections through understanding the physical actions involved in creation. The physical skills and Indigenous technologies that exists within each work are connected to researchers in profound ways.

Although this chapter is fundamentally about research practices, it must also acknowledge another aspect of the COVID-19 crisis which this writing addresses. The pandemic adversely affected Indigenous peoples across Australia. Cut off from seeking out community members, fear for Elders vulnerable to the virus and the sudden cessation of normal connections to our families and friends created an environment where many were locked inside their homes. For many Indigenous people living in urban and regional environments, the loss of connection to other people was more than just loneliness. It was a form of isolation that worked its way into the souls of people, allowing no place for the fear of the unknown and the uncertainty of the future to go anywhere but internally. Making connections, reaching out, stepping outside of isolation, and reclaiming some sense of community strength became crucial very quickly for an entire people with a history of institutional neglect and abuse.

The case study presented here is through the generosity and permission of a group of First Nation women[1] who met every Friday – from April 2020 and throughout the process of writing this article – in order to learn about traditional Aboriginal basket weaving in Australia. Permission to consider the workshops for publication was sought first and was given the green light by the members. We all felt that the workshops did a good job demonstrating not only a methodology for learning in a time of crisis but also a vehicle for underscoring the ethics and cultural considerations of working with First Nations material culture. It should be noted that throughout this chapter, First Nations will be used when talking more broadly about Indigenous peoples across the globe, in recognition of their unceded sovereignty and their continued existence. When specifically referring to makers in Australia, the term Aboriginal will be used.[2]

This chapter is written from the perspective of two First Nations researchers and cultural practitioners. As such, it is appropriate to introduce who we are before proceeding. For First Nations peoples, telling about who we are and where we come from is a crucial part about establishing relationships and connections. 'The protocol for introducing one's self to other Indigenous people is to provide information about one's cultural location, so that connections can be made on political, cultural and social grounds and relations established' (Moreton-Robinson, 2020). Additionally, self-reflexivity and self-awareness needs to be part of any academic project (see Herzfeld, 1997; Clifford and Marcus, 2010) but particularly in writing in order to position the voices and views being prioritised in the work. The how of that learning is equally if not more important to what is being learned. The passing of knowledge is part and parcel of both the how and the why. These narratives are an important process of identity sharing, creating connections that translate across space and time. 'Who we are to each other situates us and allows us to know each other as First Nations peoples' (Stolte et al, 2020: 179), and to that end, we introduce ourselves as follows.

Gretchen Stolte is a descendant of the Wallowa Band of the Nimi'ipuu (Nez Perce) tribe and has lived in Australia for over a decade. In the Nimi'ipuu tradition of naming lineages as identifiers of Indigenous identity, her father was Richard Stolte, son of Capella Smith whose mother was Josephine Foley, a Nimi'ipuu woman from the Colville Reservation in eastern Washington. Gretchen's grandmother's grandfather was Chief Ollokot, son of Old Chief Joseph of the traditional lands of the Wallowas in eastern Oregon. Gretchen has degrees in art history and anthropology, focusing on collections research and material culture among Cape York Aboriginal communities, the Torres Strait Islands, and her own cultural heritage from the Plateau Region of the American Northwest. She calls herself a material culture anthropologist.

Lisa Oliver is a proud member of the Gomeroi Nation, north-western New South Wales, Australia. She identifies herself in terms of family names (surnames) and communities. Her father is a Binge, her mother is a McGrady, and she has extended family in the communities of Tamworth, Narrabri, Moree, Boggabilla, and Toomelah. Lisa has a degree in Natural and Cultural Resource Management and is undertaking a PhD exploring the importance of Aboriginal Women's connections.

Both of us have been long-term participants of Gillawarra Arts' Friday weaving sessions and our decision to write this piece stems from a desire to share our experiences in order to highlight important cultural and ethical considerations of practice-based research through online connections. The meetings happened during the self-isolation months the entire world found itself in during the start of the COVID-19 pandemic. The initial conception of these weaving workshops started with Krystal Hurst, Worimi artist and director of Gillawarra Arts. Her desire to share her basket-weaving knowledge and bring together First Nations peoples across Australia created an enthusiastic and safe space for learning and yarning. Yarning is an Australian Aboriginal word for 'talking', an 'Indigenous cultural form of conversation' which involves sharing and exchanging information (Bessarab and Ng'andu, 2010: 37) and implies a deeper sharing of self with others. We were part of the workshops from the very beginning but our participation was never meant to be part of any formulated research project. The opportunity to share the knowledges we learned through the workshops was seen as a way to celebrate the ways in which First Nations peoples connect.

Practice-based research

Practice-based research 'has yet to reach a settled status in terms of its definitions and discourse' (Candy and Edmonds, 2018: 63) and, as such, its methodology is a bit contested (MacDonald et al, 2015; Candy and Edmonds, 2018). Exploring praxis methodologies in addition to practice-based research offers a wider area of inquiry, exploring the act of self-reflexivity upon the act itself. Forms of praxis offer 'the potential for the individual to assess the creative act from outside of the act' (Crouch, 2007: 106). Adopting a reflexive viewpoint allows 'an understanding of the creative process from a subjective viewpoint, revealing the dynamic relationship between the context, construction and the articulation of the act' (Crouch, 2007: 106). The core of practice-based methodology focuses on original research 'undertaken to gain new knowledge, partly by means of practice and the outcomes of that practice' (Candy and Edmonds, 2018: 63) but the critical thinking of the practice is crucial. This is a key difference in definitions between practice-*based* and practice-*led* approaches. Consistently in the literature, the two are defined as follows:

- If a creative artefact is the basis of the contribution to knowledge, the research is practice-based.
- If the research leads primarily to new understandings about practice, it is practice-led (Candy and Edmonds, 2018: 64).

Practice-led research develops practice – musicians become better musicians; potters improve their clay mixes and throwing techniques; instructors improve their methods of education. Whereas curators might explore means of better curating exhibitions and the display of works (practice-led),[3] material culture anthropologists might explore the techniques of artefact construction through the creation of those very artefacts (practice-based). Practice-based research is found across many disciplines including medical practitioners, where the sciences and arts meet (see Roughley et al, 2019) and in fine arts through PhD projects (MacDonald et al, 2015; Candy and Edmonds, 2018). The common thread across these different disciplines and their practice-based approaches is the idea of 'knowing through doing' (MacDonald et al, 2015: 342).

Although much of the focus of practice-based research in the arts is on the process of PhD research, this chapter proposes that this is not just a methodology for postgraduate work. Practice-based research can be part of a larger toolkit for material culture researchers if done with the appropriate cultural protocols and research ethics in mind. Instead, we see practice-based research as developing a greater sense of how to appreciate the works found in museums – the technical skills and the artistic creativity. Most importantly, one can repatriate Indigenous technologies back into the museum database if you can recognise the types of technologies being employed. Recognising the technologies of First Nations peoples is something museums are in a key place to do but not every collections manager or curator can be a proficient maker. The recognition and recording of these technologies are woefully underrepresented in museum databases despite the fact that they are important forms of cultural, environmental, and economic knowledges.

The how of an object's construction illuminates many forms of information that are 'hidden' if not understood. Understanding the techniques of construction can indicate provenance, forms of cultural change *and* exchange, forms of adaptation, the types of Indigenous technologies employed, and approaches to problem solving when considering design and limitations of resources. For example, when Indigenous peoples say our objects are our ancestors, it is both a figurative and literal truth. Making infuses an object with the creator's own body through their sweat (when an object is closely held for long periods), blood (when a finger is pierced with a needle), and hair (because who hasn't woven their hair into a work by accident?). These forms of knowledge are possible through practice-based research. Practice-based researchers and artists can make important contributions to the field of material culture research.

Connecting and exploring in women's groups

Aboriginal women have a long history of gathering for women's business, connecting physically, socially, and spiritually (Walker et al, 2012). There is a sisterhood, a collective solidarity that has supported Aboriginal women's resilience, through which we maintain our cultural identities, strength, and independence (Burgmann, 1982; O'Shane, 1993; Huggins, 1998). Aboriginal women's connections are important in providing a powerful network of female support (Huggins, 1998). These connections also lead to the challenging of historical and contemporary oppressions, which have impacted social, historical, material, and political aspects of Aboriginal women's lives. While there is a diversity of personal experiences, there is a shared positioning among Aboriginal women – they relate to each other's life experiences (Moreton-Robinson and Walter, 2009). An inherent desire to be in the company of each other might be the reason Aboriginal women join in Aboriginal women's groups to connect and satisfy, what Walker et al (2012) term a 'cultural longing' that Aboriginal women have for each other, to be together. There is a sameness, a likeness, and a social environment that allows for trusting relationships to be built (Brough et al, 2006). This has also been described as relationality or relatedness, whereby Aboriginal women are related in some way by 'descent, country, place, or shared experiences' (Moreton-Robinson, 2020: 16; Martin, 2008).

Groups provide environments for us to be relaxed, be ourselves, and take time out from our many commitments. Women's groups can also be a place for women's business to take place. We can connect for women's business and share cultural knowledge in contemporary settings. Such cultural business has several layers of accessibility depending on several factors including if someone is considered part of a cultural group or outside that group. A level of cultural knowledge can be shared with everyone, as opposed to deeper sacred knowledges that are shared only in women's ceremonies. The Gillawarra Arts Weaving Group formed at the peak of the COVID world pandemic. We were mostly strangers to begin with, looking to familiarity and comfort during what was a very scary time. Trust was built slowly; connections were made based on country and kinship. Knowledge is exchanged each Friday night in the Gillawarra Arts Weaving Group – women talk about their individual experiences and worldviews. Women's weaving practice improves, and connections deepen. Weaving is a way that Aboriginal women connect with their ways of being, doing, and knowing. Connecting with Country, their Ancestors, themselves, and their people. Aboriginal women's ways of being (ontology) is derived from our connection to Country and is specific to individual nation/groups. Some of us believe Ancestral beings created the land and all living things (including humans), as well as the moral rules for us to follow (Moreton-Robinson, 2013). Our ways of knowing (epistemology) refers to theory of knowledge, who can be knowledgeable, and what knowledges are valued over others (Martin, 2003; Walter, 2013). Our axiology (ways of being, doing, and knowing) refers to a set of morals and ethics that guide our search for knowledge and determine which knowledge is worthy of searching for (Wilson, 2001; Moreton-Robinson and Walter, 2009; Moreton-Robinson, 2013). These are the elements that connect us as Aboriginal women.

Our axiology also determines the nature of knowledge shared and the rules of engagement. Cultural protocols are taught to us by our families and communities, which informs how we act within the group and the respect we hold for each other and the knowledge shared. Social norms and cultural protocols guide our behaviour within the group. No one person talks for the group – each member is equal and valuable as the next.

Sharing knowledge is an important activity in the weaving workshops because this is how one learns a technique. However, even in a workshop setting, the sharing of knowledge requires one to follow cultural protocols. Anthropologists have written extensively about First Nations cultural protocols, especially with Australian Aboriginal peoples. Some of us teach weaving lessons to others. Lisa Oliver was first taught to weave with Lomandra in 2010 by the Boolarng Nangamai (Together Dreaming) weavers from Gerringong, New South Wales. Boolarng Nangamai is an artists' cooperative of Indigenous artists promoting art and culture. In 2010, they travelled to communities across NSW to teach Aboriginal communities traditional basket weaving in the aim of reviving the practice. Her most significant weaving and cultural lessons came from weaving with this group and the Yinarr Maramali weavers based in Tamworth NSW. Oliver learned how to harvest Lomandra for weaving coil baskets, but most importantly she learned the role respect plays in the weaving process. Both these groups talk of respect for Country, respect for the native grasses, and respect for each other. There also needs to be respect for the teacher or knowledge holder and their knowledge.

After attending numerous basket-weaving workshops held by non-Indigenous weavers, Oliver decided to teach her own version of a weaving workshop embedded with her personal cultural values and learnings. Oliver was frustrated that the non-Indigenous workshops failed to acknowledge First Nation weavers and country. For her, creating a workshop meant educating non-Indigenous people in what Oliver calls 'respectful' or 'mindful' weaving. She aims always to make people aware that there are Aboriginal weavers that reside and still carry out weaving practices on their Country. For example, Oliver lives on Quandamooka Country (Redlands, Brisbane) and at the beginning of her workshops, she acknowledges the Quandamooka People, the Traditional owners of the land upon which she weaves. Oliver also acknowledges the Carmichael family on Minjerribah country, who are skilled weavers still practising their traditional weaving. This is how she pays respect to the Ancestors, Country, and its people. Then Oliver introduces herself, locating herself in terms of Country and kinship. Next, it is essential to acknowledge her teachers. For her, Oliver is adhering to the cultural protocols by following these steps. When teaching workshops to other Aboriginal women, she includes more personal and private information, because she feels like Aboriginal women's weaving circles are more trusting. With non-Indigenous weavers she only shares 'public' knowledges and only those knowledges allowed and learned through the cultural process with her people. Oliver cannot say that she is teaching 'culture'; what she is trying to teach is the importance of connections, being connected to each, and connected to their respective Countries (traditional lands) and Ancestors. Basket making is the vessel for teaching these values – while people's hands are busy their ears are open and the conversation flows freely. It feels amazing to pass on the basket-weaving technique to other Aboriginal women, and even more interesting to see how they use it to make connections to their own culture. Then later they can use the basket to tell a story; baskets tell so many stories.

Baskets and their stories

Turning to the baskets themselves, there are several ways in which we might appreciate them. 'Baskets bring pleasure to people. Some seek out the technical aspects of processes and materials while others look at the finished design' (Hamby, 2010: 7). Their style, shape, and technical proficiency are the most visible and easily accessible aspects to any audience but for baskets have been slow to be appreciated by researchers and anthropologists.

> Baskets in most cultures, whether made by indigenous [sic] people or not, have been considered craft objects. ... Art historians, critics and writers of anthropology of art have ignored baskets because in their opinion these items were not considered to be art. ... baskets have been viewed as utilitarian objects ... not been seen as ceremonial objects with religious significance. (Hamby, 2010: 8)

Another factor in the reception of baskets is that 'they are mainly made by women with the majority of anthropological interest in men's objects and weapons' (Hamby, 2010: 8). Basket-weaving practices are gaining new understandings as strong, Aboriginal women are stepping forward and showing how weaving is connected to country and culture.

Materials for the baskets are wide ranging. The most common material for beginning basket weavers is raffia. Readily available at all craft stores, although in variable quality, raffia is also cheaper than other materials, easily home-dyed, and fairly easy to manipulate. Other commercially available materials include wool yarns, rope, and macramé cord. One of the main goals of the workshops though was to explore traditional fibres found in nature. Plant exchange has a long history between Aboriginal groups with plants needing to dye weaving materials part of extensive network exchanges (Hamby, 2010: 110). One example commonly found in the northern regions of Australia includes the pandanus family of plants (*Pandanus spiralis*). Among the southern regions of the country, common weaving materials include wetland grasses like those in the *Cyperaceae* family (bulrush), the *Asparagaceae* family (lomandra), and pine tree needles as found among the *Lagarostrobos* family. An appreciation of material emerged with the ability to manipulate it into shapes and styles pleasing to the eye and to the touch.

Beyond the aesthetics and those aspects visible to the eye, the weaving of baskets and thus the baskets themselves present additional pieces of evidence on the experience of First Nations women in post-colonial societies. These experiences range from the exploration of Ancestral knowledges to the connection to country and land to the finding of place and people. Doing is experiencing and the practice of traditional weaving connects all the workshop participants to their Ancestral lines as well as to each other. The experiences of the women participating in the workshop are presented here in their own words, without editing. These words sit next to their basket creations, connecting those thoughts and reflections to the baskets themselves. The baskets presented here then come to symbolise more than an ability to weave and make. The baskets themselves are testaments to the endurance, viability, and strength of First Nations women today, yarning to their audience their stories and their construction.

The baskets are presented here as objects of beauty, utilising forms and materials that were readily available by their creators without any pattern.

Creators responded to the materials, crafting their baskets in a wide variety of shapes and colours while listening and talking with other women, all experiencing different aspects of a cultural journey.

Tracey Armstrong

The awakening of the weaving workshop is now part of my life journey in helping me repair fractures. The energy of working the basket in my hands provides a deep sense of my ancestors. While weaving I feel the songlines bringing me to Glen Helen homestead where my mother was born. I allow my mind to travel in her journey as a stolen-generation survivor. Through Jay Creek where all that remains is a field of white wooden crosses. Onto the Bungalow in Alice Springs seeing the floor she slept on with other inmates. I imagine Groote Eylandt and the beautiful Emerald River. Finally to Mulgoa NSW where her teenage years were lived.

I too am a survivor by forced adoption. I was extremely lucky to have found my mum and spent the last nine years with her. My daughter also attends the workshop. She listens to the stories and dreams of finding her culture. The weaving group consists of super talented indigenous women. The knowledge they hold and what we share is so powerful. The embrace of my sisters are like warm hands wrapping around me and I feel safe and protected. I feel the connection to truth and the sacredness of the workshop.

Sarah Carter

I can recall during my school years being asked to colour in the Aboriginal Flag for a project about cultural backgrounds. While I always knew and acknowledged my Aboriginal identity, I could not say more on traditions or mob. Like most, our Aboriginal connection was lost in Australia's history. My family, especially my mum, has worked hard to reconnect us and find where our country is.

What I have gained from this wonderful weaving group is a further connection. I have been fortunate to learn the different weaving techniques from all these talented women. Weaving has resonated with me, as I have always loved to express my creative side, but now I have depth and meaning. I am learning techniques which have been passed down for years, and it is sacred information which I am honoured to be part of. I have felt embraced by my sisters and the online platform has allowed our relationships to build across each country. This is incredibly special during a year with such uncertainty. I do hope our bond continues to grow, yarning, listening to stories, and weaving together, as this group has strengthened my culture within me.

Figure 5.1: Tracey Armstrong, Sarah Carter, and Jessica Fulton

Note: **Row 1:** Tracey Armstrong, from left to right: (1) coil woven basket with raffia and emu feathers; and (2) lomandra coil woven basket; and (3) raffia coil woven basket. **Row 2:** Sarah Carter, from left to right: (1) woven raffia basket with natural seeds and emu feathers; (2) coiled wall hanging, dyed raffia and yarn (detail); (3) twined raffia basket with natural seeds. **Row 3:** Jessica Fulton, from left to right: (1) coil woven wall hanging in raffia; (2) twined basket in native plant materials; and (3) coil woven basket in native plant materials with black crow and maireener shell necklaces. The necklaces are named, left to right, Mother and Daughter and Me, the Girls and Mum.

Jessica Fulton

I'm Jessica Fulton – I am 33 years old. I am a proud palawa daughter to a strong palawa mother, both born and raised in nipaluna lutruwita. I am mother of two strong palawa girls aged 14 and 11. Our bloodline comes from Fanny Cochrane Smith. I have a strong passion for being out on country, practising culture while being guided on this journey with my elders, family, and community. I began my passion for practising culture in my teens. I was privileged to have the late Aunty Leonie Dickson by my side, along with her sister Aunty Verna Nichols, who continues to make sure Leonie's wishes are kept for me to continue this journey on for myself and my daughters. Of late I have also had the privilege to learn and be guided by Jeanette James – I truly feel so blessed to have such strong passionate Aboriginal women to learn from.

Lisa Oliver

Weaving has allowed me to connect with my true self, others, Country, and the Ancestors. For a long time weaving has also been for healing in

Figure 5.2: Lisa Oliver and Gretchen Stolte

Note: **Row 1:** Lisa Oliver: (1) Madagascan and raffia from the Philippines – long- and short-stitch basket; (2) lomandra – coil- stitch basket base; and (3) vintage wool, cotton, raffia, and emu feather – coil basket. **Row 2:** Gretchen Stolte: (1) vegetable-dyed Madagascan raffia with cone and coquina shells; (2) detail of the beginning technique called the magic circle with detail of the blanket stitch; and (3) a trio of baskets of wool wrapped over rope.

stressful times. For so many of us COVID created isolation like we have never experienced before; the women's weaving group on Friday nights was a true gift and helped me cope with the stress and isolation. I've never felt so connected to my weaving practice and to the other women in the group. The group is like a basket itself; the women are the individual strands that have been woven together to make the basket strong and resilient. The basket is the group and holds knowledge and stories of who we are and our personal experiences. I hope that we can continue to connect and create more baskets together well into the future. My love for weaving grows each week, as does my connection with my weaving sisters.

Gretchen Stolte

Like many of the other women in the group, colonial histories have disconnected many of us from our traditional lands, cultural knowledges, and practices. Online learning and connecting is one of the many ways in which Native peoples can connect to both community and to traditional cultural practices. As a Nimi'ipuu woman away from country and community, I have found the weaving group to be crucial in both maintaining my mental health during the global pandemic and learning Native weaving practices that connected me to my cultural heritage. There was something to look forward to, activities to enjoy, and learning new skills that all stimulated an overworked and emotionally exhausted brain. The ability to recognise the technologies of my Ancestors and appreciate their carefully crafted works is both an inspiration and a new way of seeing that helps heal the heart.

Ethical considerations and limitations

The use of practice-based research can illuminate the many ways in which objects are created and offers some insight into the technologies employed by Aboriginal makers. For material culture researchers, the practice of weaving gives additional insights into both the materiality and cultural nature of object making. Anthropologist Louise Hamby, a weaver turned researcher, produced one of the most comprehensive and respectful works on Aboriginal basket making in Australia (2010). Through her own practice-based research, Hamby brings out how 'sacred bathi' (containers) have a spiritual power, derived from the ancestors, which Yolngu call märr. Spiritual objects are removed from the ordinary or mundane objects in their perceived believed capacity to cause effects in the contemporary world' (2010: 20). Although an accomplished researcher, much of what makes Hamby's work so innovative is through her additional insight as a weaver. Hamby learned their weaving on Yolngu country, through deep immersion with Aboriginal weavers. As illustrated in this chapter through Lisa Oliver's approach to teaching and through Hamby's published accounts, the how of learning is a key component of practice-based research methodologies when examining Aboriginal material culture. The study presented here focuses on both practice-based research and the importance of women's groups in developing social networks of support during times of crisis. An important note must be made, however, that gender-diverse people and marginalised genders were not discussed as it was beyond the scope of the chapter to have those discussions with workshop participants. It is recognised that the use of the term 'women's groups' does exclude gender-diverse people and therefore represents a very real limitation of the outcomes of this research. Further research on how other online networks support and empower marginalised peoples during times of crisis is required and this research should be viewed as a single step in a much longer road of inquiry.

The major take-away from this analysis remains fundamentally true in that the bringing of people together during times of stress to engage in practices that create foundational knowledges of First Nation practices and material culture traditions not only aids the material culture researcher but also emotionally strengthens and fortifies people during times of disaster and crisis. The COVID crisis acted as a window on past crises and online practice-based research aids in the survivorship of, and healing for, First Nation peoples. The amazing stories attached to these baskets attest to the power of online social groups and practice-based knowledge creation that builds community and allows us to survive during times of crisis.

Acknowledgements

This publication would not have been possible if not for Krystal Hurst and her generous sharing of her cultural knowledge, time, and expertise. We extend our deep appreciation to her dedication in bringing us all together and creating a space for connecting and collaborating. Deepest appreciation and thanks also go to the weavers of our Friday night weaving group for your support and enthusiasm and your friendship. We also thank our Elders and communities who make us who we are today.

Lisa Oliver would like to extend appreciation and thanks to Dr Gretchen Stolte for the invitation to contribute to this chapter. We have established a great friendship through weaving online. I also pay respects to all my weaving teachers, Boolarng Nangamai, and Yinarr Maramali for your generosity and support.

Gretchen Stolte would like to thank Lisa for coming on board this project and lending her insight and support. I also want to extend my gratitude to Kellen Trenal and his generous sharing of cultural knowledge. Qe'ciyéw'yew! This writing was funded by the Berndt Foundation at the University of Western Australia.

Notes

[1] See the final section of this chapter for further discussion on women, gender-diverse people, and marginalised genders.

2   Torres Strait Islanders are another major First Nations group in occupied Australia and
     this research recognises them as well. They were not part of the workshop group but the
     authors acknowledge their own unique weaving traditions.
3   Example used in Candy and Edmonds, 2018: 65.

References

Bessarab, D. and Ng'andu B. (2010) 'Yarning about yarning as a legitimate
    method in indigenous research', *International Journal of Critical Indigenous
    Studies*, 3(1): 13.

Brough, M., Bond, C., Hunt, J., Jenkins, D., Shannon, C. and Schubert,
    L., (2006) 'Social capital meets identity: aboriginality in an urban setting',
    Journal of Sociology, 42(4): 396–411.

Burgmann, M. (1982) 'Black sisterhood: the situation of urban aboriginal
    women and their relationship to the white women's movement', *Politics*,
    (17): 23.

Candy, L. and Edmonds, E. (2018) 'Practice-based research in the creative
    arts: foundations and futures from the front line', *Leonardo*, 51(1): 63–9.

Clifford, J. and Marcus, G. (2010) *Writing Culture: The Poetics and Politics of
    Ethnography*, Los Angeles, CA: University of California Press.

Crouch, C. (2007) 'Praxis and the reflexive creative practitioner', *Journal of
    Visual Art Practice*, 6(2): 105–14.

Hamby, L. (2010) *Containers of Power: Women with Clever Hands*, Richmond,
    Victoria: Utber & Patullo Publishing.

Herzfeld, M. (1997) 'Anthropology: A practice of theory', *International Social
    Science* Journal, 49(153), 301–318.

Huggins, J. (1998) *Sister Girl*, St Lucia: University of Queensland Press.

MacDonald, S. and Malins, J. (2015) 'Special issue: practiced-based
    research in art and design', *International Journal of Education Through Art*,
    11(3): 339–43.

Martin, K. (2003) 'Ways of knowing, being and doing: a theoretical
    framework and methods for Indigenous and Indigenist research', *Journal
    of Australian Studies*, 27(76): 203–14.

Martin, K. (2008) *Please Knock Before You Enter: Aboriginal Regulation of
    Outsiders and the Implications for Researchers*, Brisbane: Post Pressed.

Moreton-Robinson, A. (2013) 'Towards an Australian indigenous women's
    standpoint theory', *Australian Feminist Studies*, 28(78): 331–47.

Moreton-Robinson, A. (2020) *Talkin' up to the White Woman: Aboriginal
    Women and Feminism* (20th Anniversary edn), St Lucia: University of
    Queensland Press.

Moreton-Robinson, A. and Walter, M. (2009) 'Indigenous methodologies
    in social research', in M. Oxford (ed) *Social Research Methods: An Australian
    Perspective*, South Melbourne: University of Melbourne Press.

O'Shane, P. (1993) 'Aboriginal women and the women's movement',
    Refractory Girl: A Women's Studies Journal, 69.

Roughley, M., Smith K., and Wilkinson, C. (2019) 'Investigating new areas of art-science practice-based research with MA Art in Science programme at Liverpool School of Art and Design', *Higher Education Pedagogies*, 4(1): 226–43.

Spencer, S. (2011) *Visual Research Methods in the Social Sciences: Awakening Visions*, Florence: Taylor & Francis.

Stolte, G. (2020) *Aboriginal and Torres Strait Islander Art: An Anthropology of Identity Production in Far North Queensland*, Sydney: Routledge.

Stolte, G., Zaro, N., and Zaro, K. (2020) 'Kebi Paser: the small hill approach to research, ethics and cultural protocols', in George, L., Tauri, J., and MacDonald, L. (eds) *Indigenous Research Ethics: Claiming Research Sovereignty Beyond Deficit and the Colonial Legacy*, Bingley: Emerald Publishing, 177–88.

Walker, M., Fredericks, B., and Anderson, D. (2012) 'Understanding Indigenous Australian women's social and emotional wellbeing and wellness through yarning: the Indigenous Women's Wellness Program', *International Indigenous Development Research Conference 2012*. Nga Pae o te Maramatanga, University of Auckland.

Walter, M. (2013) *Social Research Methods*, South Melbourne: Oxford University Press.

Wilson, S. (2001) 'What is an indigenous research methodology?', *Canadian Journal of Native Education*, 25(2): 175–9.

Communicating crisis research with comics: representation, process, and pedagogy

Gemma Sou and Sarah Marie Hall

Introduction

The move towards creative research outputs within academia has seen a recent and rapid uptake of mediums such as comics, zines, film, podcasts, and theatre to translate and engage the wider public in academia (Arevalo et al, 2020). These mediums can both be powerful and enlightening ways to communicate research findings, though they also come with distinct challenges (Hall et al, 2021). In this chapter we discuss the process and potential of communicating crisis research in creative forms, using the example of comics. More specifically, we draw upon our own experiences of developing creative research outputs and explore this process by looking at the comic, *After Maria: Everyday Recovery from Disaster*. This comic translates Gemma Sou's ethnographic research on how low-income Puerto Rican families recovered from the impacts of Hurricane Maria, which devastated the Caribbean island in September 2017. Our aim is to use the *After Maria* example as a means of developing critical discussions about the representational politics, pedagogy, and process of translating crisis research into comic form.

We argue that communicating crisis research via comics is a highly democratic process because it ensures your research is accessible to your participants as well as the wider public. Relatedly, the production of comics also enables a more participatory research process whereby participants can shape how their story is told. Comics are also uniquely positioned to produce a politics of representation that challenges reductive, dehumanising, and apolitical narratives about crisis-affected people that often circulate in mainstream media (Scott, 2014), and in academic research (Tuck, 2009). Furthermore, comics offer powerful rhetorical power as they are uniquely able to distil complex ideas into engaging and highly learnable forms (Chute, 2016).

We begin by outlining the communicative capacity of comics, before giving further details on the development of *After Maria*. We then detail practical issues, learning spaces, and representational challenges, before offering some conclusions.

Comics

A comic is generally an illustration that employs metaphor and/or storytelling to clearly communicate an idea to a broad audience (McCloud, 1994). Comics that centre on and tackle political, social, and economic issues are known as 'serious' comics. These developed in the 1960s and 70s, largely in New York and San Francisco, and were independently created and produced. They have origins in underground and politically left movements that sought to challenge mainstream ideas and understanding of social and political issues (Chute, 2016). With 'serious' comics, creators shifted away from the notion that comics had to be action-packed, silly, formulaic, or even slightly inclined towards children through their focus on superheroes and villians, for example. Serious comics produce complex, textured, and even absurdist storylines. They are avant-garde; they are political; and they are taboo-shattering. They tackle issues such as disaster (Neufeld, 2016); war (Sacco, 2003); sex (Road, 2012); genocide (Stassen, 2006); mental health (Bechdel, 2007); inequality (Sulaiman, 2017); illness and disability (Bell, 2014); queerness (Tamaki, 2014); and civil rights (Lewis and Aydin, 2016).

Inspired by the notion that comics can deal with 'serious', real-world issues, an increasing number of academics have communicated their research in comic form. In public health research, comics have long been recognised as an effective tool for reaching lots of different populations for education on subjects like cancer (Krakow, 2017), fitness (Tarver et al, 2016), and diabetes (McNicol, 2014) to name only a few. There is also a comics series focusing on 'graphic medicine' – both by and for doctors, nurses, and patients (Graphic Medicine, nd). Other examples include *Positive-Negatives* (Positive Negatives, nd), *A Vision for Emberá Tourism* (Theodossopoulos, 2019), *Lissa* (Hamdy and Nye, 2017), *Gringo Love* (Carrier-Moisan, 2020), *Mentawai!* (Pendanx and Juguin, 2019), *Love in a Time of Precarity* (Taylor, 2019), and *Little Miss Homeless* (Earle-Brown, 2020). We now outline how Gemma came to use comics in her research, and provide more detail on the *After Maria* comic.

The *After Maria* comic

For many years Gemma has read graphic novels and comics that tackle 'serious' issues, and was intrigued about their political potential in research. This included an appreciation of the sensitivity of the storytelling power of comics and their ability to synthesise and communicate complex social narratives into understandable, engaging, and beautiful stories. In collaboration with the London-based illustrator, John Cei Douglas (see www.johnceidouglas.com), Gemma produced a 20-page comic based on her one-year ethnographic research project, which explored the recovery of low-income Puerto Rican families that were affected by Hurricane Maria in 2017 (Sou and Cei Douglas, 2019). This project investigated the everyday social, cultural, political, and economic factors that shape family recovery during the first year after a major disaster (Lindell, 2019).

She collected data in the neighbourhood Ingenio, a community of 4,415 persons across 1,529 households with a 66 per cent poverty rate (US Census Bureau, 2018). Ingenio is a peri-urban, coastal community in Toa Baja municipality, located 13.5 km from Puerto Rico's capital, San Juan. Hurricane Maria caused major structural and water damage to the majority of houses in Ingenio and recovery from state actors was limited (see Sou et al, forthcoming). Data collection began on 16 October 2017 (27 days after Hurricane Maria hit) and concluded on 13 September 2018 (almost one year after the hurricane). Data were collected through five visits that were equally spaced throughout the period. She carried out in-depth, semi-structured interviews with each household head during each visit, and she also interviewed local and national government officials, as well as domestic and international non-governmental organisations (NGOs). Extensive observation and visual methods (that is, photography and videos) were also conducted, and she consulted pertinent disaster recovery policies and data, as well as census data. The comic tells the story of a fictional family, yet the narrative, dialogue, and experiences of the characters are entirely based on the data collected. As such, *After Maria* ties together the main findings and experiences of all of the Puerto Rican families that Gemma spoke to. The comic also includes ten extra pages with further reading about the causes and recovery of disasters, discussion points, references, and information about the authors.

It was surprisingly simple to find a graphic artist. Gemma pitched her comic idea on a Facebook page for UK-based graphic artists and was met with many inquiries. She asked two of her favourite artists to sketch a scene that she had scripted, and from there she decided to work with the very talented John Cei Douglas. Using her in-depth ethnographic data, Gemma wrote the script (with support from Kneece, 2015), which included the dialogue, narration, perspective, information about what is happening in the scene, characters' emotions, and even the mood/ambience, which all helped John to create the visual story. The script was written to ensure that each individual page communicated at least one major finding from the research. For example, the gendered impact of disasters; loss of identity and sense of home; weak state capacity to support household recovery; and the increase in community solidarity. Although these are weighty topics, graphic illustration is well suited to distil complex ideas into six or seven panels of images as we will discuss later on. Once the script for the first 16 pages was complete, John began final illustration.

The *After Maria* comic shown in Figure 6.1 was made freely available online (in English and Spanish) in May 2019, and over 1,500 physical copies were sent to educators and academics across the world. The comic has received significant international attention, being featured in the *Guardian* UK newspaper, numerous blog spaces, interactive exhibitions, festivals, and Gemma has enjoyed being invited to speak about the comic on several podcasts and events. Educators working at high school, undergraduate, and postgraduate level in over 20 countries have also used it as a teaching resource. Disciplines are varied and include geography, anthropology, development studies, gender studies, media studies, and English literature. Individuals working in NGOs have also used it as a resource to facilitate discussions with communities affected by disasters when conducting participatory workshops.

Working with artists and participants

Unless you are a talented artist, producing a comic is an inherently democratic process because it requires researchers to work collaboratively and dialogically in order to effectively translate research findings into an engaging and accessible visual narrative. Though, as a researcher it is fundamental to ensure the integrity of the research and of those being represented and to avoid ethnographic errors. In other words, it is critical that the accuracy of the research findings is not lost through their translation into a visual story. As such, researchers must relinquish some control over their research outputs if they are to take full advantage of the visual narrative form of comics.

Further to this, a central aim of producing the *After Maria* comic was to ensure an ethical portrayal of research participants by foregrounding nuanced representations of their experiences and personalities, as we discuss later. Working with these principles, collaboration with an artist stimulates a creative dialogue between the researcher who gathers and analyses data, and the artist who must distil and communicate these complex ideas in accessible as well as engaging ways. Reconciling these two approaches was challenging and exciting in equal measure. This process also allows researchers to work more creatively themselves, which can be a welcome break for academics for whom sharing findings can often be reduced to writing articles, chapters, and books – a relatively lonely activity for many.

Initially there was a lot of back and forth between Gemma and John concerning the script, which is made up of text – what is read (dialogue, captions, thought, and sound), and visuals – what is seen (the action of the story, the artwork, the layout). These two components work together to generate energy within the script and thus within the story. Gemma wanted

Figure 6.1: *After Maria: Everyday Recovery from Disaster*

to ensure the integrity of the research findings and the voices and personalities of the people she spoke to. At the same time, John brought his expertise in visual storytelling and was fantastic at suggesting what dialogue to leave out, or what perspective to draw a scene from to take advantage of visual storytelling. Gemma's first attempt at scripts/storyboarding depended heavily on dialogue and captions to drive the narrative. This is not surprising because as academics, we are accustomed to words and text being the primary way that we communicate and receive ideas. Yet, collaboration with an illustrator pushes researchers to make shrewd decisions about which findings we want the public to engage with and understand as focusing on a select number of findings will ensure the comic works narratively and aesthetically.

An artist's expertise in graphical storytelling is invaluable as it ensures that the visuals and the spatial organisation of information, rather than the text, drive the story. For example, a character's emotion, whether anger, fear, shock, or delight, can be communicated through facial expression, body language, shading, or even the angle and perspective of the image, rather than explicitly stating this in dialogue or captions. For instance, in Figure 6.2, the central family in *After Maria* have just discovered the extent of damage caused by Hurricane Maria. The characters' feelings of vulnerability and despair do not need to be didactically spelt out for the reader. Instead, the image conveys this through the body language (embracing one another, slumped shoulders) and facial expressions of characters, set in a landscape of destruction. The wide, bird's-eye view perspective also makes the characters appear small, which cleverly signifies the family's initial sense of helplessness in relation to the enormity of the problem they faced after the hurricane.

The ability to be economical with text is a key benefit of visual storytelling (Aiello and Parry, 2019). Therefore, it is critical to collaborate with an experienced artist who is sensitive to your research findings and who has the skill and intuition to know how to distil ideas into images. As such, it is important to work with an artist who feels comfortable in making these suggestions to you as a researcher. This can result in a healthy dynamic where researchers and artists share, push, pull, and compromise as necessary in the pursuit of a visual representation of research. Artists require sufficient freedom so that they can communicate the researchers' script and ideas in the most appropriate and effective way for their particular artistic medium.

Another exciting element of producing a comic is that they offer a more democratic opportunity for research participants to influence and understand the work of academics. For instance, Gemma consulted with research participants to receive their feedback and input on the text, dialogue, images, narratives, and purpose of the comic. In practice, after each field visit to Puerto Rico, Gemma would write a script for approximately four pages of the comic, or three months of the one-year ethnography. John would then roughly sketch these four pages (see Figure 6.3), and Gemma would show this to research participants on her subsequent field visit. This allowed her to gather feedback from those who were directly affected by Hurricane Maria, and amend the comic accordingly.

Research participants felt more comfortable directing, critiquing, and suggesting ideas for an output that visually conveys environments, events, dialogue, experiences, and people they are familiar with and recognise. When people can literally 'see' themselves, they are more likely to feel invested.

Figure 6.2: *After Maria*, p 6, panel 8

In contrast, academic jargon and theoretical obfuscation often found in journal articles and books may quickly marginalise research participants from engaging in meaningful feedback (Detweiler, 2014; Pinker, 2014). Moreover, it is not widespread academic practice for researchers to gather research participants' feedback on traditional academic outputs. As such, producing comics can subvert the traditional and asymmetrical researcher–'researched' relations, as research participants become active collaborators in the process of knowledge production and communication. Moreover, a comic may also be far more useful to research participants than a research report, book, or journal article. There is also something about the physicality and durability

Figure 6.3: Rough sketches of *After Maria*

of a print copy of a comic that lends both legitimacy and longevity to the research it presents. It is less likely to be lost somewhere in the wilds of the endless Internet, or trapped behind the pay wall of an academic journal, but can be found on a shelf for future generations to discover.

Learning about crises with comics

Historically, there has been an association between comics and a kind of subpar literacy, as if comics reading could not be 'real' reading. This is because of the widespread notion that visual literacy is somehow less complicated than verbal literacy, which comics also require (Glasgow, 1994). In this line of thinking, which is prevalent today, the visual is immediate, sensual, and obvious. Contemporary comics, however, ask us to reconsider several dominant commonplaces about images, including that visuality stands for a subpar literacy. Comics, in fact, are mediums that involve a substantial degree of reader participation and visual literacy to decode narrative meaning and stitch together meaning. Comics are site-specific forms of literature that have their own vocabulary: gutters, panels, tiers, balloons, bubbles, bleeds, splashes, perspectives, shading. These are all elements that carry meaning and which exist meaningfully in relation to one another in the space on the page. To produce them requires learning a new syntax, a new way of ordering ideas. And the visual content of comics that once signalled a 'lesser-than' literacy is now an integral part of our contemporary daily lives, as so much of our primary media intake, especially online, combines the verbal and the visual, often with complexity we have learned to navigate quickly (Avgerinou and Pettersson, 2011; Hattwig et al, 2013).

For instance, blank spaces are central to comic storytelling – they are where the reader fills in the blank between pictured moments, participating imaginatively in the creation of the story. And different readers do this and experience this blank space differently. Too much text and being bluntly told exactly what is happening can kill the reader's imaginative engagement with the narrative (Kneece, 2015). Comics provide enough text and images so readers will imaginatively connect parts of the story. Comics are as much about what can be pictured, and what cannot be or will not be pictured, which is left to the reader's imagination. The images are also able to make their own contribution to the making of the story, as an image is always capable of provoking a narrative response in the mind of the reader. In other words, the reader is supposed to infer the story not only from the textual and verbal indications that are given, but also from the elements of the image (Baetens, 2008). For a reader navigating the space of the page, reading comics can feel less directive and linear than reading most prose narrative. This way of reading stimulates both analytic and creative activity in the brain, a process that has been shown to enhance understanding (Mayer and Sims, 1994). Not only can this process potentially augment learning, but it can also facilitate empathy between author and reader by offering a portal into the individual's experience (Williams, 2011).

As such, comics offer new pedagogical avenues that can contribute to and support traditional teaching from academic texts. They combine the power of ethnographic research, with the unique aesthetic elements of illustrations, as a sequential art, using pages, panels, visuals, dialogue, captions, and lettering to tell a story. Comics also use the visual medium to express non-human environmental elements in a form that is not overly didactic. This approach makes comics excellent for critical analysis, because readers can use their wider understanding of theories, concepts, and ideas they have learnt in class, or elsewhere, to unpack the stories images, text, dialogue, and narratives. For example, in Figure 6.4, Natalia, the protagonist, is thinking about how she misses the way life and her home were before the hurricane (shaded panels denote daydreaming and memories). Readers familiar with Blunt and Dowling's (2006) notion of home will recognise how the loss of material items such as furniture and family photographs, as well as familiar sounds such as the radio and television, rupture Natalia's sense of homeliness, familiarity, normality, and even sense of identity. This undermines her material and emotional attachment to home as well as disrupting her sensory experiences of home (Burrell, 2014; Sou and Webber, 2019). By critically reading visual texts, students become more careful observers (Naghshineh et al, 2008).

Figure 6.4: *After Maria*, p 16, panels 2, 3, and 4

I didn't miss the things so much...
I missed what used to be.

This way of teaching is appreciated by students, who increasingly request different and more visual approaches to teaching.

The visuality of comics is also one of the main reasons why they are so engaging and accessible to 'non-experts'. This is significant because academic writing is often criticised for being overly complicated and impenetrable to anyone outside a small circle of experts (Kamler and Thompson, 2014). Yet, an effective comic can convey complex ideas in an accessible form without oversimplification. Their visual narrative form can illuminate obscure concepts, and create a metaphor that can be much more memorable than a straightforward text-based description of the concept itself. In fact, pedagogical and psychological studies show that the comic form has significant impact on readers' knowledge acquisition and content understanding (Sousanis, 2019). This is not only because comics are engaging, but also because they are uniquely able to present complicated ideas in a more accessible and understandable way because of their visual storytelling form, regardless of the reader's prior knowledge of the particular topic at hand. This is especially important in the context of crises, when personal experiences, vulnerabilities, and sensitivities are at stake, and arguably it becomes more important for researchers to share these findings to highlight the injustices that crises expose.

Representing research on crises and human vulnerability

Media representations of crises, whether in TV, film, news outlets, and NGOs' fundraising or advocacy campaigns, tend to rely on aesthetics of suffering and highly emotive imagery that depicts crisis-affected groups as defeated and broken (Lewis et al, 2014; Sigona, 2014). A common trope is to focus on the misery of children, women, the elderly, and those who are injured or sick, which convey ideas of helplessness, as they tend to be internationally recognised as 'symbols of distress' (Manzo, 2008). This is because they are deemed to be passive and as having less agency, and are therefore 'more deserving' of our sympathy and support (Johnson, 2011). This reifies and reproduces essentialist and reductive narratives about crisis-affected populations, who are often the most low-income and socio-politically marginalised groups in society. A notable and infamous illustration of this approach was the photo taken of the dead body of Aylan Kurdi, a small Syrian boy who washed ashore in Turkey.

However, over-reliance on documenting the suffering of people results in apolitical and ahistorical narratives that decontextualise and simplify the causes and experiences of crises, and how they can be addressed. Crises are simply seen to exist as there is marginal engagement with the broader structural factors that insidiously and gradually create crises and shape people's unequal experiences (Hattori, 2003; Hojer, 2004; Scott, 2014). There is also a reliance on images of large crisis-affected groups, which portrays people as lacking any individualising features, because people are aggregated into large abstract groups; for example, refugees, dying hospital patients, disaster victims. This homogenises people, and denies their unique personalities, voices, personal experiences, and identities (Chouliaraki, 2013).

Tuck (2009: 409) also argues that scholarly research on crises and marginalised groups is often guilty of narrowly focusing on documenting the agony and troubled lives of crisis-affected people, or what she calls 'damage centred research'. This surreptitiously invites vulnerable and oppressed people to speak but to 'only speak from that space in the margin that is a sign of deprivation, a wound, an unfulfilled longing. Only speak your pain' (hooks, 1990: 152). This kind of research reinscribes a one-dimensional notion of people as depleted, ruined, and hopeless. Tuck urges researchers to reformulate the ways that research is framed and to reimagine how findings might be translated; calling for researchers to focus on documenting not only the painful elements and suffering of crises but also the wisdom, hope, vision, and lived lives. Such an axiology can depathologise the experiences of crisis-affected communities and upend commonly held assumptions of ignorance and paralysis within crisis-affected peoples (Hattori, 2003; Hojer, 2004; Chouliaraki, 2006; Scott, 2014).

The technological form and subversive culture of comics are particularly well placed to construct narratives that challenge the reductive and dehumanising representational practices that circulate in mainstream media and damage-centred research. In *After Maria*, a priority was to construct nuanced representations of the families in Puerto Rico, by bringing through their voice, personalities, personal relationships, and hidden everyday personal experiences of disaster that are seldom revealed in mainstream media or much academic research. This is an inherently ethical endeavour that directly challenges the focus on damage, pain, and suffering in mainstream media and crisis research. Comics afford this because they focus on character-driven narratives and the creation of three-dimensional characters who express their emotions and unique personalities, which drive the narrative without being too intrusive. For example, *After Maria* portrays families in Puerto Rico as complex human beings who have pasts, presents, and imagined futures, as dignified in work clothes, as members of families, neighbourhoods, and churches, as simultaneously serious, humorous, and energetic. Comics enable researchers to avoid fetishising damage and homogenising suffering, as they are equipped to celebrate the wisdom, heterogeneity, hope, and ingenuity of affected groups (Vizenor and Lee, 1999; Grande, 2004; Brayboy, 2008). We propose that comics are a powerful medium to steer academic and public representations of crises away from essentialist narratives of damage, passivity, and victimhood.

For example, in Figure 6.5 we see two characters joking and laughing about their son tiring of humanitarian relief food. These small moments, and some might say, insignificant moments, are unlikely to be covered in mainstream media or many studies of disasters; yet, comics celebrate and lend themselves to the inclusion of 'unspectacular' moments (Chute, 2016). Inclusion of 'unremarkable' moments foreground the unique personalities of characters and allow one to represent research participants as far more than a 'miserable' and defeated victim of disaster. The ability to showcase nuanced representations of research participants also allows researchers to highlight the ability of crisis-affected people to navigate adverse contexts. In fact, the culture of comics insists on narratives that place individual characters' agency and capacity at the forefront (Kneece, 2015). This allows comics to challenge the reductive idea that people are passive and helpless victims of crises. In this sense, the comic form allows researchers to construct much denser representations of research participants and their contexts than is possible in text-based mediums (Sousanis, 2019).

However, when representing crises in comics it is important that researchers do not fall into the trap of romanticising people's 'resilience'. Overly focusing on the capabilities of people (or lack of) as the analytical explanation for the causes, impacts, and recovery from crises moves responsibility for risk towards affected populations, while the broader political, economic, social, and environmental structures that shape crisis are obscured. Such a narrative is apolitical and ahistorical, and opens up a space for neoliberal policies that shift responsibility away from the state and towards families (Felli and Castree, 2012; Harrison, 2013). We insist that crisis comics must highlight the ways in which crisis-affected groups are routinely and systematically marginalised from formal state support, which is succinctly illustrated in two panels from *After Maria* found in Figure 6.6.

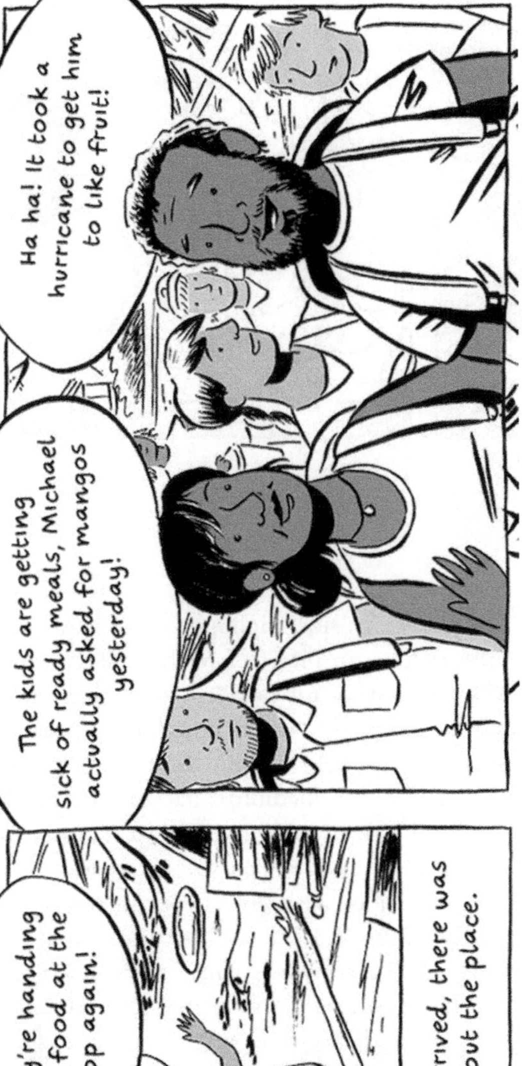

Figure 6.5: *After Maria*, p 9, panels 1 and 2

Figure 6.6: *After Maria*, p 3, panels 1 and 2

Conclusion

The outputs of crisis research do not typically consist of creative outputs such as comics. Yet, our discussion highlighted how the respective crafts of illustrator and researcher can intersect really well in the translation of crisis research into a visual story for broader uptake beyond academia. As researchers of crises, we are used to unearthing, interpreting, and analysing stories, then communicating these via journal articles, book chapters, or perhaps even blogs. That is, via mediums that are principally text based. Comics provide a new and intriguing register to translate and distribute research findings. They allow us to engage our creative sides, stop us in our tracks, and force us to consider what aspects of our research we think the general public should be aware of. It is a revelatory process that creates a space for researchers to engage research participants in research communication.

Communicating crisis research is an inherently ethical endeavour, which places participants at the very heart of the research process, allowing them to maintain control over how their story is told. We suggest it is important that academics learn ways of communicating findings about crisis research that are appropriate and enjoyable for their participants, and comics represent one such avenue. The storytelling form of comics also provides ample opportunity for researchers to create more ethical representations of participations which move away from reductive portrayals of participants as faceless and voiceless victims of crises. Finally, while comics are still sometimes blanketed as escapist, today it is clear that many comics gesture towards the opposite: a participatory, even slowed-down practice of consumption that allows readers to access complex ideas via an engaging and highly learnable form.

References

Aiello, G. and Parry, K. (2019) *Visual Communication*, London: Sage.

Arevalo, V. et al (2020) 'Storylines for practice', *Sustainability Science*, 1–20.

Avgerinou, M. and Pettersson, R. (2011) 'Toward a cohesive theory of visual literacy', *Journal of Visual Literacy*, 30(2): 1–19.

Baetens, J. (2008) 'Graphic novels', *English Language Notes*, 46(2): 77–88.

Bechdel, A. (2007) *Fun Home*, Boston: Houghton Mifflin Harcourt.

Bell, C. (2014) *El Deafo*, New York, NY: Amulet.

Blunt, A. and Dowling, R. (2006) *Home (Key Ideas in Geography)*, Abingdon: Routledge.

Brayboy, B. (2008) ' "Yakkity yak" and "talking back" ', in M. Villegas, S. Neugebauer, and K. Venegas (eds) *Indigenous Knowledge and Education*, Cambridge, MA: Harvard Education Press, pp 339–46.

Burrell, K. (2014) 'Spilling over from the street', *Home Cultures*, 11(2): 145–66.

Carrier-Moisan, M. (2020) *Gringo Love*, Toronto: University of Toronto Press.

Chouliaraki, L. (2006) *The Spectatorship of Suffering*, London: Sage.

Chouliaraki, L. (2013) *The Ironic Spectator*, London: John & Sons.

Chute, H. (2016) *Disaster Drawn*, Cambridge, MA: Harvard University Press.

Detweiler, E. (2014) 'Why inaccessibility?', *Impact of Social Sciences Blog*.

Earle-Brown, H. (2020) *Little Miss Homeless*, [online], available at: https://issuu.com/harriet_eb/docs/little_miss_homeless_book_template_2

Felli, R. and Castree, N. (2012) 'Neoliberalising adaptation to environmental change', *Environment and Planning A*, 44(1): 1–4.

Glasgow, J. (1994) 'Teaching visual literacy for the 21st century', *Journal of Reading*, 37(6): 494–500.

Grande, S. (2004) *Red Pedagogy*, Lanham, MD: Rowman and Littlefield.

Graphic Medicine (nd) https://www.graphicmedicine.org/ [accessed 17 September 2020].

Hall, S., Sou, G., and Pottinger, L. (2021) 'Ethical considerations for creative research', in Von Benzon et al (eds) *Creative Methods for Human Geographers*, London: Sage.

Hamdy, S. and Nye, C. (2017) *Lissa* (Vol 1), Toronto: University of Toronto Press.

Harrison, E. (2013) 'Bouncing back?', *Critical Social Policy*, 33(1): 97–113.

Hattori, T. (2003) 'Giving as a mechanism of consent', *International Relations*, 17(2): 153–73.

Hattwig, D., Bussert, K., Medaille, A., and Burgess, J. (2013) 'Visual literacy standards in higher education', *Libraries and the Academy*, 13(1): 61–89.

Höijer, B. (2004) 'The discourse of global compassion', *Media, Culture & Society*, 26(4): 513–31.

Holland, E. and Dahlman, C. (2017) 'Graphic geopolitics', *Geopolitics*, 22(1): 204–14.

hooks, b. (1990) *Yearning*, Boston, MA: South End Press.

Johnson, H. (2011) 'Click to donate', *Third World Quarterly*, 32(6): 1015–37.

Kamler, B. and Thomson, P. (2014) *Helping Doctoral Students Write*, London: Routledge.

Kneece, M. (2015) *The Art of Comic Book Writing*, New York: Watson-Guptill.

Krakow M. (2017) 'Graphic narratives and cancer prevention', *Health Communication,*, 32(5): 525–8.

Lewis, D., Rodgers, D., and Woolcock, M. (2014) *Popular Representations of Development*, London: Routledge.

Lewis, J. and Aydin, A. (2016) *March* (Vol 3), Georgia: Top Shelf Productions.

Lindell, M. (ed) (2019) *The Routledge Handbook of Urban Disaster Resilience*, London: Routledge.

Manzo, K. (2008) 'Imaging humanitarianism', *Antipode*, 40(4): 632–57.

Mayer, R. and Sims, V. (1994) 'For whom is a picture worth a thousand words?', *Journal of Educational Psychology*, 86(3): 389–401.

McCloud, S. (1994) *Understanding Comics*, New York: HarperPerennial.

McNicol S. (2014) 'Humanising illness', *Medical Humanities*, 40(1): 49–55.

Naghshineh, S. et al (2008) 'Formal art observation training improves medical students', *Journal of General Internal Medicine*, 23(7): 991–7.

Neufeld, J. (2016) *AD: New Orleans after the Deluge*, New York: Knopf.

Pendanx, J. and Juguin, T. (2019) *Mentawai!*, Paris: Futuropolis..

Pinker, S. (2014) 'Why academics stink at writing', *The Chronicle of Higher Education*, 26 September, available from: https://www.chronicle.com/article/why-academics-stink-at-writing/.

Positive Negatives (nd), https://positivenegatives.org/comics-animations/ [accessed June 16 2020].

Road, C. (2012) *Spit and Passion*, New York: Feminist Press at the City University of New York.

Sacco, J. (2003) *Palestine*, London: Jonathan Cape.

Scott, M. (2014) *Media and Development*, London: Zed Books,.

Sigona, N. (2014) 'The politics of refugee voices', in E. Fiddian-Qasmiyeh (ed) *The Oxford Handbook of Refugee and Forced Migration* (1st edn), Oxford: Oxford University Press, pp 369–82.

Sou, G. and Cei Douglas, J. (2019) *After Maria: Everyday Recovery from Disaster*, Manchester: University of Manchester.

Sou, G. and Webber, R. (2019) 'Disruption and recovery of intangible resources during environmental crises', *Geoforum*, 106: 182–92.

Sou, G., Shaw, D., and González, F. (2021) 'A multidimensional framework for disaster recovery: longitudinal qualitative evidence from Puerto Rican households', *World Development*. 144.

Sousanis, N. (2019) 'Articulating ideas and meaning through the use of comics', *LEARNing Landscapes*, 12(1): 33–8.

Stassen, J. (2006) *Deogratias, a Tale of Rwanda*, New York: First Second.

Sulaiman, H. (2017) *Freedom Hospital: A Syrian Story*, Paris: Editions çà et là/ARTE Editions.

Tamaki, M. (2014) *This One Summer*, New York: First Second.

Tarver T. et al (2016) 'A novel tool for health literacy', *Journal of Hospital Librarianship*, 16(2): 152–9.

Taylor, F. (2019) 'Love in the time of precarity', available from: https://loveinthetimeofprecarity.wordpress.com/

Thébaud O. et al (2017) 'Managing marine socio-ecological systems', *ICES Journal of Marine Science*, 74: 1965–80.

Theodossopoulos, D. (2019) 'A vision for Emberá tourism', *Entanglements: Experiments in Multimodal Ethnography*, 2(2): 7–26.

Tuck, E. (2009) 'Suspending damage', *Harvard Educational Review*, 79(3): 409–28.

US Census Bureau (2018) Puerto Rico, available from: https://www.census.gov/quickfacts/PR (accessed 11 November 2020).

Vizenor, G. and Lee, A. (1999) 'Postindian conversations', Lincoln: University of Nebraska Press.

Williams, I. (2011) 'Autography as auto-therapy', *Journal of Medical Humanities*, 32(4): 353–66.

PART III

Digital methods

7

Developing a Collaborative AutoNetnographic approach to researching doctoral students' online experiences

Richard McGrath, Holly Bowen-Salter, Emma Milanese, and Phoebe Pearce

> Out of adversity comes opportunity.
>
> Benjamin Franklin

Introduction

2020 was a year few will forget. The COVID-19 global pandemic resulted in massive changes to people's lives, particularly in relation to the use of online communication tools. While video conferencing and communication tools had been used before the global 2020 COVID-19 crisis, this increased across all aspects of society, including healthcare (Lee, 2020; Wosik et al, 2020), business (Obrenovic et al, 2020), education (Dhawan, 2020), entertainment and recreation (Agostino, Arnaboldi, and Lampis, 2020; Son et al, 2020b), and for personal use (Farooq, Laato, and Islam, 2020). Schools and universities rapidly shifted to online learning modalities (Garbe et al, 2020; Rapanta et al, 2020). In tertiary education, this presented both challenges and opportunities. One challenge was to continue to support learning in an engaging environment. However, this also provided research opportunities focused on the impact and benefits of online learning as well as opportunities to develop innovative research methodologies aligned to an online world.

This chapter reveals the development of one such methodology, Collaborative AutoNetnography. The development of a Collaborative AutoNetnographic methodology stemmed from an online initiative created to support doctoral students during COVID-19. Discussions by Higher Degree by Research (HDR) candidates during online sessions related to the potential of conducting a research project focused on their experiences concerning the initiative.

We begin this chapter by reviewing the context within which the initiative was developed. We then discuss the various individual methodologies that we drew upon to develop Collaborative AutoNetnography and discuss how the research methodology was implemented, including reflections of key enablers, barriers, and ethical aspects.

Background

A key public health response to COVID-19 was to impose physical and social distancing restrictions on all citizens (Lewnard and Lo, 2020). In Australia these restrictions were imposed across the country in late March 2020. These restrictions resulted in people being required to spend much of their time at home, with only some limited opportunities to venture to other locations, primarily for food and medical care (Australian Broadcasting Corporation, 2020). While the use of physical and social distancing was viewed as the most appropriate approach in relation to containing the spread of COVID-19 (Kissler et al, 2020), psycho-social issues related to social isolation became apparent (Banerjee and Rai, 2020), the most obvious being loneliness. Feelings of loneliness due to isolation from others, community, and society has been identified as having a detrimental effect on an individual's mental and social well-being (Cacioppo and Patrick, 2008; Stickley and Koyanagi, 2016) as well as being a risk factor for several mental health disorders including anxiety, depression, stress, and insomnia (Wilson et al, 2007; Hawkley and Cacioppo, 2010; Cacioppo et al, 2011; Leigh-Hunt et al, 2017).

Also, the spread of COVID-19 into Australia occurred after one of the largest bushfire seasons experienced by many Australian communities which in turn had been preceded by several other climactic disasters, including long periods of drought, cyclones, and flooding. As Shakespeare-Finch et al (2020) point out, the Australian public had for some time been experiencing a plethora of crises that were impacting their physical and mental health.

The impact of social isolation due to COVID-19 has affected several population groups, including older people (Brooke and Jackson, 2020), families (Usher et al, 2020), as well as youth and young adults (Australian Bureau of Statistics, 2020; Li et al, 2020). Most notable among this latter group has been the impact of COVID-19 on tertiary students (Gallagher, Doherty, and Obonyo, 2020; Konstantopoulou and Raikou, 2020; Son et al, 2020a). While supporting undergraduate tertiary students became an area of importance for many Australian universities during the COVID-19 pandemic (Johnstone, 2020), support for HDR[1] students was limited. It could be argued that as Australian universities view HDR students as more self-sufficient due to the nature of their study,[2] the impact of not being able to physically attend a university campus was less compared with undergraduate students, and thus universities did not need to provide as much direct support.

Prior to the COVID-19 pandemic, studies had shown social isolation can occur for HDR students during candidature (Ali and Kohun, 2006; Ali, Kohun, and Levy, 2007; Janta, Jugosi, and Brown, 2014). Social isolation during HDR candidature can have an impact on students' academic performance leading to some failing to complete their studies (Jiranek, 2010). Several reasons have been suggested as to why and how social isolation can occur for HDR candidates. This includes the type and/or role of the students' academic discipline, which can also be linked to opportunities to engage with peers, as well as the nationality status of the HDR student.

In relation to HDR candidates' academic discipline, studies have shown that HDR students in the physical sciences and technology are less likely to experience social isolation compared with students studying in the social sciences and humanities (Deem and Brehony, 2000). It's been argued that this may be due to the nature and role within these academic disciplines, with HDR candidates involved in the physical sciences and technology being members of structured research teams while those studying in the social sciences and humanities conduct projects different to their supervisors (Chiang, 2003). As a result, those involved in physical sciences and technology 'teams' are more likely to have frequent contact with other researchers compared with those involved in the humanities and social sciences (Deem and Brehony, 2000; Chiang, 2003; Janta, Lugosi, and Brown, 2014). Essentially, physical sciences and technology HDR candidates have an opportunity to be involved in research-focused 'Communities of Practice'. These 'Communities of Practice' provide collegial support beyond research experience as they also assist with developing academic identities. As Trede, Macklin, and Bridges (2012: 378) point out, 'collaborative, dialogic learning from practice enables and facilitates professional identity development'.

Before COVID-19, the majority of HDR peer support groups (often developed as 'writing groups') had been established within universities and involved face-to-face sessions (Aitchison and Guerin, 2014; Beasy et al, 2020; Tremblay-Wragg et al, 2020). It's been identified that HDR writing groups have been established for numerous reasons, such as ensuring student progress to completion (Maher, Fallucca, and Mulhern Halasz, 2013), dissertation dissemination (Lehna et al, 2016), and to develop social connections and collegial scholarship (Tyndall et al, 2019). However, due to COVID-19 the ability for tertiary institutions to provide this form of HDR support became unfeasible. It has been argued that to overcome impacts of physical distancing restrictions on HDR candidates there is a need to develop and support virtual, online activities to a level similar to on-campus interactions (Wang and DeLaquil, 2020).

An example of such an initiative is the Social Isolation Prevention Sessions (SIPS) group. SIPS has been a daily Zoom group which began at the outset of the COVID-19 pandemic in Australia to support Australian HDR candidates. SIPS is run completely by volunteer HDR researchers, for HDR researchers. While initially SIPS was administered by a single individual (one of the authors of this chapter), regular attendees have taken on ownership of the sessions, allowing for administration to be conducted by HDR candidates from various universities throughout Australia, without affiliation to any singular institution or field of study. All authors of this chapter were involved as participants in SIPS sessions, with HBS and RM attending all sessions as primary facilitators, while EM and PP attended some sessions.

Initially SIPS followed the Pomodoro Technique (Cirillo, 2009) for working periods, allowing 25 minutes for each set working period. However, to allow for flexibility and in response to attendee feedback, this moved to a voting system, allowing attendees to vote for whether a 25-minute or 45-minute working session with majority rules. SIPS has been designed to be a combination of working and socialising. Unlike other Shut Up and Write sessions, SIPS has been designed to focus on the 'social isolation prevention' component. While there is an understanding by SIPS attendees that working on their thesis is important, there is an emphasis on the philosophy that 'your thesis is not more important than you are'. As such, SIPS sessions attempted to be as flexible as possible to allow members the opportunity to get the support they need from their peers.

As part of this flexible accommodation, attendees could enter or exit any time during the three-hour SIPS sessions to allow for the lifestyle factors such as teaching or family commitments or supervision meetings. Sometimes, such as when there are major political or environmental changes in response to the COVID-19 pandemic, there has been a minimalisation of 'working' sessions, and a majority of the session is spent talking, supporting each other, and working through common concerns/providing advice. SIPS also aims to provide people the opportunity to discuss issues within their studies as they arose which are not specific to the COVID-19 pandemic. For example, some people have worked through supervision issues, others have had a chance to practise a presentation and get feedback from the rest of the attendees, and some have talked through issues with their employment and balancing this with their studies.

As identified at the outset of this chapter, a topic that was raised by attendees was the idea of conducting a research project focused on the impact and benefits of the SIPS sessions. While the topic of conducting a research project involving attendees continued across several sessions, there was no direct input into how the research would be conducted or any underpinning methodology to guide the research process. As participants and facilitators of SIPS sessions we formed a research team to undertake designing and implementing a research-based project. We decided that we would start by exploring potential methods and methodologies that could be useful to guide a study involving SIPS attendees. Due to the nature of the online writing sessions developing as a 'Community of Practice' (Shacham and Od-Cohen, 2009) whereby attendees supported each other with completing self-identified writing outcomes, the adoption of a collaborative research methodology was deemed the most appropriate. In addition, we identified the need to adopt a methodology that enabled attendees the opportunity to reflect on their own experiences from being involved in SIPS sessions.

Methodological exploration

As a team we began exploring methodology literature that encapsulated the collaborative nature of SIPS as well as providing an opportunity for participants to reflect on their own experiences. This resulted in the team exploring three key methodologies; first, autoethnography, followed by collaborative autoethnography, and then netnography. The next section of this chapter provides a brief overview of each methodology as well as identifies the elements we viewed would be of use to explore the experiences of SIPS attendees.

Autoethnography

Autoethnography is a research approach that allows the author to write in a highly personalised style, seeking to describe and systematically analyse the personal experiences of the author, in order to understand societal phenomenon (Ellis, Adams, and Bochner, 2011). Autoethnography seeks to acknowledge the complicated link between the personal and the cultural and to make room for non-traditional forms of inquiry and expression (Wall, 2006). Mendez (2013) explains that autoethnography can range from research about personal experiences of a research process to parallel exploration of the researcher's and the participants' experiences, and/ or the experience of the researcher while conducting a specific piece of research. According to Jones (2007), autoethnographic texts are reflexive and self-critical and strive to create an emotionally and intellectually charged engagement of selves, bodies, texts, and contexts. To create such texts, autoethnographers adopt the conventions of literary writing, calling upon the power of personal narrative and storytelling to conjure how selves are constructed, disclosed, silenced, implicated, and changed in the acts of telling and reading (Jones, 2007).

Thompson-Lee (2017) and Denejkina (2017) point out that there are two forms of autoethnography – evocative and analytical. Evocative autoethnography 'focuses on emotion, evocation of emotion, and self-expression' (Denejkina, 2017: 3) that allows the researcher to examine themselves, their identity, and emotions as well as experiences and how these may be impacted by social and cultural structures (Haynes, 2017). Analytic autoethnography seeks to analyse and generalise the data rather than provide personal reflections and stories of experiences (Anderson, 2006; Borders and Giordano, 2016). Anderson (2006: 387) points out those who adopt an analytic autoethnographic approach analyse data seeking to stimulate 'theoretical development, refinement, and extension' which can then be used to further encourage conversations.

A key aspect of autoethnography is that it can provide a voice to the voiceless (Denzin, 2013) and provides flexibility as it can serve different purposes across different studies (Denejkina, 2017). There are many advantages of this methodology. One of the main advantages of personal narratives is that they provide access to the researcher's life, therefore acquiring rich data quickly and easily. However, this advantage also entails a limitation as, by using personal narratives, the research is also limited in its conclusions (Mendez, 2013). We also identified that autoethnography tended to be single participant/researcher focused. As such there was a need to explore a collaborative or group version that could draw from the advantages of an autoethnographic approach.

Collaborative autoethnography

Further exploration led us to identifying collaborative autoethnography as being an underpinning methodology that could overcome the individualistic limitation of autoethnography as it involves both the individual reflection or narrative, followed by interpreting data collectively and collaboratively within a team.

Expanding upon autoethnography as a qualitative research method, collaborative autoethnography is the paradoxical act of engaging in the study of the self, in a collective (Chang, Ngunjiri, and Hernandez, 2016). Importantly, collaborative autoethnography allows for two levels of reflection – the individual, through initial autoethnographic reflection, followed by the interpreting this data collectively and collaboratively, within the context of sociocultural, economic, and ecological settings (Chang, Ngunjiri, and Hernandez, 2016). This layered act of reflection and interpretation of purposeful, intentional storytelling has been argued to act as a pathway for transformative learning, especially for students in higher education (Blalock and Akehi, 2018).

Within higher degree research, there have been several uses of collaborative autoethnography to better understand how candidates engage with leadership training (Hargons et al, 2017), mentoring (Duffy et al, 2019), and their roles as a researcher and as a participant (Cicek et al, 2020). Beyond that, doctoral work has been increasingly allowing collaborative writing (Chang, Ngunjiri, and Hernandez, 2013; Blalock and Akehi, 2018) suggesting greater use and understanding of collaboration.

Doctoral writing groups provide many opportunities for this collaboration (Aitchison and Guerin, 2014; Vacek et al, 2019), but beyond that, provide social structures needed to support doctoral candidates to complete their studies (Spaulding and Rockinson-Szapkiw, 2012). Vacek et al (2019) conducted a collaborative autoethnographic investigation into a doctorial writing group which emerged from their doctoral programme in 2018 and sought to understand how the group practice of doctoral writing contributed to the successes and failures of the candidates involved. Findings from this study suggested that it was necessary for writing groups to consider how they can support the writing ecology and maintain flexibility within group practices to accommodate for the lifestyle changes that many doctoral candidates undergo. However, these groups also met in person for a considerable period, and while there were some elements of these groups which broached into a digital sphere, much of their strengths were from physical interactions.

To date there has been limited use of collaborative autoethnography within a digital environment. As the SIPS initiative was solely based on connections and interactions occurring online, we viewed it necessary to investigate qualitative research methodologies that focus on online communities. This led us to exploring netnography.

Netnography

Netnography is a very specific form of qualitative research methodology that focuses on online communities and online cultures. Netnography draws from ethnographic research techniques and recognises online communities are constructed by group members (Costello, McDermott, and Wallace, 2017). A major aspect of netnography is the inclusion of researcher engagement with their online community (Kozinets, 2015). The development of netnography as a specific methodology was recognised as a new approach as online social platforms, and the way people interact on them is different to the everyday world and face-to-face connections (Kozinets, 2015).

Online social media platforms are largely developed and enhanced by the members who are committed to investing their time to this form of community (Costello, McDermott, and Wallace, 2017). As netnography is more of a naturalistic approach to research, data is captured through researcher and member observation (Kozinets, Dolbec, and Earley, 2014). Netnography allows for the collection and analyses of digital communication artefacts (such as chatroom texts or images) through digital platforms.

As a methodological approach, netnography appeared to be very adaptive and had the potential to be useful in respect to a study exploring the experiences and views of SIPS participants. We viewed that adopting aspects related to netnography would enable us to observe the interactions between participants and identify the participants ability to take ownership of the sessions. Netnographic research is also suitable for dealing with sensitive and personal topics (Kozinets, 2010), and while SIPS does not provide participants the opportunity to be anonymous during sessions, it has created a community where participants are comfortable sharing their experiences with one another.

After adopting key aspects of netnography as SIPS was being constructed, we found using a methodology that had a focus with online communities and researcher participation was a useful methodological approach. Consequently, we decided to draw from both collaborative autoethnography and netnography resulting in a Collaborative AutoNetnographic approach to explore the impact and benefits of attendees being involved in SIPS.

Collaborative AutoNetnography

Essentially, we define Collaborative AutoNetnography as a methodology that involves two or more people working as a team, both as participants and researchers, to explore share reflexive stories concerning online experiences, that ensures a balance between the narratives of individuals with the collective online experiences. We put forward that the use of a Collaborative AutoNetnographic approach will assist with developing a deeper understanding of the cultural norms and process that are being created within online communities.

Data collection involved participants writing personal reflections of the impact and benefits they perceived from their involvement in SIPS. Participants were not constrained with any specific word count limits to their personal reflection stories. Self-reflection narratives were initially sent to the research team to be collated and redistributed to all participants to review. Participants were invited to select their own pseudonyms which were applied prior to redistribution of stories to all involved in the study. The core research team then provided participants with basic instructions regarding thematically analysing reflection stories. This included seeking participants to first read through each story and make notes of the core ideas they perceived arose from each story. Participants were advised that they could identify as many core ideas they felt were relevant to each story and that no idea was 'wrong'. Participants were then asked to 'collate' their ideas into general themes. Again, participants were advised that there was no right number of themes or theme titles. The research team gave participants four weeks to conduct their analysis.

Participants were then encouraged to discuss the heuristic commonalities across the reflection narratives to identify themes during a SIPS session. As a collective, attendees involved in the research project discussed theme names, sub-themes within themes, and interpreting connections between themes. Consensus concerning themes and sub-theme identification was reached when all participants agreed.

Overcoming issues from adopting a Collaborative AutoNetnographic study

Adopting a Collaborative AutoNetnographic approach had unique barriers, enablers, and ethical issues that emerged as the study was being developed and implemented. Ethical considerations such as inclusion and exclusion criteria; participant and researcher well-being; and issues of power between individuals were initially discussed among the research team and then with SIPS attendees. As the idea of conducting a research project was initially raised by SIPS attendees, all of whom were doctoral candidates, discussion regarding ethical issues was not foreign. All agreed that any person who had attended more than one SIPS session would be invited to be involved in the study.

As Geist-Martin et al (2010) point out, autoethnographic studies can be risky because they are inherently about revealing deep personal thoughts and experiences. Adopting a collaborative approach to the study assisted with managing ethical risks associated with participant/researcher well-being as well as concerns related to power between individuals. As the study was conducted while participants continued to be involved in the regular SIPS sessions, this enabled participants to strike a balance between encouraging others to share personal views and experiences, while also developing a safe space to reduce any forms of distress or discomfort. The sharing of experiences and feelings had become a normalised aspect of SIPS sessions. For some, SIPS sessions allowed them to 'vent their feelings' about a range of topics, including the impact of COVID-19 on their daily lives, issues with doctoral studies, university resources access limitations, as well as pressures regarding online undergraduate teaching. This openness of discussing a variety of personal topics and experiences during SIPS sessions created concerns among some participants about the level of sensitivity in their reflections. They indicated they wanted to be open about their experiences and session discussions and how SIPS how assisted them with specific issues but didn't want some discussions (for example, issues with their universities) to be recorded in their reflections as this could result in them being identifiable. Participants were consistently advised they could decide the level of detail in their reflection stories as well as indicating all information provided by them would remain anonymous, with any data used in future journal publications or conferences not containing information about specific tertiary institutions or academic staff names.

As with any research project, data collection can be fraught with issues (such as limited responses/respondents); however, there were no major difficulties in relation to obtaining reflective stories. While most SIPS attendees provided reflexive stories within a set time frame, a few took a little longer. Those who did not provide a reflexive story by the initial research deadline were openly supported and encouraged by those who had, with a number of attendees indicating that they initially found writing their reflections was a little difficult but that once they got started, they found it much easier to complete.

Another barrier that appeared to be overcome during the implementation of the Collaborative AutoNetnographic study was related to each participant's experiences with qualitative research. While some members of the writing group had limited prior experiences of qualitative methodologies, others were conducting their doctoral studies within qualitative approaches. This barrier was again overcome due to the collaborative approach adopted throughout the study resulting in those doctoral students conducting qualitative studies 'training' and supporting those aligned within quantitative approaches.

Conclusion

As stated at the outset of this chapter, 2020 will be a year few will forget. While the COVID-19 global pandemic has resulted in unprecedented societal problems and disruptions, it has also provided an opportunity to explore and develop innovative practices across several fields. As a result of physical distancing restrictions imposed on communities, the shift to using online digital communication technologies became imperative, particularly in the tertiary education system. The identification and development of SIPS was born out of an understanding of the social isolation that doctoral students can face at any time during their studies and exasperated by COVID-19. While 'writing groups' have been used by universities to support doctoral students these are usually established within individual institutions due to the face-to-face nature of such initiatives. To our knowledge there are very few cross-institutional, multi-disciplinary support groups for doctoral students. The evolution of SIPS by doctoral students, for doctoral students during the COVID-19 crisis, indicates such initiatives are useful for some; however, as there is no overarching organisational support it is not clear whether such initiatives are sustainable into the future.

As a result of SIPS involving doctoral students, the topic of conducting a study focusing on the experiences and perceptions of attendees arose naturally. From this initial discussion among SIPS participants the need to adopt an appropriate methodology became apparent. Consequently, a

Collaborative AutoNetnographic methodology was developed and trialled with attendees. A key value of adopting this approach is that it aligned with the nature and norms of the collective. Sharing feelings and frustrations, highs and lows, successes and challenges became normalised during regular SIPS sessions. Adopting a research methodology that continued to support this collective norm appeared not only appropriate but also necessary to ensure those involved in the study felt safe and secure in relation to providing personal, in-depth reflective stories.

The methodological approach we have identified in this chapter should be viewed as a guide rather than a set of rules in relation to Collaborative AutoNetnography. As Denejkina (2017) points out, autoethnographic studies provide flexibility as they can serve different purposes across different studies. We would argue that our identification of Collaborative AutoNetnography continues this tradition. We would argue, however, that the adoption of this particular methodology should be firmly located with a participatory research approach, much like those who adopt a Participatory Action Research approach. Conducting online research with members of groups can be challenging, particularly if a study is seeking in-depth reflections. While a value of using a Collaborative AutoNetnographic approach can provide deep understandings of an online culture, adopting an approach that aligns with the expectations and norms of an online group is paramount. The development of Collaborative AutoNetnography emerged from the culture of the online environment that became the focus of the study. This was achieved, in part, by the involvement of the authors as regular participants of the online community. Essentially, we were insiders. We would advise future researchers contemplating using a Collaborative AutoNetnographic approach to be aware of not only the online group norms but also their situation in relation to the online group.

While other qualitative researchers may have developed similar approaches during the COVID-19 pandemic, we are not aware of this methodological approach being discussed in previous academic literature. We encourage other researchers in the future to draw on our ideas presented in this chapter to further push the boundaries concerning the adoption of collaborative qualitative methodologies within an increasingly digital world. We also encourage those involved in establishing and/or managing doctoral student 'writing groups' to create safe spaces through which the voices of those involved in those programmes can be heard.

Notes

[1] In Australia those studying in Master by Research and PhD degrees are referred to as HDR students.

[2] Australian HDR students primarily work with their supervisor(s) throughout their degree with either very limited or no requirement to be involved in any scheduled coursework.

References

Agostino, D., Arnaboldi, M., and Lampis, A. (2020) 'Italian state museums during the COVID-19 crisis: from onsite closure to online openness', *Museum Management and Curatorship*, 35(4): 362–72.

Aitchison, C. and Guerin, C. (eds) (2014) *Writing Groups for Doctoral Education and Beyond: Innovations in Practice and Theory*, London: Routledge.

Ali, A. and Kohun, F. (2006) 'Dealing with isolation feelings in IS doctoral programs', *International Journal of Doctoral Studies*, 1(1): 21–33.

Ali, A., Kohun, F., and Levy, Y. (2007) 'Dealing with social isolation to minimize doctoral attrition – a four stage framework', *International Journal of Doctoral Studies*, 2(1): 33–49.

Anderson, L. (2006) 'Analytic autoethnography', *Journal of Contemporary Ethnography*, 35(4):373–95.

Australian Broadcasting Corporation (2020) 'Australia's social distancing rules have been enhanced to slow coronavirus – here's how they work', available from: https://www.abc.net.au/news/2020-03-20/coronavirus-covid-19-scott-morrison-enhanced-social-distancing/12075532

Australian Bureau of Statistics (2020) *Household Impacts of COVID-19 Survey*, Cat no 4940.0, Canberra.

Banerjee, D. and Rai, M. (2020) 'Social isolation in Covid-19: the impact of loneliness', *International Journal of Social Psychiatry*, 66(6): 525–7.

Beasy, K. et al (2020) 'Writing together to foster wellbeing: doctoral writing groups as spaces of wellbeing', *Higher Education Research and Development*, 1–15.

Blalock, A. and Akehi, M. (2018) 'Collaborative autoethnography as a pathway for transformative learning', *Journal of Transformative Education*, 16(2): 89–107.

Borders, L. and Giordano, A. (2016) 'Confronting confrontation in clinical supervision: an analytical autoethnography', *Journal of Counseling & Development*, 94(4): 454–63.

Brooke, J. and Jackson, D. (2020) 'Older people and COVID-19: isolation, risk and ageism', *Journal of Clinical Nursing*, 29(13–14): 2044–6.

Cacioppo, J. and Patrick, W. (2008) *Loneliness: Human Nature and the Need for Social Connection*, New York: W.W. Norton.

Cacioppo, J., Hawkley, L., Norman, G., and Berntson, G. (2011) 'Social isolation', *Annals of the New York Academy of Sciences*, 1231(1): 17–22.

Chang, H., Ngunjiri, F., and Hernandez, K. (2013) *Collaborative Autoethnography*, Willow Creek, CA: Left Coast Press.

Chang, H., Ngunjiri, F., and Hernandez, K. (2016) *Collaborative Autoethnography*, London: Routledge.

Chiang, K. (2003) 'Learning experiences of doctoral students in UK universities', *International Journal of Sociology and Social Policy*, 23(1/2): 4–32.

Cicek, J., Paul, R., Sheridan, P., and Kuley, L. (2020) 'Researchers explore their roles as participant-researchers in characterizing the lived experiences of graduate students in engineering education research in Canada: a collaborative autoethnography', *Canadian Journal of Science, Mathematics and Technology Education*, 1–18.

Cirillo, F. (2009) 'The Pomodoro technique', available from: http://pomodorotechnique.com

Costello, L., McDermott, M., and Wallace, R. (2017) 'Netnography: range of practices, misperceptions, and missed opportunities', *International Journal of Qualitative Methods*, 16: 1–16.

Deem, R. and Brehony, K. (2000) 'Doctoral students' access to research culture – are some more equal than others?', *Studies in Higher Education*, 25(2): 149–65.

Denejkina, A. (2017) 'Exo-autoethnography: an introduction', *Forum: Qualitative Social Research*, 18(3): 1–12.

Denzin, N. (2013) *Interpretive Autoethnography*, London: Sage.

Dhawan, S. (2020) 'Online learning: a panacea in the time of COVID-19 crisis', *Journal of Educational Technology Systems*, 49(1): 5–22.

Duffy, J., Wickersham-Fish, L., Rademaker, L., and Wetzler, E. (2019) 'Using collaborative autoethnography to explore online doctoral mentoring: finding empathy in mentor/protégé relationships', *American Journal of Qualitative Research*, 2(1): 57–76.

Ellis, C., Adams, T., and Bochner, A. (2011) 'Autoethnography: an overview', *Forum: Qualitative Social Research*, 12(1): 273–90.

Farooq, A., Laato, S., and Islam, A. (2020) 'Impact of online information on self-isolation intention during the COVID-19 pandemic: cross-sectional study', *Journal of Medical Internet Research*, 22(5): e19128.

Gallagher, H., Doherty, A., and Obonyo, M. (2020) 'International student experiences in Queensland during COVID-19', *International Social Work*, 0020872820949621.

Garbe, A., Ogurlu, U., Logan, N., and Cook, P. (2020) 'Parents' experiences with remote education during COVID-19 school closures', *American Journal of Qualitative Research*, 4(3): 45–65.

Geist-Martin, P. et al (2010) 'Exemplifying collaborative autoethnographic practice via shared stories of mothering', *Journal of Research Practice*, 6(1): M8.

Hargons, C., Lantz, M., Reid Marks, L., and Voelkel, E. (2017) 'Becoming a bridge: collaborative autoethnography of four female counseling psychology student leaders', *The Counseling Psychologist*, 45(7): 1017–47.

Hawkley, L. and Cacioppo, J. (2010) 'Loneliness matters: a theoretical and empirical review of consequences and mechanisms', *Annals of Behavioral Medicine*, 40(2): 218–27.

Haynes, K. (2017) 'Autoethnography in accounting research', in Z. Hoque, L. Parker, M. Covaleski, and K. Haynes, (eds) *The Routledge Companion to Qualitative Accounting Research Methods*, London: Routledge.

Janta, H., Lugosi, P., and Brown, L. (2014) Coping with loneliness: a netnographic study of doctoral students', *Journal of Further and Higher Education*, 38(4): 553–71.

Jiranek, V. (2010) 'Potential predictors of timely completion among dissertation research students at an Australian faculty of sciences', *International Journal of Doctoral Studies*, 5(1): 1–13.

Johnstone, M. (2020) 'Online mass exodus: how Australian unis are coping with COVID-19', *IT News*, available from: https://www.itnews.com.au/news/online-mass-exodus-how-australian-unis-are-coping-with-the-covid-19-pandemic-539630

Jones, S. (2007) *Autoethnography*, Wiley Online Library, available from: https://onlinelibrary.wiley.com/doi/full/10.1002/9781405165518.wbeosa082 .

Kissler, S., Tedijanto, C., Lipsitch, M., and Grad, Y. (2020) 'Social distancing strategies for curbing the COVID-19 epidemic', *medRxiv*, available from: https://www.medrxiv.org/content/10.1101/2020.03.22.20041079v1

Konstantopoulou, G. and Raikou, N. (2020) 'Clinical evaluation of depression in university students during quarantine due to Covid-19 pandemic', *European Journal of Public Health Studies*, 3(1), doi: http://dx.doi.org/10.46827/ejphs.v3i1.65

Kozinets, R. (2010) *Netnography: Doing Ethnographic Research Online*, London: Sage.

Kozinets, R. (2015) 'Netnography: seeking understanding in a networked communication society', available from: https://www.researchgate.net/profile/Robert_Kozinets/publication/325942107_Netnography/links/5c8fc3fa92851c1df94a0bed/Netnography.pdf

Kozinets, R., Dolbec, P., and Earley, A. (2014) *Qualitative Data Analysis*, London: Sage.

Lee, A. (2020) 'COVID-19 and the advancement of digital physical therapist practice and telehealth', *Physical Therapy*, 100(7): 1054–7.

Lehna, C., Hermanns, M., Monsivais, D., and Engebretson, J. (2016) 'From dissertation defense to dissemination: jump start your academic career with a scholar mentor group', *Nursing Forum*, 51(1): 62–9.

Leigh-Hunt, N. et al (2017) 'An overview of systematic reviews on the public health consequences of social isolation and loneliness', *Public Health*, 152: 157–71.

Lewnard, J. and Lo, N. (2020) 'Scientific and ethical basis for social-distancing interventions against COVID-19', *The Lancet Infectious Diseases*, 20(6): 631–3.

Li, S., Beames, J., Newby, J., Maston, K., Christensen, H., and Werner-Seidler, A. (2020) 'The impact of COVID-19 on the lives and mental health of Australian adolescents', *medRxiv*, pre-print, available from: https://www.medrxiv.org/content/10.1101/2020.09.07.20190124v1

Maher, M., Fallucca, A., and Mulhern Halasz, H. (2013) 'Write on! through to the Ph.D.: using writing groups to facilitate doctoral degree progress', *Studies in Continuing Education*, 35(2): 193–208.

Mendez, M. (2013) 'Autoethnography as a research method: advantages, limitations and criticisms', *Colombian Applied Linguistics Journal*, 15(2): 279–87.

Obrenovic, B., Du, J., Godinic, D., Tsoy, D., Khan, M., and Jakhongirov, I. (2020) 'Sustaining enterprise operations and productivity during the COVID-19 pandemic: "Enterprise Effectiveness and Sustainability Model"', *Sustainability*, 12(15): 5981–6008.

Rapanta, C., Botturi, L., Goodyear, P., Guàrdia, L., and Koole, M. (2020) 'Online university teaching during and after the Covid-19 crisis: refocusing teacher presence and learning activity', *Postdigital Science and Education*, 1–23.

Shacham, M. and Od-Cohen, Y. (2009) 'Rethinking PhD learning incorporating communities of practice', *Innovations in Education and Teaching International*, 46(3): 279–92.

Shakespeare-Finch, J. et al (2020) 'COVID-19: an Australian Perspective', *Journal of Loss and Trauma*, 25(8): 662–72.

Son, C., Hegde, S., Smith, A., Wang, X., and Sasangohar, F. (2020a) 'Effects of COVID-19 on college students' mental health in the United States: interview survey study', *Journal of Medical Internet Research*, 22(9): e21279.

Son, J., Nimrod, G., West, S., Janke, M., Liechty, T., and Naar, J. (2020b) 'Promoting older adults' physical activity and social well-being during COVID-19', *Leisure Sciences*, 1–8.

Spaulding, L. and Rockinson-Szapkiw, A. (2012) 'Hearing their voices: factors doctoral candidates attribute to their persistence', *International Journal of Doctoral Studies*, 7(1): 199–219.

Stickley, A. and Koyanagi, A. (2016) 'Loneliness, common mental disorders and suicidal behavior: findings from a general population survey', *Journal of Affective Disorders*, 197: 81–7.

Thompson-Lee, C. (2017) *Heteronormativity in a Rural School Community: An Autoethnography*, Rotterdam: Sense Publishers.

Trede, F., Macklin, R., and Bridges, D. (2012) 'Professional identity development: a review of the higher education literature', *Studies in Higher Education*, 37(3): 365–84.

Tremblay-Wragg, É., Mathieu Chartier, S., Labonté-Lemoyne, É., Déri, C., and Gadbois, M. (2020) 'Writing more, better, together: how writing retreats support graduate students through their journey', *Journal of Further and Higher Education*, 1–12.

Tyndall, D., Forbes III, T., Avery, J., and Powell, S. (2019) 'Fostering scholarship in doctoral education: using a social capital framework to support PhD student writing groups', *Journal of Professional Nursing*, 35(4): 300–4.

Usher, K., Bhullar, N., Durkin, J., Gyamfi, N., and Jackson, D. (2020) 'Family violence and COVID-19: increased vulnerability and reduced options for support', *International Journal of Mental Health Nursing*, 29(4): 549–52.

Vacek, K., Donohue, W., Gates, A., Lee, A., and Simpson, S. (2019) 'Seeking balance within personal writing ecologies: a collaborative autoethnography of a doctoral student writing group', *Studies in Continuing Education*, 1–15, DOI: 10.1080/0158037X.2019.1703670.

Wall, S. (2006) 'An autoethnography on learning about autoethnography', *International Journal of Qualitative Methods*, 5(2): 146–60.

Wang, L. and DeLaquil, T. (2020) 'The isolation of doctoral education in the times of COVID-19: recommendations for building relationships within person-environment theory', *Higher Education Research and Development*, 1–5.

Wilson, R. et al (2007) 'Loneliness and risk of Alzheimer disease', *Archives of General Psychiatry*, 64(2): 234–40.

Wosik, J. et al (2020) 'Telehealth transformation: COVID-19 and the rise of virtual care', *Journal of the American Medical Informatics Association*, 27(6): 957–62.

8

The ethical implications of using digital traces: studying explainability and trust during a pandemic

Natasha Dwyer, Hector Miller-Bakewell, Tessa Darbyshire, Anirban Basu, and Steve Marsh

Introduction

Digital technologies give researchers new opportunities to access the most personal thoughts of those who use them. The ethics and implications of using data from peoples' everyday interactions have recently become a mainstream topic of concern (Lucivero, 2020). In some contexts, such as governance, it can be argued that algorithmically-generated decisions are valued over individuals' and communities' expertise (Danaher, 2016). As with other projects described in this book, our work is being carried out during the COVID-19 pandemic. The crisis has highlighted the ethical complications that occur when vulnerable individuals requiring information are surveilled in a rapidly changing environment. Currently, worldwide legislative changes are determining how data-intensive technologies, including forms of data collection and surveillance, are used. Recent history indicates that once the initial threat has passed, legislation remains and becomes the 'new normal' (Lodders and Paterson, 2020).

Organisations, including universities, are establishing mechanisms for collecting and managing stakeholder data, which will remain in place after the pandemic. The collected data will become part of the hidden curriculum, the subtle messages students receive about what an institution values, and the nature of the power relations inherent in its interactions (Kayama et al, 2015). In this chapter we outline and engage with the ethical practices involved in performing such data collection, with a particular focus on the use of chatbot transcripts.

We particularly highlight the impact of crisis scenarios on 'information anxiety' (Blundell et al, 2014) in undergraduate students and evaluate the potential of chatbots as a tool to improve information literacy. Chatbots can be used to enable individuals to seek information ranging from functional to personal, including information that may be sensitive or personal in nature.

As students adapt to the new normal of education during crisis, individuals can suffer from information anxiety as they seek assurance to help deal with new and changing circumstances. In the case of the COVID-19 pandemic, these include increased digital learning, increased working off-campus, and increased social isolation. Information overload (Soroya et al, 2021) can contribute significantly to information anxiety as organisations seek to provide guidance and support across many different topics. This can result in confusion if it is difficult to search the information that a given individual prioritises. In times of crisis, the need for tools that increase information literacy and enable effective filtering becomes apparent. The extremity of a crisis situation highlights the concerns we should have with technology in more 'everyday' situations (Troshynski et al, 2008).

Here, we use transcripts from a chatbot in a university setting to inform a project exploring explainable artificial intelligence (XAI) and trust. XAI is a practice that seeks to provide those engaging with automated systems with some insight into the rationale behind a given decision-making process. However, this chapter does not primarily deal with our research findings with respect to XAI and trust, but offers to give an account of the ethical issues we have encountered while collecting this data. During the COVID-19 pandemic, the shift to online education and activities has exacerbated ethical questions; for example, through the introduction of practices such as digital proctoring in learning assessment and track and trace systems. These practices are invasive and disrupt the experience of individual students in unprecedented ways (Zeide, forthcoming). Monitoring may impact on trust relations in learning environments, affect students' educational experience, and shape graduates' expectations of work life. Chatbots are an example of the displacement of professional expertise occurring in the learning environment, as personalised learning systems are developed. Crises drive rapid technological innovation and the increase in home learning as the COVID-19 pandemic has progressed has resulted in digital technologies increasingly replacing in-person services such as student support. In a crisis, individuals have less choice, and trust may become a luxury, there is more pressure and less opportunity to seek input and support for decisions. As Zeide (forthcoming) writes: 'Transparency is not just important for algorithmic and school accountability, but also for students' ability to exercise agency over their own education.' If those responsible for the design of digital technologies do not adopt ethical practices, there is a risk of acclimatising students to accept invasive digital surveillance cultures, practices that are becoming increasingly significant in their education and future work environments. We do not wish to contribute to this culture.

The chapter closes with an exploration of strategies that can guide an ethical use of digital data traces. As digital researchers have established (see Chang (2018) for an overview), even though digital technologies are fraught with risk, we need the involvement of practitioners who can critique and suggest development processes that are fairer and more trustworthy. Additionally, students need to be aware of the complexities and the potential of technology to be used for benefit or harm in order to be prepared for a world where digital technology inhabits ever more of our private lives and thinking. As Lodders and Paterson (2020) predict, some of the invasive digital technologies that have been deployed in this time of crisis, such as contact tracing, will experience 'scope creep', moving from required-for-now to a new normal. In the education context, we need technology controllers to carefully consider how we move forward out of the crisis, evaluating which practices are beneficial to students and which should be deactivated.

Project context: XAI and trust

To provide context to our chapter we now briefly explain our wider project. Our broader research aim is the design of trust-enabling systems that enable users to make informed decisions and determine their own level of trust or comfort in a digital system (Dwyer et al, 2013; Basu et al, 2019). In this case we are studying XAI, artificial intelligence systems that explain to users the internal state of a system so that the user can understand the system's logic. Authors such as Pasquale (2015) and Danaher (2016) point out that the 'black box' phenomenon of AI, where humans are put 'out of the loop', make AI systems impenetrable (and thereby untrustworthy) to humans. XAI attempts to compensate for this ethical risk by explaining the box's contents to users, thereby generating trust. We wish to explore the type of explanations people want and how they ask questions of a system (Miller et al, 2017).

An explanation needs to be tailored to a particular learner's needs, their priorities, and what they are already familiar with (Miller et al, 2017). The role of trust is central. Trust, in this context, means that a learner will cross the threshold of uncertainty and accept an explanation, sometimes unthinkingly, and so may rely on untrustworthy systems (Hoffman et al, 2018). In a crisis, trust can work as a shield, allowing individuals to receive information from trusted institutions and so continue their work or learning in a difficult situation without the mental load of filtering what to trust and what information should be rejected. Thus trust can make individuals vulnerable and put them in a position where they may be taken advantage of (Moliner-Tena et al, 2018; Kye and Hwang, 2020). There is evidence to suggest that explanation mechanisms are not widely adopted because many are regarded as unethical or untrustworthy (Miller et al, 2017). To address this trust gap, we might seek to incorporate trust indicators such as highlighting a system's purpose, process, and performance, so that users might utilise these to determine trustworthiness (Sanneman and Shah, 2020). Purpose refers to how much the system is used for the reasons it was originally designed. Process is how appropriate an AI system is in the context in which it is being used. Finally, the dimension of performance is an exploration of how predictable and reliable a system is.

There is research outlining ways to embed explanation mechanisms into systems to assist users. For instance, Kulesza et al (2015) argue that developers should beware of overwhelming users. Explanations can be fraught and make an interaction more complex and bewildering, putting off users who may be worried about their lack of domain knowledge. There are questions that researchers generally agree a successful explanation model should address, including: how does the system work? What did it just do? Why did it do what it did? Who is impacted by the decision? Who needs to understand the decision? What level of explanation is required?

Hoffman et al (2018) add an important contribution to our methodology in studying XAI: 'The property of "being an explanation" is not a property of statements, it is an interaction.' Explaining is not an abstract task undertaken by a developer to help others understand their work in the form of a one-way broadcast; explaining is a conversation between those involved in a system. To the list of questions to which an XAI responds, we wish to add: what are you doing with the data from my current interaction?

Studying users and the questions they might have for a system

We are using transcripts from a chatbot to inform our research. The chatbot we are using is designed for and by university students attending Victoria University in Australia. The purpose of the chatbot is to provide a novel information pathway for students, written by existing students. The chatbot was originally planned to be used as a support tool for students attending university on campus. The student experience moved to a remote setting and in Australia, as we write, there are no plans to move back to the classroom and our chatbot will need to support students coming into the university who may have little understanding of university. Chatbots use AI, an underlying system that tries to predict what the user wants. These systems aim to be proactive in reducing the effort required from users in order to interact and achieve their aims (Winkler et al, 2020). Students are involved in each stage of the design. Some students have scripted responses for the chatbot; for instance, explaining academic expectations. Informal observations of interactions with our chatbot suggest that topics our students think are important include: dealing with stress, accessing resources and support when the university buildings are closed, coping with assignment-driven anxiety, making friends and connecting with others, and dealing with homesickness and boredom. The popular press has told us that the stress of young people is much higher during the pandemic and our informal observations of interactions with the chatbot echo this. Students give consent for their anonymised data to be used; however, previous research argues that the act of ticking 'yes' to a consent form does not necessarily mean that users have understood that they might be surveilled (Basu et al, 2019). The act of consenting represents a transfer of power (Basu et al, 2019). Additionally, students may not feel they should select what they would privately prefer, when asked by a university member about consenting to be involved in a data-gathering exercise because they fear their decision may impact their marks. During a crisis, individuals may be more likely to agree, as discussed previously, because their ability to negotiate with systems may be diminished (Moliner-Tena et al, 2018; Kye and Hwang, 2020).

It is easy to see that the topics students want to talk about can be personal and that their disclosures could reveal protected characteristics. For instance, a student might like to ask 'Are there any LGBTQ+ societies?' or 'Is there a wheelchair ramp for this entrance?' Research indicates that the data users provide to a chatbot can be more personal than what they might reveal in an interaction with a human such as a study advisor (Brandtzaeg and Følstad, 2018). Individuals feel more freedom to be candid with a machine because they feel that they will not be judged. For instance, a stressed student might want to know how to simply pass a unit and may feel embarrassed about not wanting to excel. We can see from the emotional nature of some of the domains our students are interested in, such as loneliness and boredom, that they may become vulnerable to disclosing personal information about the state of their mental health.

Chatbots can assist students to make sense of the university experience, especially when the information pathways that usually assist students have been constrained by the pandemic. Like other universities, Victoria University has been under pressure to adapt to delivering education remotely. Students themselves are isolated, unemployed, and facing uncertainty. New students at a university have traditionally had the resources of a physical campus – in particular, the serendipitous presence of other students – to help them navigate the new (pedagogic, bureaucratic, cultural, geographic) system they are in. Evaluating the trust mechanism in this context will enable us to determine what is required to enable a positive trust relationship between a student and the chatbot. As Troshynski et al (2008) point out, we learn about more average everyday thoughts and feelings during a crisis because the dynamics around technology are highlighted. Before we can do that, we must first reflect on the ethical challenges entailed by using chatbot transcripts and then return to the issue of what an ethical research process might look like.

Using chatbot transcripts as a data collection tool: ethics of using the traces of new technology

New technologies promise new methods of observing, collecting, and accessing users' inner worlds, sometimes at scale. But they also have a 'darker side' (Ryan and Tynen, 2020). From an ethical perspective, as technology and possibilities change so quickly, it is not sufficient to rely on the advice of government and institutional guidelines or legal frameworks (Legewie and Nassauer, 2018). As technology expands into more areas of individuals' private lives, there will always be new questions to tackle to ascertain an ethical methodology (Thompson et al, 2020). Crisis periods drive a proliferation of technological solutions designed to address a suite of social challenges. The COVID-19 pandemic has driven significant changes in the education space and digital technologies are being used for online learning, online assessment, and student support. It is unlikely that there would have been such a significant pivot towards a digital experience without the crisis context, and many of the technologies are introduced with the aim of monitoring students without significant time being spent assessing the fairness or long-term mental health impacts for individual students. We argue that the use of chatbot transcripts, produced through sometimes highly personal conversations between a human and a machine, is a form of monitoring. There are ethical implications from utilising monitoring as a research tool that we will now unpack.

Surveillance and monitoring form the 'generalized condition of watching and being watched' (Knox, 2010). 'Surveillance capitalism' is a relatively new term to describe the way market forces use data gathered from surveillance activities to promote their own interests (Zuboff, 2019). For instance, an organisation might learn about the behaviour of those who interact with it in order to promote more of its services to them. According to Zuboff (2019), the forms of digital technologies that can be used for surveillance are varied and if the data is easy to access, the technology becomes more attractive. The need for a digital interface for learning in this crisis has provided an opportunity to rapidly introduce data collection systems that might otherwise have spent longer in development or been rejected outright for ethical reasons. Digital chatbot transcripts represent data that could prove very attractive to surveillance capitalism, since system users are providing their thoughts in written form, ready to be searched and categorised.

Universities have always utilised surveillance to monitor students, staff, and their results (Watters, 2017). Lyon calls this practice in education 'surveillance culture'. As forms of digital experience, due to the COVID-19 pandemic, are blurring individuals' boundaries between work, study, and private lives, Collier and Ross (2020) argue that people working in universities need to be more critical of tightening relationships between surveillance culture and surveillance capitalism. How can privacy rights be established and maintained? We argue that educators need to pay attention to the messages they are giving students about the use of technology so that students are informed about ethical practices now and in their lives after university.

Educational environments have an explicit curriculum that includes the subjects and the rules of conduct (Perry-Hazan and Birnhack, 2018). But there is also the 'hidden curriculum' – the subtle messages to students about the values and codes of behaviour of an institution (Kayama et al, 2015). By utilising chatbot transcripts, even with consent, are we providing students with a hidden curriculum of what Furedi (2006) describes as a 'morality of low expectation'? Are we giving students the message that performing research on data, that has been retrieved from a technology they used to seek personal assistance, is acceptable? Does this acclimatise them to surveillance society? Duffy and Chan (2019) describe the ways college students already adapt their behaviour in response to the assumption that their social network accounts will be viewed by those who will have an impact on their lives, such as future employers. We argue that 'scope creep' of digital technologies introduced during the pandemic is reasonably likely as universities have invested time and money in their development and are gaining valuable monitoring data that might not have been available outside the crisis context. If this is the case, the new normal will include acclimatisation to technologies that support surveillance society.

The impact of the hidden curriculum does not finish once a student's course is complete. Students carry with them an understanding of the world shaped by their university experience and the power structures they have engaged with. Arguably, they are vulnerable and the world of work that today's students will enter will be very different from that of previous generations. Remote work in some form is here to stay, as it has been demonstrated to work for employers and employees. There is a larger talent pool to select from and office costs can be saved when employees work from home. The features that we see today in remote work culture were accelerated by COVID-19, resulting in a blurring of work and leisure, in both time and space. Workers' personal domains were encroached upon (McParland and Connolly, 2020). 'Log in, log out' times became blurred and work happened in our bedrooms. Employee monitoring was predicted in 80 per cent of companies by 2021 (Vatcha, 2020). This could include monitoring of typing patterns to ensure workers are functioning at the correct speed, location records, and device tracking so employers know where employees are working from. Other data traces left by employees that can be recorded include call logs, response speed to messages, and search histories. An extreme case is software that uses webcams to take screenshots of employees so they can be reviewed in a 'wall of screens' and checked for correct behaviour and location. There are always justifications that workplaces can provide for monitoring practices, such as providing security, combating insider trading, and improving the design of systems (Vatcha, 2020).

Are we acclimatising the users of our chatbot to accept the power imbalances and hierarchy associated with monitoring and surveillance, such that the traces of their interactions can be used in a range of circumstances? This risks enforcing the distinction between the observed, who provide the data, and the observers, who collect it (Knox, 2010). Those who collect data and undertake research choose whose concerns are represented in their data, who is given access to the data, and how the data is interpreted and applied (Kaufmann and Tzanetakis, 2020). Thompson et al (2020) point out that digital technologies give the observer invisibility: those providing the data are sometimes completely unaware that they are creating data traces for analysis, and that findings from the data can have an impact on their everyday life.

If surveillance causes distrust, leading to a drop in performance, will employees of the future be blamed for the decrease in productivity and take on this blame personally? Distrust can cause anxiety (Cofta, 2006), hinder communication exchanges (Botan, 1996), and curtail motivation (Frey, 1993), making it difficult to function in these new environments. Knox (2010) argues that monitoring practices may become self-fulfilling prophecies, and cause the erosion of trust that they were installed to prevent. Little research has been undertaken into the mechanics of these emerging workplaces (Vatcha, 2020); however, it is known there is already a power imbalance, in that junior employees are being monitored more frequently and intensely than senior members of an organisation (Frey, 1993).

Are we, as researchers using digital tools, no better than social media networks that soften their users to accept continually expanding privacy boundaries? Southerton and Taylor (2020) explain how social media networks operate a cycle of continually violating privacy, sharing users' data in a variety of ways and then re-establishing comfort with a user, making disclosure a habit for individuals. It becomes 'normal' for a user to release data without concern for privacy, the value of data, or the implications of sharing. We can see that norms for acceptable data disclosure are continually shifting, normalising increased sharing. Similar patterns are seen in workplace practices. Facial recognition software and tracking devices were not acceptable until recently. Trust is intertwined with these choices because the actions of data sharing are 'sufficiently cushioned by the familiarity of process or place' (Pink et al, 2018).

Trust is an essential ingredient of learning and is changed by the practice of watching (Ryan and Tynen, 2020). The dynamics of trust change the quality of dialogue and exchange and also the 'intellectual risk-taking' entailed in education and learning relationships (Hai-Jew, 2006). Monitoring has an impact on knowledge production, the process of individuals having the time and space to consider their own understandings and collaborate with others. Foucault (1995) argues that watching is the 'manifestation of distrust' because uncertainty is increased and the data gathered from watching allows for categorising; that is, the segmenting of different types of individuals based on generalised behaviour or types of responses. Categorisation can be harmful because the practice enables prejudicial judgements: 'There's no such thing as flattering stereotypes – only flattening stereotypes' (Raji, 2020). Without trust, there cannot be comfortable relations between individuals, communities, and learning environments that are required for learning to flourish.

Developing a chatbot in a university environment is clearly fraught; it entails entering into surveillance culture and asking those who use our chatbot to trust us. We are presenting a 'hidden curriculum' that gives students messages about what the relationship between those using technology should be. But as authors such as Drucker (2012) argue, it is not enough just to critique technology. Practitioners must engage with it and make their own projects accordingly, if we are to have a hope of highlighting and challenging problematic technology and making future designs more inclusive and less exploitative. McPherson (2012) adds that we also need students and graduates who possess both 'critical and digital literacies'. We will now explain what researchers using forms of digital technology that enable data can do to make surveillance culture visible, taking steps towards an ethical practice.

Suggestions for ethical XAI research and practice

There are measures that can be put in place so that technology owners are worthy of users' trust, can communicate trustworthiness, and ethically use data. Our aim is not to treat the users of our system as 'ill-informed dupes of repressive power' (Southerton and Taylor, 2020) but as students who will be entering a post-crisis world when they exit the university environment.

Collecting non-identifiable data and asking for as little personal disclosure as possible should be built into the design of a chatbot conversation. Another initial measure is to provide a statement in a visible part of the project interface so that potential users of our chatbot are aware of our use of data, so that our monitoring is visible. As Weiser (1999) points out, a problem with some technology implementations is that they disappear. 'They weave themselves into the fabric of everyday life until they are indistinguishable from it.'

Although it is difficult to create awareness of research without risking an interruption to the flow of the interaction (Thompson et al, 2020), visibility of research methods needs to be part of research interactions, as an issue of informed consent (Basu et al, 2019), a practice that attempts to share information, acknowledge power imbalances, and allow healthy relationships between users of a system, whether they are researchers, educators, or technologists. As mentioned earlier, trusted relationships are key to comfortable learning environments. There needs to be a clear statement that is as succinct as possible, reducing friction for users.

Chatbots necessarily provide an opportunity for dialogue with the user. With this in mind a chatbot must, within its own system:

- **Inform** the user of the data collection process.
- **Answer** questions the user has about data collection and its purpose.
- **Respect** the user's requests for privacy.
- **Minimise** the data collection.

A chatbot needs to explain the details of data collection processes in stages. The advantage of a chatbot is that there is a dialogue between user and system, allowing the user to request additional information as required. The chatbot should, in particular, be able to answer questions such as: 'What data are you collecting?' and 'Why are you collecting this data?' It needs to be able to act on the instructions: 'Show me the data you have collected from me', 'Stop collecting my data', and 'Delete data collected from me'. We are striving for this functionality in our project. In practical terms, it is difficult to achieve these aims entirely. The technology we are using to prototype our system is IBM Watson Assistant. IBM has well-developed policies stating that developers own the data they generate. However, it is more difficult to delete data or to stop the collection of an individual's data so that the interactions are not recorded in the system. As Ginart et al (2019) point out, deleting data from a machine learning system is an oxymoron. Machine learning systems learn from potentially every interaction, so to claim that data has been deleted can be a falsehood. Kara (2018) points out that this problem lurks in all forms of data collection; a researcher might delete material from their data set, whether it be paper surveys or audio files of an interview, but this deletion does not erase the data and interaction from the 'hearts and minds' of those who collected the data. Data collection is a complex process since the systems are designed for corporate organisations who tend to gather as much information on their users as possible. Our current design approach is to be clear about the limitations of what we can offer with regard to data privacy.

An additional technique to enable informed consent is a procedure by which users can ask questions about the data and the processes of research. Some AI systems do not have the facility to allow questions within their own interface (Miller, 2019) but there are other ways to provide a forum for questions. For instance, a form on a website with a list of responses to previous questions provides a means to follow up on issues. There should be an option of anonymity for those posting, so that there is no identifiable data to put at risk. There needs to be ways for potential users to ask questions and engage without having to use the tool itself. Users may need some sort of orientation to be able to ask questions, a skill that may be useful for our students in their lives post-university. Questions about data and privacy may not occur to some users. In this instance, access to questions other users have asked might be helpful. For instance, how is the monitoring information stored and who has access to it? How is monitoring information used to make decisions? How can concerns about monitoring and data usage be heard? How can your monitoring processes impact me? This knowledge may be useful in the future for our students during their careers.

Conclusion

This chapter has explored the ethical concerns raised by our broader research into chatbot transcripts for studying trust and XAI. These concerns have been exacerbated through the rapid introduction of monitoring technologies during the COVID-19 pandemic and concerns about the life of these technologies beyond the crisis context. The pandemic pivoted work and learning environments online, and if aspects of remote interaction remain in the new normal the research into data collection, like ours, could be ethically fraught. We argue that using the traces of digital interactions from new digital tools is a form of monitoring, and that this then impacts on trust relations and knowledge production, additionally acclimatising students to a world of work within which surveillance practices are becoming embedded. The pandemic has dramatically increased the adoption and capability of surveillance technology, and there is a strong risk that this technology will become the new normal before it has been properly critiqued.

In addition to our earlier statement that an ethical chatbot must Inform, Answer, Respect, and Minimise, we also suggest that any surveillance system should provide users with ways to question and resist. Especially when it comes to our education system we do not want those we work with to be ill-informed dupes of repressive power.

References

Basu, A., Marsh, S., Darbyshire, T., Dwyer, N., and Miller-Bakewell, H. (2019) 'Empowering people with informed consent', 4th International Conference for Data for Policy: Digital Trust and Personal Data, London.

Blundell, S. and Lambert, F. (2014) 'Information anxiety from the undergraduate student perspective: a pilot study of second-semester freshmen', *Journal of Education for Library and Information Science*, 55: 261–73.

Botan, C. (1996) 'Communication work and electronic surveillance: a model for predicting panoptic effects', *Communications Monographs*, 6(4): 293–313.

Brandtzaeg, P. and Følstad, A. (2018) 'Chatbots: changing user needs and motivations', *Interactions*, 25(5): 38–43.

Chang, E. (2018) 'Playing as making', in D. Kim and J. Stommel (eds) *Disrupting the Digital Humanities*, Santa Barbara, CA: Punctum Books.

Cofta, P. (2006) 'Distrust', *Proceedings of the 8th International Conference on Electronic Commerce: The New E-commerce: Innovations for Conquering Current Barriers, Obstacles and Limitations to Conducting Successful Business on the Internet*, New Brunswick, 250–8.

Collier, A. and Ross, J. (2020) 'Higher education after surveillance?', *Postdigital Science and Education*, 2(2): 275–9.

Danaher, J. (2016) 'The threat of algocracy: reality, resistance and accommodation', *Philosophy & Technology*, 29(3): 245–68.

Drucker, J. (2012) 'Humanistic theory and digital scholarship', *Debates in the Digital Humanities*, 150: 85–95

Duffy, B. and Chan, N. (2019). ' "You never really know who's looking": imagined surveillance across social media platforms', *New Media & Society*, 21(1): 119–23.

Dwyer, N., Basu, A., and Marsh, S. (2013) 'Reflections on measuring the trust empowerment potential of a digital environment', *IFIP International Conference on Trust Management*, Malaga, 127–35.

Foucault, M. (1995) *Discipline and Punish: The Birth of the Prison* [1975], trans A. Sheridan, New York: Vintage, 1, 977.

Frey, B. (1993) 'Does monitoring increase work effort? The rivalry with trust and loyalty', *Economic Inquiry*, 31(4): 663–70.

Furedi, F. (2006) *Culture of Fear Revisited*, Bloomsbury, Bloomsbury Publishing.

Ginart, A., Guan, M., Valiant, G., and Zou, J. (2019) 'Making AI forget you: data deletion in machine learning', *Advances in Neural Information Processing Systems 32: Annual Conference on Neural Information Processing Systems*, Vancouver, 3513–26.

Hai-Jew, S. (2006) 'Operationalizing trust: building the online trust student survey (OTSS)', *Journal of Interactive Instruction Development*, 19 (20): 16–30.

Hoffman, R., Mueller, S., Klein, G., and Litman, J. (2018) 'Metrics for explainable AI: challenges and prospects', *arXiv: 1812.04608*.

Kara, H. (2018) *Research Ethics in the Real World: Euro-Western and Indigenous Perspectives*, Bristol: Policy Press.

Kaufmann, M. and Tzanetakis, M. (2020) 'Doing Internet research with hard-to-reach communities: methodological reflections on gaining meaningful access', *Qualitative Research*, 20(6): 927–44.

Kayama, M., Haight, W., Gibson, P., and Wilson, R. (2015) 'Use of criminal justice language in personal narratives of out-of-school suspensions: black students, caregivers, and educators', *Children and Youth Services Review*, 51: 26–35.

Knox, D. (2010) 'A good horse runs at the shadow of the whip: surveillance and organizational trust in online learning environments', *The Canadian Journal of Media Studies*, 7: 07–01.

Kulesza, T., Burnett, M., Wong, W.-K., and Stumpf, S. (2015) 'Principles of explanatory debugging to personalize interactive machine learning', *Proceedings of the 20th International Conference on Intelligent User Interfaces*, Atlanta, 126–37.

Kye, B. and Hwang, S. (2020) 'Social trust in the midst of pandemic crisis: implications from COVID-19 of South Korea', *Research in Social Stratification and Mobility*, 68: 100523.

Legewie, N. and Nassauer, A. (2018) 'YouTube, Google, Facebook: 21st century online video research and research ethics', *Forum Qualitative Sozialforschung/Forum: Qualitative Social Research*, 19(3).

Lodders, A. and Paterson, J. (2020) 'Scrutinising COVIDSafe: frameworks for evaluating digital contact tracing technologies', *Alternative Law Journal*, 45(3): 153–61.

Lucivero, F. (2020) 'Big data, big waste? A reflection on the environmental sustainability of big data initiatives', *Science and Engineering Ethics*, 26(2): 1009–30.

McParland, C. and Connolly, R. (2020) 'Dataveillance in the workplace: managing the impact of innovation', *Business Systems Research: International Journal of the Society for Advancing Innovation and Research in Economy*, 11(1): 106–24.

McPherson, T. (2012) 'Why are the digital humanities so white? Or thinking the histories of race and computation', *Debates in the Digital Humanities*, 1: 139–60.

Miller, T. (2019) 'Explanation in artificial intelligence: insights from the social sciences', *Artificial Intelligence*, 267: 1–38.

Miller, T., Howe, P., and Sonenberg, L. (2017) 'Explainable AI: beware of inmates running the asylum', International Joint Conference on Artificial Intelligence, Workshop on Explainable AI (XAI), Melbourne, 36: 36–40.

Moliner-Tena, M., Fandos-Roig, J., Eestrada-Guillen, M., and Monferrer-Tirado, D. (2018) 'Younger and older trust in a crisis situation', *International Journal of Bank Marketing*, 36(3): 456–81.

Pasquale, F. (2015) *The Black Box Society*, Cambridge, MA: Harvard University Press.

Perry-Hazan, L. and Birnhack, M. (2018) 'The hidden human rights curriculum of surveillance cameras in schools: due process, privacy and trust', *Cambridge Journal of Education*, 48(1): 47–64.

Pink, S., Lanzeni, D., and Horst, H. (2018) 'Data anxieties: finding trust in everyday digital mess', *Big Data & Society*, 5(1): 1–14.

Raji, I. (2020) 'Handle with care: lessons for data science from black female scholars', *Patterns*, 1(8): 1–3.

Ryan, C. and Tynen, S. (2020) 'Fieldwork under surveillance: rethinking relations of trust, vulnerability, and state power', *Geographical Review*, 110(1–2): 38–51.

Sanneman, L. and Shah, J. (2020) 'Trust considerations for explainable robots: a human factors perspective', arXiv preprint, arXiv: 2005.05940.

Soroya, S., Farooq, A., Mahmood, K., Isoahoi, J., and Zara, S. (2021) 'From information seeking to information avoidance: understanding the health information behavior during a global health crisis', *Information Processing & Management*, 58(2): 102440.

Southerton, C. and Taylor, E. (2020) Habitual disclosure: routine, affordance, and the ethics of young peoples social media data surveillance', *Social Media+ Society*, 6(2): 1–11.

Thompson, A., Stringfellow, L., Maclean, M., and Nazzal, A. (2020) 'Ethical considerations and challenges for using digital ethnography to research vulnerable populations', *Journal of Business Research*, 124: 676–83.

Troshnski, E., Lee, C., and Dourish, P. (2008) 'Accountabilities of presence: reframing location-based systems', *Droit et cultures. Revue internationale interdisciplinaire*, 61: 171–93.

Vatcha, A. (2020) 'Workplace surveillance outside the workplace: an analysis of e-monitoring remote employees',*iSCHANNEL*, 15(1): 4–9.

Watters, A. (2017) 'The weaponization of education data', *Hack Education* [online].

Weiser, M. (1999) 'The computer for the 21st century', *ACM SIGMOBILE Mobile Computing and Communications Review*, 3(3): 3–11.

Winkler, R., Hobert, S., Salovaara, A., Söllner, M., and Leimeister, J. (2020) 'Sara, the lecturer: improving learning in online education with a scaffolding-based conversational agent', *Proceedings of the 2020 CHI Conference on Human Factors in Computing Systems*, Honolulu, 1–14.

Zeide, E. (forthcoming) 'Robot teaching, pedagogy, and policy', in M. Dubber, F. Pasquale, and S. Das (eds) *The Oxford Handbook of Ethics of AI*, Oxford: Oxford University Press.

Zuboff, S. (2019) *Surveillance Capitalism and the Challenge of Collective Action. New Labor Forum*, Los Angeles, CA: Sage, 10–29.

9

The use of objects to enhance online social research interviews

Maged Zakher and Hoda Wassif

Introduction

The ongoing COVID-19 health emergency, and the restrictions that it has placed on research, led many researchers to the re-evaluation of how social research interviews need to go online and how these can be enhanced. The online space presents a platform that brings participants and researchers together in an environment owned by both regardless of who hosts the online session. Online methods are likely to continue through emergencies and crises in general and beyond, and this calls for innovative ways to enhance online research interviews.

This chapter discusses a study of a series of online interviews where interviewees were invited to bring an object of personal value with the aim to facilitate a discussion on 'happiness in lockdown'. The selected topic served as a vehicle to explore this approach to online interviews while contextualising it in a crisis situation. It also helped to anchor the discussion around a positive theme in the middle of a global crisis. The study aimed at exploring the dynamics observed and the type of thematic materials gathered in this research context. The focus is to investigate the research technique and explore the benefits and challenges of using objects in social research interviews online.

As participants select objects related to the research, they are given some control to steer the discussion. Hennigar (1997) discussed the shift in thinking when artefacts are placed at the centre of the conversation, and the participant's own values, beliefs, and views about the world could be explored in more depth resulting in what Rubin and Rubin (2012: 95) call an 'extended conversation'. The purpose of such a conversation is to explore in depth some themes of relevance to the interviewee through their choice of objects. Using thematic analysis (Braun and Clarke, 2006), we explored the richness, depth, and genuineness of the materials gathered in object-based online research interviews.

The chapter details the research process, discussing the benefits and challenges of using objects as enhancing tools in social research interviews conducted online. It considers how participants chose their items, how the tool compares with other enhancing tools, and some methodological implications. The chapter concludes with our reflection as interviewers offering advice to researchers who may choose to use this enhancing technique in their online interviews.

Online interviews and social research

Online interviews have been widely used in social research as the medium of choice over face-to-face interviews when the latter were practically and/ or ethically difficult to conduct. With the restrictions on movement in most parts of the world as a result of COVID-19, working from home has meant that many face-to-face meetings have shifted to online platforms that have been improving massively with more enhanced functionalities: options to record, share the screen, use breakout groups, among many other features.

This advancement in online meetings has spilled over to social research interviews which may have been considered, by some, as second best when face-to-face interviews were the standard. Others were calling for the use of online interviews to benefit from some features available in online platforms (Hanna, 2012). As more people used online media to connect with others due to the COVID-19 pandemic, regular conversations using these platforms became more familiar not only in professional settings, formal meetings, and job interviews, but also for informal, family-and-friends connections. This may have led to online meetings including interviews becoming more standard, or at least no longer second best or as an option only for tech-savvy participants.

Online platforms may have lost the novelty they once had since this crisis, in a way, forced many to use such media. The familiarity with the media used, the ease and the multiple contexts they are used in, may have led to them being the first medium of choice to meet with someone in almost all capacities, including research interviews. Conducting the interviews online provides an opportunity for interviewers and interviewees each to be comfortable in a familiar environment, cutting down on the travel costs, and allowing for recording of the video interaction (Hanna, 2012). This has made online interviews relatively easier to conduct and record without the invasiveness of a physical video- or audio-recorder. It is, however, argued that such familiarity may raise the need for tools to enhance online research interviews so they can become more engaging and interviewee-focused.

Enhanced interviews

Using Zakher's (2018: 212) definition, '[a]n enhanced interview aims at a flowing conversation that can produce rich and varied data, and, therefore, can be defined as an interview that starts as an interviewee-centred, interviewee-empowering dialogue contextualised in interviewee-relevant themes and progresses to include an equally interested and fully engaged interviewer'. While conventional, semi-structured, in-depth interviews including online interviews can produce rich, genuine, and deep data, an enhanced interview uses an enhancing tool with the aim to anchor the dialogue in a contextualised and conversation-like environment. Examples of interview-enhancing techniques include: photo-elicitation (Harper, 2002; Smith et al, 2012), diaries (Alaszewski, 2006), using proverbs (Weber et al, 1998), the use of videos taken by participants (Cherrington and Watson, 2010), maps, life stories, among other tools (Kara, 2015). Moreover, key to the definition is the element of contextualisation in interviewee-relevant themes which requires a rethink of the tool used to enhance the interview.

This chapter reports on a set of qualitative interviews where we invited each participant to bring an item of personal relevance to them; the item needed to be linked to their idea of happiness during lockdown. The aim was to explore the dynamics of using objects chosen by participants in the online interview setting and to assess the benefits and challenges of the technique.

Method

Following ethical approval and an email invitation, 13 participants agreed to take part in this study. We invited participants to bring to the online interview an item that represented happiness in lockdown. The Information Sheet included some examples of possible objects such as mobile phones, charms, photos, plants, prayer mats, baking trays, exercise equipment, musical instruments, and so on.

The online interviews were conducted and video-recorded on Microsoft Teams resulting in more than nine hours of data (an average of 42 minutes per interview). Participants were two males and 11 females who lived in the UK during lockdown, and interviews were conducted one-on-one by the two authors. Each participant was asked to show the item(s) he/she brought and to talk about how the item(s) related to their happiness during lockdown. Some participants brought more than one item while others talked about some items they would have brought along with the one they chose for the interview.

The conversations started with a focus on the item where the participants explained what the item was and how it related to their happiness. The conversation then naturally continued based on the themes the participants mentioned (for example, their time with family, gardening, online shopping, work, and the online interview itself). Each participant was designated 'P' (1 to 13).

Findings and discussion

Choice of object

The range of items brought included a LEGO model (P9), lap tray (P10), white board (P12), smart phone (P3, P5, and P13), remote control (P11), art projects (P6 and P7), gardening tools (P2 and P10), film projector (P1), children's books (P8), and a sewing machine (P4).

The question 'How did you select this item for our interview?' was part of the initial conversation with each participant with the following observations:

> *The ease with which each of the 13 participants chose their item differed.* For example, P12 had forgotten to bring the item to the screen at the start of the interview, and when reminded of the research participation invite, she apologised for forgetting but ran without hesitation to bring an item. She said that she knew exactly what she would discuss (a white board she used with her children to establish some routine and to bond over a range of activities during lockdown). This is an example of someone who found it very easy to bring an item of personal relevance at a few seconds' notice. On the other hand, P5 reported on having taken some time to decide on what to bring to the interview. She discussed it with her daughter and decided to bring her mobile phone.

Participants shared their ideas and their elimination process for selecting their items, judging their own selection:

> 'We did a lot of cooking, I thought about bringing a recipe book, but I thought that will be fake, because I looked up everything online.' (P5)

Others wanted to choose something worthy to reflect:

> '[U]sing my time wisely.' (P7)

Some participants reported trying to guess what others may bring to the interviews:

> 'I thought people may bring iPads.' (P7)

In all cases, it was noticed that participants were not put on the spot to answer a series of interview questions, as could be the case in some research. They had the chance to explore what to bring to the interview, and this, in turn, meant that they had the opportunity to reflect on the theme of the research.

It may have been more challenging to other interviewees who decided to bring more than one item to the interview (P7 and P10, for example). In all 13 interviews, no one opined that they could not think of an item or that they could not bring at least one item to the interview. It is argued that no matter how long it takes for participants to select an object to talk about, it is almost always guaranteed that each participant will have something in their environment that they can talk about.

When participants articulated their thought process behind their choices, they mentioned thinking about how the interviewer would perceive them in view of their selected object:

'I toyed with the idea of a bottle of wine [as my item] but [it] will make me look like I have an alcohol problem [laughter].' (P5)

'I have my idea about how I am perceiving this [the object], but this may not come across to the other person, what does it say about me, does a projector mean that I am a lazy person staying in bed watching TV or does it mean that I was creative?' (P1)

Such comments were explored, and participants were asked to elaborate on them, which, again, added an element of honesty and genuineness to the discussion. After all, many interviewees could be giving socially desirable answers; the fact that they are bringing a real item that they have can, to a certain extent, facilitate an honest discussion. In all cases, such comments reflect the expectation that cherished items can tell something about people. This may highlight the credibility of using such a tool in comparison with some other tools that may be seen by some participants to be used randomly to trigger a conversation.

It was clear that some *pre-interview investment* took place with reflection and consideration:

'I looked around and then thought what did we actually do [during lockdown] ... we did a lot of reading.' (P8)

Participants referred to how the selected object reminded them of their time in lockdown which some remembered with some sadness (P7 with art work) and others how their chosen object helped them cope with their anxiety (P6), increase their productivity (P12), stay connected with the family (P12 and P13), or practise a hobby (P10 and P11). Even with participants who ended up with an object different from what they had first planned, there was an opportunity to get to know them more through their talk about their thought process:

'I immediately went to the dogs and I had a debate because they are not objects ... my mind goes straight to the dogs as they bring me joy but they are not objects ... so moved on to choose an object.' (P4)

Participants came to the interview with some preparation and demonstrating excitement in anticipation of sharing their selected items. We had some similar sense of looking forward to what each would bring to the interview, which we reflect upon in a later section in this chapter.

Such pre-interview investment on the part of the interviewee also meant that they had some *control over the conversation*. It was their item that would be the focus of the dialogue, and it was they that could tell us what the item meant to them and how it was connected to their happiness in lockdown. This interviewee control is recommended in the interview literature; after all, interviewers conduct individual interviews because they are interested in each interviewee's beliefs, values, and attitudes. It is, however, believed that some interview settings lend themselves more to interviewee–centred conversations than others. While some may argue that sending the interview schedule to the participants prior to the interview allows them to know what to expect, it does not compare to giving them the opportunity to steer the conversation through an item that only they know about prior to the interview.

This pre-interview investment and the perceived control over the conversation can *relieve some of the interviewee's uncertainty before the interview*. Being invited to an interview on 'happiness in lockdown' in the abstract may cause some unnecessary ambiguity that can be mitigated through this technique. Hurdley (2006) argues that discussing objects is unique in terms of the opportunities it gives for narratives, which can be a challenge in other methods. Participants bringing items to an interview already have much to say by nature of owning the item.

Using this enhancing tool compared with others

More affordable

Qualitative interviewers have a range of options to enhance their interviews. They can bring photos and/or items to the interview to anchor the discussion around them. They can also ask participants to build or create an artefact (such as a LEGO model, a playdough figure, a photo, or a drawing). Whether it is the interviewer or the interviewee who (co-)creates, builds, or selects the anchoring point of the discussion depends on the research question. Qualitative interviewers, however, acknowledge that not all enhancing tools can in fact enhance social research interviews (whether online or otherwise) because the tool needs to be interviewee-relevant if it is to lend itself to richer, deeper, and genuine conversations. For example, being invited to build LEGO models may be stressful for some who do not enjoy this type of activity while others may prefer to write a song or express themselves in drawings.

The pressure that some interviewees may be under to draw, build a model, take a photo, produce a figure, and so on may not enhance but hinder the interviewing process. Although researchers using LEGO, drawings, and photo-elicitation usually highlight the fact that it is the conversation rather than the product itself that is the focus, participants still need to go through the product phase, and that in itself may cause unnecessary feelings of inadequacy. This could be a barrier if the participant's confidence in their own creativity is low (Rainford, 2020). Asking participants to simply bring an item can be perceived to be less demanding.

Moreover, the pressure of having to talk about whatever LEGO model was built or the simple art produced, does in fact affect the discussion. It could be argued that asking participants to bring an item of their choice is easier to do than asking them to build, create, or draw something. It is also less limiting in terms of the discussions triggered in comparison with having to justify and talk about a drawing, a LEGO model, a photo, for example.

More possibilities in an online format

Adding to this flexibility is the endless possibilities of the range of items that can be shown on the screen in online interviews. While a participant in a face-to-face conversation may be able to bring a token item, they may not be able to bring larger objects such as a sewing machine, gardening tools, or pets! The online platform allows for almost all items to be shown on the screen (regardless of the size of the item) and possibly in their home environment. In a study on work–life boundaries by Whiting (2016), participants used video cameras to capture during their days any events that may trigger a conversation on work–life balance. One participant captured his first few moments right after waking up, and it was interesting to see a participant, still in bed, reflecting on his day ahead. This flexibility of a video camera at home, and the same is mirrored in an online interview, adds to the genuineness of interviews done in the participants' home environment. Asking participants to bring items of relevance to them may trigger genuine conversations that go beyond what would be expected in a non-enhanced online interview.

More interviewee control over the conversation

Asking participants to bring something of their choice allows them more freedom compared with some other approaches that have been outlined previously. It also allows for more naturally occurring discussions around their choices, in comparison with what could be a forced conversation around something that is introduced by the interviewer.

Our reflection as interviewers

Qualitative research literature, especially within the interpretative paradigm, acknowledges the role of interviewer as someone who works together with an interviewee to co-create the knowledge (Finlay, 2002; Gubrium and Holstein, 2002; Webster et al, 2014). This means that the 'conversation with a purpose' (Kara, 2018) that is the qualitative interview works better when both sides are engaging in and contributing to the conversation with the aim of co-constructing knowledge that in turn helps answer the research question(s). Here are some of our reflections and observations as interviewers in this research.

We were always looking forward to the next interview, with *a sense of anticipation* of what each interviewee would bring, and this sense of anticipation kept the research interesting. There was always a new angle, idea, or observation in each interview, even though they all discussed the same theme of happiness in lockdown.

Preparation for each interview was relatively easy; the only thing we needed was to ensure that the platform was working well and recording was taking place. Kara (2015: 83) maintains that 'once the system is set up, electronic interviews take much less time to administer than face-to-face interviews and remove the need for travel or transcription'. This was made even easier with the onus on each participant to bring something to discuss. In comparison with the need to prepare photos, proverbs, or other prompts, this technique meant that minimal preparation was needed for each online interview.

During the interview setting itself, it was almost always *easy to build rapport*; this is due to the fact that there was always something to talk about, namely the selected item. Whatever the item was, an interviewer is almost always ready with a "Wow! Tell me about this, please!" The expectation of a not-seen-before item and how it links to the participant's life taps into the curiosity of qualitative researchers and provides for a safe setting where there will always be a point of discussion. The qualitative interview literature highlights the ease with which participants can respond to specific questions in comparison with abstract notions (Rubin and Rubin, 2012). Asking questions about the item, how it works, when the participant uses it, how he/she selected it, and so on, can all be safe questions to at least start off the conversation in preparation to get to deeper and richer ideas around happiness, satisfaction, struggles, and other more abstract concepts. Rapport may have been enhanced by the fact that we knew most of the interviewees before embarking on this research; however, having a specific item on the screen made it easy to start the conversation asking about the details of the chosen item. Rapport may have also been easy to build through good interviewing techniques, active listening, and being genuinely interested in the participants' input; however, we believe that having an item as the focus (at least at the start of the interview) gave easy access to more engagement and smooth conversations.

As interviewers, it was also *easy to recall the interviews by linking the items to the participants*. In co-writing this chapter, it was rather easy to remember who brought what to the interview, triggering a chain reaction of also remembering the thrust of the conversations and how each reflected on their happiness during lockdown. In other non-enhanced interviews, this could be a challenge, especially after some interviews where one could find it difficult to recall who said what. Some studies have reported on the observation that memories and items can be linked (for example, Beckstead et al, 2011), and it is believed that this observation adds to the genuineness of this enhancing tool which means parts of the interviews mimic real-life conversations around items (such as gifts, memorabilia, and so on.) We acknowledge that such an advantage could be lost once the number of interviews exceeds a certain point where, perhaps, the most exciting items are remembered while the mundane ones may be forgotten. However, we believe that we are more likely to remember conversations that are anchored around objects than ones based on a dialogue alone.

Methodological advantages and limitations

Based on the object-based online interviews conducted for this study, we believe that this enhancing technique has some advantages over non-enhanced online interviews and over some other enhancing techniques too. Advantages include the *flexibility* it offers; this flexibility is in terms of the wide range of objects that participants can choose from, which also include a range of sizes that can only be available in online interviews. It also provides an opportunity for almost every participant to take part in the research without the need to be artistically inclined.

Additionally, having an item in the conversation can *relieve participants of the pressure of being in the spotlight* while still keeping them at the centre. While qualitative research is after the participant's experience, priorities, and interests, and all efforts should be made to have an interviewee-centred conversation, sometimes the spotlight being on the participant can cause much pressure, especially if participants are already in a challenging crisis situation. Having an item that both interviewer and interviewee focus on can help participants to feel freer to discuss the item rather than discuss the participant. This can be even more useful in sensitive topics where participants may need to distance themselves somehow from the focus of the interview. While talking about something tangible can lead to discussions about the item owner, being able to hold an item, show it on the screen, discuss it, laugh about some of its features, and so on can allow for this space for a less self-conscious conversation, not putting participants under unnecessary pressure. As objects and artefacts could also mean different things to different people, objects almost gave permission to participants to talk about their families (P1, P4, P5, P8, P9, P10, P11, P12, and P13), their work environment (P2, P5, P6, P7, P8, and P12), and their struggles with ill health and/or anxiety (P3, P4, and P7) among other things.

The observations discussed previously point to the enhancement abilities of using objects in online interviews in mainly three areas of qualitative interviewing: depth, richness, and genuineness. *Depth* was witnessed as the discussions went beyond superficial answers that can generally be socially desirable, reaching some more complex issues. The detailed conversations around the items brought a range of layers to the dialogues with real-life stories around the items. It echoes what Rowsell (2011: 341) said about artefacts that 'brought family narratives and attachments to life'.

Richness is related to the wide range of topics and themes that could be co-constructed in interview settings (Rubin and Rubin, 2012). While the theme, happiness in lockdown, was investigated, the range of ideas, interests, and values gathered in the data demonstrated such richness linked to the variety of the items brought in to the interviews. We argue that this is due to the flexibility and endless possibilities provided by our invitation to take part in this research where participants could bring any items that they felt relevant, which can lead to different types of conversations around the research topic. It will be interesting for future research to explore the difference in perceived richness of data with and without the use of objects.

Genuineness is demonstrated through the use of real objects that carried some relevance to each participant. Instead of giving idealistic answers to hypothetical questions, participants literally brought to the interviews items from their own lives. While some selectivity is expected, which is typical of almost any conversation, the fact that each interviewee was discussing something authentic that was purchased/obtained not for research purposes can, in a way, push the conversation towards a real dialogue, akin to that in an informal conversation.

On the other hand, there are some challenges with this methodological approach. The technique would work better with researchers who are more comfortable with *uncertainty*. Not knowing what each participant would bring to the interview may cause inexperienced interviewers some worry. Interviewers who prefer to prepare well for their interviews may find themselves taking a back seat waiting for each participant to steer the conversation in a direction they prefer, based on the item they bring to the interview. This could be especially challenging if the research is about a sensitive topic.

The depth achieved in the conversation as a result of discussing one object can also result in *missing other topic-related themes that could otherwise be triggered by other objects.* Commenting on the interview, P12 mentioned that she may have covered her ideas about the white board in detail, but she may have missed mentioning other themes that the board did not naturally trigger. Experienced interviewers will need to be alert and wisely guide the conversation back to the main topic if the item of choice seems to prompt less useful details.

Another challenge is the fact that *items that are exciting to a participant may be irrelevant and/or uninteresting to the interviewer*. Participants who demonstrate their excitement about a certain painting or gardening tools or musical instruments need responders who are keen to hear about them. However, this could provide for an 'information gap' (Abell and Myers, 2008) that gives participants the licence to explain in detail what the item does and/or how exciting it is. While the research is rarely ultimately interested in the very items, it is through the discussion of the items that researchers can explore the thought processes, priorities, and attitudes of the interviewees. It could, therefore, be argued that the less the interviewer knows about an item, the more the interviewee has to say about it − the richer and more detailed the conversation can be.

We acknowledge that one should be mindful of the challenges attached to access to the resources that facilitate online interviews in general, as there are still some people who do not have reliable Internet access for many reasons. Such divide could play a part in the choice of method that caters to the individual participants' circumstances.

Advice to researchers using the tool

Interview researchers interested in using objects to enhance their online research interviews need to make sure that their pre-interview *instructions are clear*. Providing potential research participants with the nature and size of item, the topic and the expected nature of the conversation can help many participants choose their objects and can decrease any anxiety that some may face.

Researchers using this tool need to be able to *tolerate ambiguity* and be ready for the interviewee to lead the discussion based on the item they choose. Gaining experience in interviewing allows interviewers to deal favourably with uncertainty while *maintaining the needed focus* on the theme under discussion. Interviewers may also be presented with items that they may deem irrelevant, and as in natural conversations, the more an interviewer shows their interest in the conversation, the interviewee (and the item in this case), the more favourable the conversation will be.

Getting the conversation moving is key to richer data, as participants are more likely to share honestly and in detail their opinions, perceptions, and so on. This calls for inquisitive interviewers who are *open to knowing about hobbies, ideas, and artefacts of interest to their participants*. This, however, may mean that certain items brought to the interview may challenge the interviewer's typical view of the item, its relevance, use, or value. Whether the item is interesting in and of itself, the onus is on the experienced interviewer to make sure that the dialogue captures what is important to the participant in relation to the research topic.

Conclusion

In this chapter, we reported on a set of qualitative interviews conducted online, at the time of the COVID-19 pandemic-related lockdown. We conducted the online interviews with the use of objects as an interview-enhancing tool. The benefits and challenges of using objects as enhancing tools were discussed, and we also explored issues around how participants chose their items, how the tool compares with other enhancing tools, and some methodological implications. The chapter also presented our reflection as interviewers and provided some advice to researchers who may choose to use this enhancing technique in their online interviews. We have found that using objects of personal value to participants can enhance social research interviews conducted online, giving participants control, adding an element of newness, and anchoring the conversation around interviewee-relevant themes.

Although this research was conducted during a time of crisis, the transferability of the enhancing technique can be of value to online interviews conducted at any time. We believe that adding objects to online interviews can now be part of the toolbox available to qualitative researchers.

References

Abell, J. and Myers, G. (2008) 'Analyzing research interviews', in R. Wodak and M. Krzyżanowski (eds) *Qualitative Discourse Analysis in the Social Sciences*, London: Palgrave Macmillan, pp 145–61.

Alaszewski, A. (2006) *Using Diaries for Social Research*, London: Sage.

Beckstead, Z., Twose, G., Levesque-Gottlieb, E., and Rizzo, J. (2011) 'Collective remembering through the materiality and organization of war memorials', *Journal of Material Culture*, 16(2): 193–213.

Braun, V. and Clarke, V. (2006) 'Using thematic analysis in psychology', *Qualitative Research in Psychology*, 3(2): 77–101.

Cherrington, J. and Watson, B. (2010) 'Shooting a diary, not just a hoop: using video diaries to explore the embodied everyday contexts of a university basketball team', *Qualitative Research in Sport, Exercise and Health*, 2(2): 267–81.

Finlay, L. (2002) ' "Outing" the researcher: the provenance, process, and practice of reflexivity', *Qualitative Health Research*, 12(4): 531–45.

Gubrium, J. and Holstein, J. (2002) *Handbook of Interview Research: Context and Method*, Thousand Oaks, CA: Sage.

Hanna, P. (2012) 'Using internet technologies (such as Skype) as a research medium: a research note', *Qualitative Research*, 12(2): 239–42.

Harper, D. (2002) 'Talking about pictures: a case for photo elicitation', *Visual Studies*, 17(1): 13–26.

Hennigar, S. (1997) 'Teaching yourself to teach with objects', *Journal of Education,* 7(4): 80–91.

Hurdley, R. (2006) 'Dismantling mantelpieces: narrating identities and materializing culture in the home', *Sociology*, 40(4): 717–33.

Kara, H. (2015) *Creative Research Methods in the Social Sciences: A Practical Guide*, Bristol: Policy Press.

Kara, H. (2018) *Conversation with a Purpose*, [online], available at: https://drhelenkara.files.wordpress.com/2018/06/conversation-with-a-purpose.pdf [accessed 29 October 2020].

Rainford, J. (2020) 'Confidence and the effectiveness of creative methods in qualitative interviews with adults', *International Journal of Social Research Methodology*, 23(1): 109–22.

Rowsell, J. (2011) 'Carrying my family with me: artifacts as emic perspectives', *Qualitative Research*, 11(3): 331–46.

Rubin, H. and Rubin, I. (2012) *Qualitative Interviewing: The Art of Hearing Data* (3rd edn), London: Sage.

Smith, E., Gidlow, B., and Steel, G. (2012) 'Engaging adolescent participants in academic research: the use of photo-elicitation interviews to evaluate school-based outdoor education programmes', *Qualitative Research*, 12(4): 367–87.

Weber, E., Hsee, C., and Sokolowska, J. (1998) 'What folklore tells us about risk and risk taking: cross-cultural comparisons of American, German, and Chinese proverbs', *Organizational Behavior and Human Processes*, 75(2): 170–86.

Webster, S., Lewis, J., and Brown, A. (2014) 'Ethical considerations in qualitative research', in J. Ritchie, J. Lewis, C. McNaughton Nichols, and R. Ormston (eds) *Qualitative Research Practice: A Guide for Social Science Students & Researchers* (2nd edn), London: Sage, pp 77–110.

Whiting, R. (2016) *Participatory Video Diaries: Digital Brain Switch Video Study*, [lecture: 'Qualitative Methods in Action'], 10 May, Birkbeck, University of London.

Zakher, M. (2018) 'The use of sacred texts as tools to enhance social research interviews', [unpublished PhD dissertation], University of Bedfordshire, 1–263.

10

Qualitative data re-use and secondary analysis: researching in and about a crisis

Anna Tarrant and Kahryn Hughes

Introduction

The COVID-19 pandemic is the biggest global crisis of an era, rewriting norms and expectations woven into the social fabric of everyday life. Perhaps unsurprisingly, questions about the differential economic, social, and relational impacts of this crisis have preoccupied social science researchers, policymakers, and service providers across the globe in 2020. The pandemic, and various forms of lockdown imposed in most majority and minority world contexts, has dramatically altered our lives, albeit in different ways. Like other times of crisis, such as the 2008–12 global economic recession, these unfolding dimensions of rupture and change preoccupy socio-historical researchers now and will do so long into the future.

Social scientists have a unique and imperative role in advancing knowledge of the unfolding impacts of COVID-19 including how these new social conditions are affecting people's lives, needs, attitudes, and behaviours. Yet the changes wrought by the crisis have also simultaneously altered the conduct of social sciences research, placing new restrictions on how new knowledge may be produced. In this chapter, we consider how the re-use of qualitative data and its preservation has become especially pertinent as part of an important repertoire of research methods. Our position entails a more nuanced ethical sensibility towards the archiving and reuse of existing research data in the context of capturing the evolving and uneven impacts of crises and understanding the social contexts from which they emerge. We therefore argue for, and raise awareness of, the tremendous value and potential for qualitative data re-use via the associated methodology of qualitative secondary analysis (or QSA) and make a case for data preservation and archiving.

We are prompted to write this chapter because, while there has been significant innovation in methods of qualitative data re-use and QSA over the past two decades, these have not traditionally been considered as part of the 'go to' methodological repertoire for qualitative, in-depth engagement (for example, interviews, participatory methods). In the early stages of the national lockdown, there was a proliferation of work newly engaging with the various potentials of digital research methods and resources for research. We contribute to these developments to ensure that sidelining of valuable and relevant resources can be avoided in the post-pandemic research landscape through the promotion of methods of qualitative data reuse. Now, more than ever, there is a need to address the under-use of existing qualitative data, particularly as lockdown and social distancing continues to complicate, and even confound, face-to-face fieldwork for the foreseeable future.

To develop our discussion, we organise this chapter around four main sections and aims. We begin by reflecting on adaptations to research methods following the imposition of lockdown and enforced social distancing in March 2020. We do so to position data re-use and secondary analysis alongside primary forms of research that often take place face-to-face, or increasingly, via digitally mediated forms of engagement. Second, we report on the multiple ways that we have engaged with existing qualitative data to generate new substantive and methodological knowledge in the formulation of new research directions. While the work we discuss pre-dates the pandemic and social distancing policy measures, recent events have illuminated the 'added value' of working with existing data for researchers working at a 'remove'. Indeed, existing data provide essential context to the pandemic and an important baseline to emergent COVID-19 specific data that is currently being generated. Third, we outline some of the opportunities and challenges that secondary analysts must consider when working with existing qualitative data and make a case for an ethical sensibility towards data re-use and preservation. We conclude with useful links to established data sets and archives both in the UK and worldwide, that provide access to baseline resources for work of this kind.

Adapting social research methods in a crisis

Opportunities for re-using existing qualitative data went largely unnoticed in the early days of the pandemic. National lockdown and enforced social distancing (for example, in the UK context, this included a minimum of 2 m between people in any social context beyond the home; mandatory masks in shops and indoor public spaces) placed unique restrictions on primary research methods, affecting how social sciences research could be conducted and knowledge produced. Meeting with participants face-to-face was prohibited, and so was ethnographic immersion in communities. Qualitative researchers, who typically travel to field sites and meet people face-to-face to generate their data and establish and maintain research connections, were pushed to consider ways that they could modify their methods. As the lockdown extended beyond a few weeks, there was a rush to produce resources to support all social researchers whose data collection and research designs were affected. Deborah Lupton's crowd-sourced document is an excellent example of collated materials that was quickly produced and widely distributed (2020). The Nippon Foundation Ocean Nexus Centre at the University of Washington, or EarthLab (2020), has also compiled a detailed list of resources suggesting alternatives for conducting primary research online. These include document and/or media and social media analysis and the use of online platforms or telephone for data generation. These new resources identify physically distant modes of connection and connectivity using mediated forms (Lupton, 2020). Qualitative data re-use is a conspicuous omission from both lists (see also Chawla, 2020; Tarrant and Hughes, 2020) and discussion among researchers more generally.

Notwithstanding the rapidity at which the research community has had to respond to these new conditions, discussions about how to conduct research have also been accompanied by newly invigorated ethical questions. These have centred on research/er burden, including whether (or not) we should conduct research at all at a time of crisis (for example, Nuffield Council on Bioethics, 2020; Fitzgibbon, 2021, this volume). Such questions were important to consider as our initial understanding is that the differential impacts of COVID-19 are falling along existing lines of inequality (we address this in more detail later in the chapter). These, and related debates, are reflective of the core set of ethical principles that underpin much social sciences research. This includes research involving marginalised and vulnerable groups, such as in our own work, where due consideration must be given to the potential impacts research engagement may have on researched communities (Emmel et al, 2007; Garthwaite et al, 2020). Given the pace of change, as well as rapid responses by funding councils to enable research about the crisis, these were, and remain, important considerations. We return to the ethical dimensions of social research in a crisis later in the chapter, albeit with an alternate focus on data preservation and archiving as imperative to a broader ethical sensibility towards participants.

How, then, are we to research those individuals and groups disproportionately affected by the impacts of COVID-19 (economic, health and well-being, etc.), where face-to-face research is both dangerous physically, as well as entailing a potentially damaging level of research/er burden? The prioritisation of how and whether researchers should adapt their primary research designs and methods, has meant that data re-use and secondary analysis, which by their very nature can also practically be conducted in a socially distanced manner, were rarely addressed or suggested as an alternative. In part, we suggest, this is linked to the relatively under-utilised and -valued nature of qualitative data re-use and secondary analysis more generally, including prior to COVID-19. This underutilisation might be prompted by a number of factors. First, it may in part be to do with a sense of what is *lost* when researchers are not involved in the formative contexts of research. We have elsewhere (Hughes et al, 2020) made the case that 'being there' – involved directly in the formative generation of data – offers distinctive insights potentially not recoverable through 'secondary' analysis. Tacit experiential and 'felt' understanding, sensory perceptions, participation in what we might describe as knowledge collectives (that is, all the stakeholders involved in any research endeavour) are integral to formative research contexts (Hughes et al, 2021). Additionally, there are also challenges at working at a temporal remove, whereby researchers may feel historically 'out of step' with the timescapes of their participants. Second, the neoliberalisation of the academy has been orientated towards 'big qual', alongside a corresponding drive towards quantifiable evidence (Edwards and Holland, 2020). 'Big qual' refers to the analysis of large volumes of qualitative data; larger than would be feasible for an individual research or small research team to generate (Jamieson and Lewthwaite, 2019). Finally, the requirement to archive data by research funders is relatively recent, as are the technological developments producing the necessary resources for inter/national opportunities to undertake QSA. We seek to remedy this oversight by explaining the possibilities for innovation that might be afforded by data re-use and QSA as key methodological tools, both for researching in and about the crisis.

Qualitative data re-use and secondary analysis

Simply put, the secondary analysis of qualitative data involves the re-use of existing data generated for previous research studies, for new purposes (Bishop and Kuula-Luumi, 2017). Although qualitative data has become more accessible through its preservation in archives, its re-use continues to be a contested methodological field that has stimulated vigorous debate. Early debate coalesced around questions of ethics, epistemology, and practical concerns related to engaging with data that had been gathered by other people. Qualitative research data were argued to be distinctive in that they could be understood to be co-constructed in the interaction between the researcher and researched (Hammersley, 2010). This approach raised ethical and epistemological questions about whether it is even possible to fully understand data as a 'secondary user' (Mauthner et al, 1998), a static framing of researchers that has since been critiqued through consideration of what it means to work at a 'remove' from data. The ethics of qualitative data re-use represents a complex analytic terrain (Hughes and Tarrant, 2020b) involving a settlement between extending the value and insights of otherwise expensive resources to produce, while also considering participant concerns, both retrospectively and prospectively (see also Neale, 2013). In 2007, Jennifer Mason significantly moved debate forwards by reconciling these questions. She advocated a shift beyond questions of whether we *should* re-use qualitative data, to questions of *how* we can. Moreover, and in the same special issue as Mason's introductory paper, the distinction between primary and secondary analysis was challenged, as was the idea that the 'construction' of data occurred solely within the researcher/researched interaction (Moore, 2007; Hughes et al, 2020). Advancing an 'investigative epistemology', Mason's intervention paved the way for greater innovation and creativity in methods of qualitative data reuse (Moore, 2007).

Developments in both infrastructure and increased investment in data resources have been integral to the burgeoning of this methodological terrain. Over two decades ago, the Qualitative Data Archival Resource (originally named QUALIDATA, and now the UK Data Service) was established, requiring researchers to make qualitative data available for re-use at a national scale for the first time (Moore, 2007; Bishop and Kuula-Luumi, 2017). As part of the global digital revolution, the last 20 years have seen large-scale international investments in archives and repositories making it possible to access a 'tsunami' of these newly configured data. The digitisation of research data, alongside an increasing imperative to reuse it by major European and UK funding councils,[1] has stimulated a more concerted and self-conscious engagement with the methodological complexities of reusing data, including those with which researchers have had no prior relationship (James, 2012). This increasing imperative has been driven by a growing recognition that existing data resources were expensive to produce and have continuing utility, especially large-scale panel studies which may ask similar questions across different international contexts, thereby providing both nationally specific findings and offering opportunities for international comparison. The re-use of qualitative data also fits with the increasing emphasis by funding councils for researchers to ensure that before they generate any additional primary data, they make themselves aware of any existing data on their topic. While QSA has been relatively overlooked in discussions of best methods to use in a crisis, in fact it is the research direction of the future for reasons we now go on to discuss.

Increased availability of qualitative research data, and the recognition of data re-use as a viable and accepted research direction, has underscored the growth of a vibrant and creative methodological field in recent years, especially in rapid innovations in methods of qualitative secondary analysis (or QSA). Such innovation includes bringing new questions to research data; developing new interpretations by analysing existing data sets; gaining new methodological insights by bringing existing studies into analytic conversation; using existing research data to inform the design of new empirical studies; or any combination of these (for example, Irwin et al. 2012; Tarrant, 2017; Davidson et al, 2019; Jamieson and Lewthwaite, 2019; Edwards et al, 2020; Hughes et al, 2020; Hughes and Tarrant, 2020a; Tarrant and Hughes, 2020; Hughes et al, 2021). While impossible to do justice to the breadth and richness of creativity in the field, it is worth mentioning here notable interventions that demonstrate the huge potential for substantive and theoretical advance, knowledge production, and methodological development. As part of the Timescapes programme of research (Neale et al. 2012), for example, Sarah Irwin and colleagues (2012) explored the potential of several strategies that involved working across differently constituted data sets that had been prepared for archiving in the new Timescapes Archive. These include an example of working between survey data and one qualitative data set; working together as primary researchers to reinterrogate their data within a new conceptual framework; and working across multiple, linked qualitative data sets generated by other researchers (Irwin et al, 2012). Ros Edwards and colleagues (2020) are also defining the virtues and developing techniques of 'big qual' or breadth-and-depth analysis for the purposes of amalgamating qualitative data sets in a programme of work which has attracted attention both in the UK and internationally (Davidson et al, 2019).

Our shared work demonstrates how data accrue value and relevance over time rather than lose it. With Jason Hughes, we elaborate three major approaches to QSA; continuous, collective, and configurative, that demonstrate how we may harness the value of different forms of 'remove' from the data (Hughes et al, 2021; see also Hughes et al, 2020). We illustrate these modes of QSA with empirical examples later, but briefly, *continuous* QSA involves asking new questions of existing data sets to (re) apprehend empirical evidence and develop continuous samples in ways that principally leverage epistemic distance from the formative contexts of the research, bringing new questions to existing data for the purposes of new investigations, and generating new questions for future research from these data sets. *Collective* QSA involves linking across research teams and studies generating research dialogues and thus principally harnessing the analytic affordances of working in new research teams, while drawing on the different knowledge and insights new team members may have about the various data sets. *Configurative* QSA considers approaches to bringing data into conversation with broader sources of theory and evidence, principally harnessing temporal distance, where foregrounding researchers' temporal 'remove' from the formative contexts of research builds in opportunities for longitudinal engagement and comparison (Hughes et al, 2021).

Building on the strategies of Irwin et al (2012), Anna Tarrant developed what we describe as *continuous* QSA in a depth-to-breadth approach involving the use of sub-samples of two data sets stored in the Timescapes Archive in her Leverhulme-funded study 'Men, poverty and lifetimes of care' (Tarrant, 2021). In this study, she developed a new empirical research design; tested new methodological techniques; theoretically sampled from data sets in collaboration with existing research team members (Tarrant and Hughes, 2020); and brought new questions to new samples to generate new insights. An example of our shared *collective* QSA is where we engaged in-depth analyses of small samples of data from two data sets, to advance new substantive and theoretical agendas made possible through a depth-to-breadth approach to analysis (Tarrant and Hughes, 2019). Finally, we revisited a data set comprised of interviews with internet gamblers conducted in 2007, in a form of *configurative* QSA. We explored the possibilities for enhanced methodological and substantive insight offered by working at a temporal 'remove' from the original study (Hughes et al, 2020). Although we do not describe these methodologies in depth here, we anticipate that they provide a starting point for those who may wish to follow up on the kinds of strategies defining this new phase of qualitative data re-use and QSA. We expect the broad panoply of methodological advances in this field to prove foundational for social researchers in the later phases of the pandemic and post-pandemic context.

In what follows, we consider engagements with existing qualitative data as vital for establishing the key contexts to social crises and our ongoing understanding of their impacts and consequences.

The role of QSA in researching in and about social crises

As already stressed, data re-use and QSA support continued fieldwork in a world where face-to-face research is currently prohibited. These methodological approaches also facilitate greater comprehension of the dynamics of the social world as it unfolds through changing socio-historical contexts. Popular and political discourse often frames the COVID-19 pandemic as an isolated, 'unprecedented' moment. However, by building on much longer research histories, aggregating existing findings and expertise across interdisciplinary collectives, we are better able to interrogate and contextualise its distinctive facets and uneven impacts while also producing a baseline for future events.

Our contributions to methods of QSA build out of involvement in qualitative longitudinal studies spanning several decades, that investigated the longitudinal dynamics of poverty and inequality as expressed in family contexts over time. These studies enabled socio-historical insight into how crises and shocks, like the global recessions of 2008 and 2012 and the subsequent political imposition of austerity, rendered low-income families and households vulnerable (for example, Emmel and Hughes, 2010; Tarrant and Hughes, 2019). National policy responses varied globally, and previous research with vulnerable families in the UK observed how austerity politics exacerbated existing inequalities, additionally creating new and asymmetrical vulnerabilities and hardships (Emmel and Hughes, 2010; Tarrant, 2018; Hall, 2019). These qualitative data provide both *historical* evidence for how families manage 'shocks' to their households engendered through such austerity policies, as well as connection with how the *present* impacts of such policies continue to shape inequalities in experiences of the current COVID-19 crisis. In this way, legacy data provide enhanced *explanatory potential* for researchers seeking to account for the disproportionate impacts of COVID-19 on individuals and groups, thus enabling researchers to avoid analytical retreat to simplistic, present-centred descriptions of these. Our work demonstrates how access to, and analysis of, existing data resources and 'data histories' increasingly preserved in archives, enhances how we address important sociological questions about the extent of continuity and change engendered by 'moments' of crisis like the pandemic.

Such an approach may also aid understanding of what is currently seen as an anomalous disproportionate representation of Black and Minority Ethnic (BAME) individuals and groups in the death rates from COVID-19. All too frequently, the 'higher than average' death rates for BAME communities are treated as almost inexplicable. However, there is considerable evidence across the social sciences that demonstrates the importance of the intersections of race and class in ways that render BAME people as disproportionately deprived and therefore more at risk of contracting the virus, and more likely to become ill from it (Nganizi, 2020; Marmot/Highfield, 2020). Thus, while we may need to be creative in how and which data we draw upon to explore these present trends, there are long social science histories which support a critical interrogation of common-sense understanding via investigation of such questions.

Finally, data do not need to be 'historical' to inform on long-term historical processes. Even in the present there are opportunities for data sharing and collaboration on data that have only recently been generated. The unprecedented *speed* at which social crises are unfolding, present new and important questions about how and whether we can capture the diverse impacts of the crisis, not only in real time, but also in ways which can inform social science understanding and knowledge in generations to come. Currently, funding is being made available much more quickly by funding councils, speedier publishing is being facilitated by academic publishers (although this in itself has exacerbated existing inequalities in the academy too), and many of the classic delays around collaboration (for example, between researchers and non-academic partners) are being cast aside in favour of rapid response. This imperative of 'rapid response' research, in rapidly changing contexts, produces a new impetus to work collaboratively. Not only is there a necessity to research the pandemic as a new phenomenon, but this is also a moment that is catalysing anticipated change (what we might currently consider unusual, and what will become the 'new normal'). To engage with the 'unprecedented' as it becomes normalised, a breadth response is essential to capture social impacts and social change in the round. Shared and amalgamated data and findings are a key resource here for researchers, ensuring they can connect with existing scholarship. Furthermore, interdisciplinary collaboration is essential in order that research can be as comprehensive as possible, and also to maximise its relevance across societies. The UK Data Service 'Data Dive'[2] event hosted in October 2020, which supports data producers, policymakers, and charities to link and share recently generated and related data sets to address critical questions about the impacts of the pandemic, is one such example.

Through this section, we have looked at the value of retrospective as well as contemporary research and engagement. We would also suggest that fundamental to recognising the explanatory power of methods of QSA using existing data to develop and support analyses of new questions, is the acknowledgement of the need and value for prospective thinking and planning in research. In effect, engaging with questions of re-use prospectively is a persuasive reason for encouraging contemporary social researchers to prioritise data preservation for the purpose of future re-use. In this way we are not only engaging with questions of current concern, but also through this, provide for longer histories of research engagement and future generations of researchers.

Data preservation and archiving as ethical sensibility

We conclude that building what we describe as an *ethical temporal sensibility* into the research mindset, one which ensures the capture of the lived experiences of those most vulnerable to being excluded or erased from social histories, can foster a collective responsibility that extends and enhances the value of our socio-historical research both now and in future (Hughes and Tarrant, 2020a; Tarrant and Hughes, 2020b).

In this context, the significance of preserving the voices of vulnerable and/ or marginalised families and communities, namely those least likely to be captured via traditional forms of political engagement and representation, is *ethically* vital in order that they are retained as part of the social record of these times (Hughes and Tarrant, 2020b; Tarrant and Hughes, 2020b). Generating and archiving data, both from and with these populations, is essential for the preservation of more holistic and socially comprehensive historical records. Endeavours towards the digital storage and curation of research data becomes more urgent in a context where participants' voices and experiences should be retained rather than silenced. The experiences of these participants are least likely to be captured, yet these are individuals who are also most likely to be further disadvantaged by social crises. A pragmatic commitment towards data preservation and curation can therefore ensure the social histories of those with least access to digital participation.

Where can I access (and archive) qualitative research data?

At the end of this chapter we provide a list of data resources that begin to represent the great diversity and wealth of social research data already 'out there' (Hughes and Tarrant, 2020) that could be used during the crisis and as a baseline. Briefly, in the UK, principal collections include:

- the UK Data Service
- the Mass Observation Archive
- the National Social Policy and Social Change Archive, University of Essex
- the Irish Qualitative Data Archive and Northern Ireland Qualitative Archive (NIQA)
- the London School of Economics Archive
- the Timescapes Archive, University of Leeds

There has also been a flourishing of international qualitative data archives, including:

- the Australian Data Archive (ADA)
- the Qualitative Data Repository at Syracuse University, US
- the Henry A. Murray Research Archive at Harvard
- the Inter-University Consortium for Political and Social Research (IUCPS) in the US

For COVID-19 specific resources, the UK Data Service has a dedicated page, listing data sets providing social context to the pandemic. These are likely to appeal to researchers across social science disciplines in their diverse thematic coverage of issues such as (un)employment, food, finance, ageing, welfare, crime and deviance, health, policy change, and so on. The 'Data Dive' workshops (mentioned earlier) are also exemplars of opportunities for researchers to engage in the secondary analysis of recently generated crisis-specific data. Collaborative secondary analysis opportunities are also being supported in the context of rapidly funded research studies, including the Nuffield funded 'Covid Realities' project[3] which, with the support of a consortium of research studies across the UK, is examining the unfolding impacts of the pandemic and policy change on low-income families. In the UK, COVID-19-related data are also being generated and preserved via the national longitudinal panel studies. A COVID-19-specific Longitudinal Research Hub called CLOSER[4] has been set up in this regard to support researchers, policymakers, and parliamentarians to access data, both now and in future.

Conclusion

In this chapter, we have sought to render qualitative data re-use and qualitative secondary analysis (QSA) more visible as relevant and innovative forms of fieldwork that can be conducted 'at a remove' (Hughes et al, 2020). These methods are not only suitable for crisis contexts where physically distanced approaches to fieldwork may be necessary but are also innovative methodologies with capacity to inform on the social impacts and effects of crises as they unfold over time.

Our ambitions to raise the profile and visibility of qualitative data availability, re-use, and secondary analysis are also underscored by concern for the future of research methodology and knowledge production. At the time of writing, social researchers are racing to document and understand the complex and wide-ranging impacts of the pandemic, linked policy responses, and their unequal impacts on lived experience. Not only has the COVID-19 crisis brought the under-use of existing qualitative data into sharp relief, but it has also demonstrated a renewed imperative for preserving diverse data resources for the socio-historical record. Regardless of whether researchers decide to engage with these methodologies in future, the crisis has especially emphasised how data concerns, including data sharing, curation, and preservation, must be carefully attended to by all researchers as part of a broader ethical sensibility among the social research community (Tarrant and Hughes, 2020b). Such an approach is likely to foster and underscore greater efforts among social researchers, enabling us to forge ground-up policy responses building out of longer and broader empirical and theoretical histories, via a collective translation of evidence. We also make a case for creating new interdisciplinary data legacies. It is our hope that, if there is any positive learning and change to come out of this crisis for the academy, we continue to recognise the potentialities (and also learn from the challenges) of working more closely together. This is not just for the benefit of developing a better understanding but also to positively influence a dynamic social world. Through the production of new data histories as a collective, we also become stewards of evidence from a contemporary crisis that will become foundational to social history.

Finally, returning to present concerns, we acknowledge that re-using and working with data generated between others is not an obvious replacement for primary research and the face-to-face encounters that make fieldwork so enjoyable and insightful. Where online methods may go some way to enabling face-to-face engagements and modes of connectivity with participants, this is not a key feature of data re-use or qualitative secondary analysis. Nevertheless, data re-use can be both a rewarding and immersive experience (and, we acknowledge, sometimes distressing and traumatic), ethically rooted and engendering its own unique forms of emotional connection with participants (Weller, 2020). Secondary analysts gain privileged insights into the diverse social worlds of participants in the communities and localities of interest, observe methodological approaches employed by other researchers, and develop a real sense of how particular experiences are lived and given meaning. As the COVID-19 pandemic unfolds in the longer-term, we argue that opportunities for this kind of immersive work need to be foregrounded both for its own value and, indeed, to enhance face-to-face and primary forms of fieldwork.

Notes

[1] A comprehensive list of archives and international resources is provided at the end of this chapter.

[2] https://ukdataservice.ac.uk/news-and-events/eventsitem/?id=5679

[3] https://covidrealities.org/

[4] https://www.closer.ac.uk/

References

Bishop, L. and Kuula-Luumi, A. (2017) 'Revisiting qualitative data reuse: a decade on', *Sage Open*, 7(1).

Chawla, P. (2020) 'Research methods to understand the "youth capabilities & conversions": the pros and cons of using secondary data analysis in a pandemic situation', in H. Kara, and S. Khoo (eds) *Researching in the Age of COVID-19, Vol 1: Response and Reassessment*, Bristol: Policy Press.

Davidson, E., Edwards, R., Jamieson, L., and Weller, S. (2019) 'Big data, qualitative style: a breadth-and-depth method with large amounts of secondary qualitative data', *Quality & Quantity*, 53: 363–76.

EarthLab (2020) 'Adapting research methodologies in the COVID-19 pandemic', [online], available at: https://earthlab.uw.edu/2020/07/adapting-research-methodologies-in-the-COVID-19 -pandemic/

Edwards, R. and Holland, R. (2020) 'Reviewing challenges and the future for qualitative interviewing', *International Journal of Social Research Methodology*, 23(5): 581–92, DOI: 10.1080/13645579.2020.1766767

Emmel, N., Hughes, K., Greenhalgh. J., and Sales, A. (2007) 'Accessing socially excluded people – trust and the gatekeeper in the researcher–participant relationship', *Sociological Research Online*, 12(2) March, http://www.socresonline.org.uk/12/2/emmel.html

Emmel, N. and Hughes, K. (2010) '"Recession, it's all the same to us son": the longitudinal experience (1999–2010) of deprivation', *Twenty-First Century Society*, 5(2): 119–24.

Fitzgibbon, A. (2021) Just because you can, doesn't mean you should. In Kara, H. and Khoo, S. (eds) *Qualitative and Digital Research in Times of Crisis: Methods, Reflexivity, and Ethics*. Bristol: Policy Press.

Garthwaite, K., Wright, K., Patrick, R., and Power, M. (2020) 'Researching poverty in the pandemic: thinking through ethical issues and challenges', available from: http://www.social-policy.org.uk/spa-blog/researching-poverty-in-the-pandemic-thinking-through-ethical-issues-and-challenges-by-kayleigh-garthwaite-et-al/

Hall, S.-M. (2019) *Everyday Life in Austerity: Family, Friends and Intimate Relations*, Basingstoke: Palgrave Macmillan.

Hammersley, M. (2010) 'Can we re-use qualitative data via secondary analysis? Notes on some terminological and substantive issues', *Sociological Research Online*, 15(1).

Hughes, K. and Tarrant, A. (2020a) *Qualitative Secondary Analysis*, London: Sage.

Hughes, K. and Tarrant, A. (2020b) 'The ethics of Qualitative Secondary Analysis', in K. Hughes and A. Tarrant (eds) *Qualitative Secondary Analysis*, London: Sage.

Hughes, K. and Tarrant, A. (2020c) 'Resources for Qualitative Secondary Analysis', available from: https://timescapes-archive.leeds.ac.uk/wp-content/uploads/sites/47/2020/04/Resources-for-QSA.pdf

Hughes, K., Hughes, J., and Tarrant, A. (2020) 'Re-approaching interview data through qualitative secondary analysis: interviews with internet gamblers', *International Journal of Social Research Methodology*, 23(5): 565–79.

Hughes, K., Hughes J., and Tarrant, A. (2021, in press) 'Working at a remove: continuous, collective, and configurative research engagement through Qualitative Secondary Analysis', *Quality and Quantity*.

Irwin, S., Bornat, J., and Winterton, M. (2012) 'Timescapes secondary analysis: comparison, context and working across data sets', *Qualitative Research*, 12(1): 66–80.

James, A. (2012) 'Seeking the analytic imagination: reflections on the process of interpreting qualitative data', *Qualitative Research*, 13(5): 562–77.

Jamieson, L. and Lewthwaite, S. (2019) 'Big Qual – why we should be thinking big about qualitative data for research, teaching and policy', LSE blog, available at: https://blogs.lse.ac.uk/impactofsocialsciences/2019/03/04/big-qual-why-we-should-be-thinking-big-about-qualitative-data-for-research-teaching-and-policy/

Lupton, D. (2020) 'Doing research methods in a pandemic', [online], available at: https://nwssdtpacuk.files.wordpress.com/2020/04/doing-fieldwork-in-a-pandemic2-google-docs.pdf

Marmot, M. and Highfield, R. (2020) 'Coronavirus: why ethnic minority groups suffer more', [online], available at: https://www.sciencemuseumgroup.org.uk/blog/coronavirus-why-minority-ethnic-groups-suffer-more/

Mason, J. (2007) '"Re-using" qualitative data: on the merits of an investigative epistemology', *Sociological Research Online*, 12(3).

Moore, N. (2007) '(Re)-using Qualitative data?', *Sociological Research Online*, 12(3).

Mauthner, N., Backett-Milburn, K., and Parry, O. (1998) 'The data are out there, or are they? Implications for archiving and revisiting qualitative data', *Sociology*, 32(4): 733–45.

Neale, B., Henwood, K. and Holland, J. (2012) Researching lives through time: an introduction to the Timescapes approach, *Qualitative Research*, 12(1): 4-15.

Neale, B. (2013) 'Adding time into the mix: stakeholder ethics in qualitative longitudinal research', *Methodological Innovations*, 8(2): 6–20.

Nganizi, S. (2020) 'COVID-19 and the role of race in health inequality', *Young Fabians*, available at: http://www.youngfabians.org.uk/covid_19_ and_the_role_of_race_in_health_inequality

Nuffield Council on Bioethics (2020) *'Research in global health emergencies: ethical issue*, available from: https://www.nuffieldbioethics.org/publications/ research-in-global-health-emergencies/read-the-short-report/ developing-an-ethical-compass

Tarrant, A. (2017) 'Getting out of the swamp? Methodological reflections on using qualitative secondary analysis to develop research design', *International Journal of Social Research Methodology*, 20(6): 599–611.

Tarrant, A. (2018) 'Care in an age of Austerity: men's care responsibilities in low-income families', *Ethics and Social Welfare,* 12(1): 34–48.

Tarrant, A. and Hughes, K. (2019) 'Qualitative secondary analysis: building longitudinal samples to understand men's generational identities in low-income contexts', *Sociology*, 53(3): 538–53.

Tarrant, A. and Hughes, K. (2020a) 'The re-use of qualitative data as an under-appreciated field of social sciences innovation and knowledge', *LSE Impact* blog, available at: https://blogs.lse.ac.uk/impactofsocialsciences/ 2020/06/08/the-re-use-of-qualitative-data-is-an-under-appreciated-field-for-innovation-and-the-creation-of-new-knowledge-in-the-social-sciences/

Tarrant, A. and Hughes, K. (2020b) 'Developing a temporal ethical sensibility for preserving and curating research data', *Digital Curation Centre Research* blog, available at: https://dcc.ac.uk/blog/developing-temporal-ethical-sensibility-preserving-and-curating-research-data

Tarrant, A. (2021) *Fathering and Poverty: Uncovering Men's Participation in Low-income Family Life*, Bristol: Policy Press.

Weller, S. (2020) 'Collaborating with original research teams: some reflections on good secondary analytic practice', available at: http://bigqlr.ncrm.ac.uk/ 2019/03/06/post26-dr-susie-weller-collaborating-with-original-research-teams-some-reflections-on-good-secondary-analytic-practice/

Wright-Mills, C. (1950) *The Sociological Imagination*, Oxford: Oxford University Press.

Links to qualitative secondary archives and other resources

Timescapes Archive: https://timescapes-archive.leeds.ac.uk

Big Qual Analysis Resource Hub: https://bigqlr.ncrm.ac.uk

UK Data Service: https://ukdataservice.ac.uk/

IQDA (2015) *IQDA Resources for Students*, Irish Qualitative Data Archive, University of Maynooth. Available at: www.maynoothuniversity.ie/iqda/data-resources/resources-students

Examples of qualitative data resources, UK and worldwide at all scales

1970s British Cohort Study: https://cls.ucl.ac.uk/cls-studies/1970-british-cohort-study/

Adam Matthew Digital collection: https://www.amdigital.co.uk/

Gender: Identity and Social Change

Australian Data Archive – https://ada.edu.au

Avon Longitudinal Study of Parents and Children –http://www.bristol.ac.uk/alspac/researchers/access/

Aylesham Community Archives and Heritage Group – _www.communityarchives.org.uk/content/organisation/aylesham

The Council of European Social Science Data Archives (CESSDA) – www.cessda.eu

Austria: WISDOM

Czech Republic: The Czech Sociological Data Archive (SDA)

Denmark: The Danish Data Archive (DDA)

Finland: The Finnish Social Science Data Archive (FSD)

France: beQuali, Reseau Quetelet

Germany: GESIS Data Archive for the Social Sciences

Hungary: Voices of the 20th Century – Archive and Research Centre

Ireland: The Irish Qualitative Data Archive, Irish Social Science Data Archive (ISSDA)

Lithuania: The Lithuanian Data Archive for Social Sciences and Humanities (LiDA)

Northern Ireland: The Northern Ireland Qualitative Archive

Poland: Archiwum Danych Jakościowych

Slovenia: Archiv Druzboslvnih Podatkov

Switzerland: The DARIS (Data and Research Information Services)

The Feminist Archive North –_https://feministarchivenorth.org.uk

The Feminist Archive South –_http://feministarchivesouth.org.uk/

Henry A. Murray Archive, Harvard University –_https://murray.harvard.edu

Hertfordshire Cohort Study – https://www.mrc.soton.ac.uk/herts/

Inter-University Consortium of Political and Social Research – www.icpsr.umich.edu/icpsrweb/

Irish Qualitative Data Archive –_www.maynoothuniversity.ie/iqda

Kirklees sound archive in West Yorkshire, which houses oral history interviews on the woollen textile industry

Lesbian Herstory Archives –_www.lesbianherstoryarchives.org

The London School of Economics Archive – www.lse.ac.uk/library/collections/collection-highlights/collections-highlights

Mass Observation Archive –_www.massobs.org.uk

Millennium Cohort Study, UCL – https://cls.ucl.ac.uk/cls-studies/millennium-cohort-study/

The National Child Development Study – https://cls.ucl.ac.uk/cls-studies/1958-national-child-development-study/

National Survey of Health and Development – https://www.nshd.mrc.ac.uk

The Northern Ireland Data Archive on Conflict and Ageism – www.ark.ac.uk/qual/

Qualitative Data Repository, Syracuse University – www.google.com/search?client=safari&rls=en&q=qualitative+data+archive+america&ie=UTF-8&oe=UTF-8

Southampton Women's Survey, University of Southampton – https://www.mrc.soton.ac.uk/sws/

UK Data Service – _www.ukdataservice.ac.uk

UK Data Service, International Qualitative Archives – https://ukdataservice.ac.uk/get-data/other-providers/qualitative/european-archives.aspx

The World Listening Project – www.worldlisteningproject.org

Understanding Society – https://www.understandingsociety.ac.uk

Wirral Child Health and Development Study – https://www.liverpool.ac.uk/institute-of-life-and-human-sciences/schools-and-departments/department-of-psychological-sciences/research/first-steps/

11

Researching older Vietnam-born migrants at a distance: the role of digital kinning

Hien Thi Nguyen, Loretta Baldassar, Raelene Wilding, and Lukasz Krzyzowski

Introduction

With transnational families increasingly performing familyhood online, social researchers have shifted their attention to digital methods and have also begun to document and analyse the role of Information Communication Technologies (ICTs) and what it means to engage these technologies (Wang, Myers, and Sundaram, 2013; Baldassar, Nedelcu, Merla, and Wilding, 2016; Alinejad and Ponzanesi, 2020; Baldassar and Wilding, 2020). ICTs are also increasingly incorporated into online research with migrants and their kinship networks across countries (Vildaite, 2019; Bryceson and Vuorela, 2002; Baldassar and Wilding, 2020), facilitating multi-sited studies without the need for costly and time-consuming travel. Online research practices became even more dominant during the COVID-19 pandemic because of globally restricted physical movement and social restrictions to minimise risk of infection. This emergency situation made our on-going face-to-face fieldwork in Perth and Melbourne, Australia, non-viable. To address this challenge, we modified research methods to conduct the study online.

In this chapter, we explore what it means for older Vietnam-born parent migrants living in Australia to access ICTs and new media as a part of the research process. We argue that conducting ethnographic research online not only provides data on migrants' transnational ageing experiences, but also facilitates digital kinning between researchers and participants. In particular, we observed how younger family members were relied upon to facilitate parent migrants' online engagement. We develop our argument with two key points. First, online social practices of participants, which are usefully conceptualised as instances of digital kinning, are defined as 'the processes of engagement with new technologies for the purpose of maintaining support networks to sustain social support and connections, maintain cultural identity, and protect social identity, which are all particularly at risk during the ageing process' (Baldassar and Wilding, 2020: 319). Second, our reflections on the challenges and opportunities of conducting ethnographic research online by using netnography (Kozinets, 2012) allows us to explore the extent to which researchers, too, are incorporated into the practices and processes of digital kinning with participants. This point emphasises the relationship between researcher and participants, which is under-examined in the literature. Older participants and the principal researcher, Hien Nguyen, share social bonds (for instance, the same virtual residential fields [social media], history of migration, social ties, cultural and religious beliefs) and these are attributing factors of digital kinning, bringing positive feelings of support and sense of belonging to migrant participants. Here, the notion of digital kinning highlights the continuum and situated relatedness of the researcher.

Our analysis highlights five stages that reflect the development of rapport online through digital kinning practices: digital encounters, online recruitment of participants, doing Internet-based ethnographic interviews, undertaking digital participant observation, and configuration of digital research rapport. We define these digital kinning research stages as 'the process of online research involving digital devices to conduct interviews and participant observation in cyberspace that facilitate kinning between researchers and participants'. We conclude by noting that this digital kinning research relationship often actively facilitates older migrants' digital literacy and supports their access to, and knowledge of, local, distant, and virtual support networks. In turn, those networks also support the online research process.

Conceptualising digital kinning as research process

There are two main models of kinship in family research. The earlier established doctrine is based on kinship as biological or genetic ontology characterised by consanguinity, descent, lineage, and affinity (Sahlins, 2011). More recent approaches instead emphasise human social relationships and ties, with kin networks understood as performative and as 'practices of becoming such as feeding or living together' (Carsten, 2020: 321). Sahlins (2011) summarises a wide range of practices that establish kin relationships and networks across cultures and societies. The practices include shared residence, lands, history of migration and cooperation, memories, political views and alliances, cultural and religious practices, close friendship ties, fosterage and adoption, and other essential reciprocal socio-economic connections. Importantly, recent research on 'families of choice' suggests that relationships that are not structured by blood offer more emotional support than traditional family relationships (Mouzon, 2014). Signe Howell, in her research on transnational adoption, coins the term 'self-conscious kinship' to describe how adoptive Norwegian parents incorporate their adopted children into their kin networks. She argues that kinship is 'something that is necessarily achieved in and through relationships with others' (Howell, 2003: 468). Sahlins (2011: 2) conceptualises this performative dimension of kinship as creating a 'mutuality of being' – 'persons who are members of another, who participate intrinsically in each other's existence'. He argues that kinship can be reinforced or reduced by the degree of people's participation in each other's lives.

The 'mutuality of being' characterised by kinship ties is clearly evident in the exchange of transnational care that occurs in contexts of migration. Kinship ties are not only biological but are also performed, negotiated, and reproduced through the development of affection which can create enduring social bonds (Souralová, 2015, 2020; Baldassar, Ferrero, and Portis, 2017). Kin ties do not exist *a priori*, but are negotiated on a daily basis through diverse activities (Sahlins, 2011).

More recently, 'digital kinning' has been introduced to highlight how the processes of kinning increasingly rely on digital media practices. Baldassar and Wilding (2020) demonstrated that mobile phones and Internet-enabled devices are used by older migrants to maintain their social ties and relationships, as well as their social, cultural, and familial identities, particularly in response to the disruptive effects of migration. Furthermore, because of the COVID-19 public health physical distancing measures, we observed that older parent migrants were forced to pivot a majority of their kinship and care practices online, which was seen as an appropriate adaptation strategy in the time of crisis.

Research methods

The context for this chapter is a qualitative inquiry into the lived ageing and aged care experiences of older Vietnam-born parent migrants living in Australia. The notion of kinship as 'doing' rather than 'being' is reflected in the well-known Vietnamese proverb, 'better a neighbour near than a brother far off'. This saying was repeated during fieldwork as participants would regularly acknowledge the expansion of their support networks beyond their biological ties as a result of their migration process, resulting from their need for mutual support in the new migrant setting. As we suggest later on in the chapter, familiarity with, and belief in this saying, facilitated the kinning processes of Vietnam-born migrants with biologically unconnected people in the host country, including the principal researcher.

Our initial fieldwork plans were adjusted in response to the outbreak of the COVID-19 pandemic. When physical fieldwork became impractical due to the high risk the virus posed to older people in particular, netnography was introduced as a viable alternative, using 'computer-mediated communications as a source of data to arrive at the ethnographic understanding and representation of a cultural or communal phenomenon' (Kozinets, 2012: 3). One of the advantages of this method was the inclusion of participants from multiple cities across Australia. It became possible to observe the ways in which older Vietnam-born migrants are using digital media in their everyday lives.

Ethnographic interviews were conducted with 22 parent migrants (12 women and 10 men, aged 54 to 91): 10 were conducted online, 9 face to face (before and after the lockdown in Western Australia), and 3 by phone. Online participant observation was undertaken with parent migrants through their own Facebook profiles (15) or their children's/partners' profiles (7).

Half of the parent migrants reported that they could proficiently use digital devices (smartphone, tablet, or laptop) to conduct online searches for desired information and engage in online platforms. The other half reported requiring assistance from their adult children or spouses to register for an online account, instal essential apps of online platforms, or search information from digital sources. Despite having either proficient or limited digital knowledge, all 22 participants stated that they could confidently use an ICT tool readily connected with the Internet to make a video/audio call through digital platforms to their distant kin and friends.

This indicates that many older Vietnam-born parent migrants have the ability to participate in online research without significant constraints, although they benefit from assistance from their family members to use ICTs and engage with new media.

Stages in the digital kinning research process

Several scholars have identified a series of stages in the kinning process (Howell, 2003; Souralová, 2015, 2020). We have identified a similar set of five stages of what we term the digital kinning research process, described as follows.

Stage 1: Digital encounters

The digital encounters stage begins when researchers prepare to conduct research online and participants first interact with the researchers using ICT tools for digital connections and communications.

Online researchers have to be tech-savvy to instal and run different apps of online platforms, and practise digital connections such as i-message, video/audio calls, and recording. In addition, researchers may have to mentor and assist participants to use ICTs and engage in virtual platforms if they lack necessary skills. Researchers should also conduct a pre-fieldwork assessment of the virtual platforms where participants are often engaged to maximise recruitment opportunities. This assessment is crucial because the usage of the digital platforms varies by factors such as age, gender, income, and educational attainment (PRC, 2019) and is influenced by the culture of Internet utilisation shaped in participants' country of origin. For instance, Chinese people prefer using WeChat and Weibo; meanwhile, Australians prefer Facebook, Instagram, and WhatsApp (CWM, 2020; DeGennaro, 2020). Facebook is the most-widely used online platform by Vietnamese people living in Vietnam, with 59 per cent of the social media users connecting with one another via Facebook (Statcounter, 2020). Hence, Facebook was targeted as the most appropriate virtual space to facilitate the digital kinning process with participants in our research.

For participants, their first online engagement might have begun a long time ago or recently, depending on their competence, accessibility, and motivation to use social media.

Of 22 participants, nearly one third stated that they had started using ICTs since they came to Australia (for less than two years). The remaining 14 participants have used ICTs and/or engaged in online platforms for five or more years. The temporal gap in using ICTs and social media implies disparities in digital literacy among older participants. We observed that the longer time parent migrants used ICTs, the more proficient they became.

For example, Huong,[1] a 63-year-old female parent migrant, has been using ICTs and engaging with Yahoo since the mid-1990s; meanwhile, Luong,[2] a 69-year-old female parent visitor, only became acquainted with ICTs and new media since her visit to Australia in 2019. Because Huong has been using ICTs since her late 30s, her ability to grasp digital literacy was vastly superior to Luong who began using the devices in her late 60s.

Our research findings reveal that the frequency of using ICTs and new media plays a major part in facilitating the digital kinning research process. Factors that influence migrant parents' frequency of use is underwritten by their strong motivation to connect with distant support networks and cultural contents, but is tempered by their poor digital skills, limited time due to care duties, and lack of/infrequent family assistance to use the tools.

Huong indicated that she spent around five hours per day online doing electronic information searches, maintaining digital interactions, and watching electronic news and video clips; meanwhile, Luong spent only around one hour per day online making essential video calls to her kin in Vietnam. Huong was confident in using ICT tools and participated in our digital research independently. In contrast, Luong has more limited digital literacy, so her participation in our research relied upon the assistance of her daughter in Australia. Moreover, as Huong spent lots of time each day on Facebook, Hien (researcher) could interact with her online easily and frequently. In contrast, there were few opportunities to practise direct online interactions with Luong because of her infrequent online engagement. Instead, Hien maintained online interactions with Luong's daughter to facilitate the digital kinning process with her, highlighting the fact that in online research, digital engagement sometimes necessitates the assistance of family members and requires the frequent use of ICTs.

Despite some older adults, like Luong, having limited digital citizenship – the ability to confidently engage with digital resources (Baldassar and Wilding, 2020) – all participants possessed at least some basic digital skills to sustain their online connections with their distant kin and social ties. For instance, they knew how to make an Internet-based video/audio call, utilise it regularly, mostly to participate in online interactions that require basic digital competences. Hence, we describe the older participants as having 'temporary residence' in the digital world. However, to acquire 'digital fluency' (Wang et al, 2013) to become 'permanent' residents or 'citizens' in the virtual world, they need to continue improving their digital literacy so that they have the skills, knowledge, and understanding required to use ICTs and new media (Hagel, 2015).

To sum up, digital encounters are the first and pivotal stage in the digital kinning research process to conduct online research effectively. In this stage, researchers should equip themselves with essential digital skills and do pre-fieldwork assessments of the virtual platforms regularly engaged with by participants to best prepare for the online research process. In particular, researchers should also e-connect with participants' adult children to facilitate participants with limited digital competences to initiate the digital kinning research process.

Stage 2: Online recruitment of participants

The second stage begins when researchers start recruiting participants virtually. As successful recruitment is imperative for the research to progress, different strategies should be employed to build initial digital rapport with potential participants.

In our research, digital research advertisements were publicised on various social media profiles of Vietnamese communities/student associations with moderators' permission. Also, a recruitment letter was distributed electronically via Hien's personal networks. Some recruitment began face-to-face and continued electronically. Owing to the coexistence of the online and offline worlds, digital recruitment was conducted through both distant (by phone) and physical (face-to-face) interactions.

On the participants' side, online recruitment begins when they are digitally contacted by researchers or researchers' social networks. To illustrate how online recruitment was facilitated, we explore the experiences of virtually recruiting Huong and Hung,[3] a 76-year-old male parent migrant. Before being e-introduced by their mutual friends, Huong (in Melbourne) and Hung (in Sydney) were unknown to us. Hien began virtual ice-breaking conversations about her research project, including scheduling interviews with Huong and Hung's wife through Facebook to build initial rapport. As Huong had been very active online for over 20 years, the online recruitment with her progressed smoothly. In contrast, it took more time to facilitate digital interactions with Hung because of his rare online engagement. The electronic recruitment of Hung was aided by his family members, namely his daughter and wife.

We found that the most effective recruitment strategy was the virtual snowball sampling method (Baltar and Brunet, 2012). This involved e-introductions to potential participants by Hien's personal networks and participants themselves on Internet-based social platforms rather than through purposive recruitment by using online advertisements.

Of Hien's online posts on ten social media profiles, she received feedback from only two people who promised to introduce her to potential participants. Meanwhile, most of the participants were recruited by virtual snowball e-referrals.

Though Hien made numerous efforts and employed different strategies to maximise the effectiveness of online recruitment, the digital kinning research process at this stage still encountered some hurdles caused by contextual, legal, cultural, religious, and social differences perceived by participants in their home and host country. These differences were also intensified by gaps in cultural capital and socio-economic backgrounds of participants and their dependency on their adult children as gatekeepers.

First, as most of the older participants in our research had limited knowledge of Australian legislation, cultures, languages, religions, and living environment, the spatial scope of their activities was usually restricted to their homes and nearby spaces. Their social connections were mainly with their established social and kin networks in Vietnam. They developed several new social ties in Australia but they did not favour new relationships with unknown people who their adult children did not recommend. Second, several older parents hesitated to participate in the research because they were afraid of saying 'wrong' things or having nothing to say. We observed that older participants from low socio-economic backgrounds with low educational attainment were more likely to refuse to participate in the research than those from higher socio-economic backgrounds with higher educational attainment. This pattern might be explained by the fact that the former cohort participated in the digital world less and later than the later cohort, so they might feel unsafe about having online conservations with Hien who they did not know well. The former cohort also tended to refuse to participate in the research if Hien said that she would like to 'interview' them. To them, the term 'interview' refers to a type of formal conversation that should only involve knowledgeable or educated people.

Thus, when older parents recognise themselves as 'uneducated', they often refuse to participate.

To tackle these challenges, Hien actively employed culturally appropriate interactions to build initial online relationships with participants, including building digital rapport with their adult children to facilitate online conversations with them. In this way, older participants were not treated as atomised individuals, but rather as members of family and social networks. With permission, encouragement, and support of their adult children, parent migrants felt safer and more confident to participate in online interviews. Also, to prevent their bias against participating in 'interviews', plain language terms, such as 'chatting' or 'everyday talk', were used instead. Furthermore, in virtual ice-breaking conversations, Hien took on the persona of a dutiful adult daughter, rather than a researcher, in keeping with Vietnamese cultural expectations about the important role of daughters in care of the elderly, thus facilitating the processes of digital kinning.

In this second stage, we conclude that the virtual snowball sampling method, utilising the virtual support networks of both researchers and participants, is the most effective way to recruit participants. To address cultural, language, and knowledge barriers that often prevent older migrants from participating in online research, culturally appropriate interactions and terminology should be employed to build initial digital research rapport.

Stage 3: Doing Internet-based ethnographic interviews

When participants join the first online ethnographic interview, the third stage of the digital kinning research process begins.

In our research, ethnographic interviews were conducted once or several times depending on participants' time availability and data collection purposes. Moreover, because of objective and subjective factors (for instance, the COVID-19 pandemic, participants' preferred interview modes), both online and offline ethnographic interviews were conducted, which enabled us to compare the two modes of interview.

We observed no difference in the quality of information gathered. The online interviews lasted longer than the face-to-face ones.

On average, an offline interview lasted from 1.5 to 2 hours; however, most of the online interviews lasted over 2 hours; some even lasted more than 4 hours. The online interviews were longer than the offline ones because of their convenience and comfortableness. Without requiring physical travelling and personal preparedness for appointed face-to-face meetings, Hien and participants had greater flexibility and time for interviews. A number of online interviews were conducted while participants were cooking, driving,[4] or gardening. As such, participants felt freer to share their life narratives.

To facilitate participants' openness and active engagement, Hien applied the Socratic or active interviewing method, which reflected a culturally appropriate interviewing approach to foster fruitful discussions on a specific research topic with participants (Bellah, Madsen, Sullivan, Swidler, and Tipton, 1985; Brinkmann, 2007).

In Vietnamese culture, older people are highly appreciated for their lived experiences and accumulated knowledge through their lifetime (Tran, 2018). If they are valued as knowledgeable people, they often feel respected and become more open in sharing their thoughts instead of acting as passive respondents. Hence, in the interview process, older participants were treated as knowledge producers who were encouraged to share their multifaceted experiences regarding their migration, social ties, cultural and religious practices, living arrangements, memories, daily routines, habits and hobbies. This depth and richness of interview discussions facilitated strong social bonds between participants and Hien.

Moreover, by facilitating older participants to voice their particular concerns, more in-depth information was gathered in our research. For instance, Huong took great pride in her homemaking, childcare, and cooking; thus, Hien encouraged her to share these experiences. Huong felt excited and respected when her shopping and homemaking tips could be shared with Hien, who is of a similar age to her daughter. Meanwhile, Hung was keen on discussing Vietnam's retirement and ageing policies knowing that Hien was working for a Vietnamese governmental body. Hien encouraged him to share his thoughts on those policies and to make recommendations for policy changes. In this way, the online interviews became more active, productive, and empowering. Older participants also felt a sense of satisfaction because their knowledge and experiences were recognised and valued.

We can learn from this stage that the quality of online research is as rich as the quality of offline research. Researchers can facilitate older migrants to participate in digital research and gain richer and more in-depth research information if appropriate interviewing methods are used. Researchers should also provide more freedom to participants to engage in 'everyday talks' even while they are doing some other activities (like cooking or gardening). In this stage, culturally appropriate interactions should continue being used to generate rich research data and to further facilitate digital kinning between researchers and participants.

Stage 4: Undertaking online participant observation

Stage four commences when researchers start to undertake online participant observation and participants or their family members allow researchers to follow and become their friends online.

After completing an interview, Hien would request participants' permission to follow them on social media. Of 22 participants, 15 were digitally observed through their own Facebook profiles and 7 others were observed through their family members' profiles.

We illustrate the fourth stage of the digital kinning research process with two illustrative cases involving Huong and Hung. Hien officially became online friends with Huong, Hung's wife, and Hung's adult daughter after their first online ethnographic interviews were done. With their permission, Hien paid weekly visits to their Facebook profiles to observe what was ongoing in their online lives. As Huong's and Hung's main concerns comprised taking care of their extended family in Australia and sustaining online connections with their distant kin and social networks, most of their posts were about their beautiful moments photographed with their grandchildren and adult children. Huong was also interested in reading English and Vietnamese news, which she loved to share on her Facebook. Meanwhile, Hung's wife and daughter preferred posting pictures about landscape, garden, and Vietnamese cuisines online, which also included Hung. Noticeably, lots of Huong's and Hung's distant family members, friends, former colleagues, neighbours, and former students (of Hung) interacted with them virtually. They might 'like' or send 'love', 'happy', 'smile', 'cheering', 'thumb up' emojis in response to Hung's and Huong's online posts. That was the way participants practised digital kinning with their distant kin and social networks.

We observed that these online interactions became more frequent during the COVID-19 pandemic because participants and their distant kin and friends faced restrictions to physical contacts and travel. Having the same fear and anxiety about COVID-19, older parents and their distant kin and social networks practised their distant and virtual care activities with each other on social media. Older parents revealed that they highly appreciated the role of ICTs, new media, and, in particular, the digital kinning processes, in promoting their social well-being despite social restrictions.

Hien facilitated the digital kinning research process in this stage by having online conversations with participants or their family members. Like their distant friends and kin, Hien followed, gave comments, and sent emojis in response to their online posts. The conversations were diverse, about daily activities or particular hobbies, which identified mutual interests with participants. Care was also taken to respect participants' mental health, and time was spent conversing with them, including about the topics that were not especially relevant to the research. We define this as a 'context-responsive' interviewing skill, which was employed to take particular care of older participants in the challenging time caused by the unprecedented circumstances of the pandemic. In fact, these 'everyday talks' had significant meaning to the older participants who could not travel far from home or have close social contacts with people because of social restrictions. The talks brought trust, more in-depth research information, and truly facilitated the digital kinning research process in the time of crisis. The contextual responsiveness was also informed by Vietnamese cultural awareness and sensitivity whereby the online conversations were conducted with the manifest respect, active listening, and sympathetic understanding that Vietnamese older people expect from descendants and younger people. In the words of Sahlins (2011), Hien and participants started to participate in each other's lives and the researcher–participant relationship was elevated to a higher level – 'digital or virtual friendship', which extends into the next stage of the digital kinning research process.

However, on undertaking online participant observation, we experienced some ethical dilemmas in using and analysing participants' online posts/interactions in cyberspace. Though we got permissions from participants and their adult children to follow them virtually, we could not get permissions from all the people who participated in online conversations with participants. Hence, it would be unethical if we used online conversations as data without permission from participants' friends and kin who generate their posts. There is a parallel to this in offline research – what Mannay (2016) calls the 'non-consenting others' who are mentioned by participants in interviews and focus groups.

To address these dilemmas, we applied ethical guidelines introduced by Eynon, Fry, and Schroeder (2011) in analysing online interactions within virtual environments. If we had any intentions of using any specific posts/conversations, Hien would first ask participants if we could use them. Hien would also ask participants to contact the person(s) engaging in their posts/conversations to obtain their consent for data reproduction. We would not use the online posts/conversations for our analysis if the participants or whoever engaged in the online posts/conversations did not consent. To keep privacy of participants and relevant parties in online social settings, any avatars, personal images, and relevant names we used were all anonymous from the audience in the analysis of research findings.

The key research experience learnt from this stage is that online participant observation, along with researchers' active online interactions with participants, would assist researchers to investigate participants' behaviours and lived experiences in the digital world. Researchers need to take ethical issues into account in using and analysing participants' online posts/interactions in cyberspace. Permission must be obtained from participants and whoever engages in the online conversations used for data analysis. On reproducing online information, researchers must strictly respect anonymity and privacy of participants.

Stage 5: Configuration of digital research rapport

After the online interviews and participant observation were complete, that may be the end of the researcher–participant relationship. However, this relationship may continue in the form of digital research rapport which denotes 'frequent Internet-based interactions and conversations between researchers and participants'.

As mentioned in Chapter 13 of this book, the Euro-Western literature rarely recognises or discusses care and aftercare in the research process. However, in our online research, care and aftercare in the form of digital kinning research practices were all crucial to build digital research rapport for the research process and follow-ups.

The 'digital' dimension of research rapport refers to the digital world where researchers and participants live their virtual lives and practise research activities; meanwhile, 'kinning' denotes active relationships that build on social bonds identified or established during the online research process which develops a sense of mutuality of being. In our research, participants and Hien share a large number of social bonds, including Vietnamese cultural values and socio-economic backgrounds, beliefs, ritual practices, a history of migration, and memories about their lives in the home and host country. In particular, the common use of Facebook to practise their virtual lives and work demonstrates that they are living in the same virtual social fields. These social bonds and mutual understandings are attributing factors of digital kinning.

Furthermore, routine practices of digital connections through Internet-based platforms enabled Hien to nurture closer relations with participants, creating a sense of social bonding (Holland, 2012) that enabled continuing aftercare. Even when the main research process ended, Hien continued to 'love' and 'care' about older participants at a distance by continuing 'everyday talks' as online friends. In turn, the older participants also loved to converse with Hien, treating her like their adult child or grandchild. Thus, the digital research rapport is not a 'one-off' but a long-lasting relationship. It turns into 'kin-like' ties which continues in both the online and offline world. Importantly, the digital research shifted power relations between researchers and participants and empowered participants as knowledge 'co-creators' of the research process.

Digital research rapport also brings mutual benefits for researchers and participants and these benefits, in turn, further promote the digital kinning process between them.

Results of our ethnographic interviews indicated that almost all 22 participants knew little or nothing about Australia's current aged care policies, services, and support networks. When interviewing them, Hien was able to inform participants about Australia's available aged care services that they could access. Also, by engaging in participants' existing virtual support networks, Hien could approach other older participants. This mutual support relationship helps facilitate the progress of online research, leveraging the research quality, and enabling participants to access available support networks that can improve their social well-being during their transnational mobility.

In this stage, by building and sustaining digital research rapport as an outcome of the digital kinning research process, researchers can reach other potential participants, facilitating the progress of online research and improving the research quality. Moreover, researchers could, in turn, inform participants about unknown available support networks to improve participants' social well-being. Digital research rapport is a type of aftercare that both researchers and participants could do when the main research process ends.

Conclusion

In this chapter, we argue the digital kinning research process plays a vital role in facilitating online research, especially in the time of crisis when people mostly rely upon social media and ICTs to access distant and virtual support networks. The process is even more effective and efficient with migrant communities who physically disperse across states and countries. When researchers and participants share social bonds, including the same virtual residential fields (social media), history of migration, social ties, cultural and religious beliefs, this facilitates digital kinning in the research process. Researchers can bring positive feelings of support and a sense of belonging to migrant participants. Digital kinning not only generates rich and unique research outputs but also configures digital research rapport at the end. This rapport, as a form of aftercare, further generates positive outcomes including the expansion of local, distant, and virtual support networks, useful knowledge, and virtual social connections for researchers and participants. We term this 'the co-creation and consumption of knowledge' that facilitates older participants' social well-being and, in turn, supports researchers to achieve their social research ends.

In conducting online research and practising the digital kinning research process with migrant communities, in particular, with older people, attention must be paid to cultural, language, and knowledge barriers that participants may face. Researchers also need to plan culturally appropriate solutions to address them. They must be tech-savvy to use different ICT tools and engage with different online platforms for reaching and assisting participants' engagement in online research. Moreover, researchers must care about ethical issues relating to using and analysing data gathered from online environments to protect participants and relevant parties who engage in online posts/conversations observed.

The digital kinning research process can be applicable to other types of online research as building and sustaining the researcher–participant rapport play a crucial role in gathering primary data and follow-ups. Few welcome further research exploring other dimensions of the digital kinning research process, including care during and after the research.

Reflective questions

- Can the digital research kinning processes be applied with different research groups, not limited to migrant communities?
- Will the digital research kinning processes negatively affect participants and researchers if the digital research rapport ends on one side when the other side does not expect that? If yes, in what ways?
- What are the ethical issues that may need to be considered in conducting online research, building and sustaining digital kinning research practices?

Notes

[1] Pseudonym
[2] Pseudonym
[3] Pseudonym
[4] It is legal to use a phone while driving if it is securely mounted and not touched by the driver; for example, using Bluetooth or voice activation. Our participants complied with these rules when participating in interviews.

References

Alinejad, D., and Ponzanesi, S. (2020) 'Migrancy and digital mediations of emotion', *International Journal of Cultural Studies*, 23(5): 621–38.

Baldassar, L., Nedelcu, M., Merla, L., and Wilding, R. (2016) 'ICT-based co-presence in transnational families and communities: challenging the premise of face-to-face proximity in sustaining relationships', *Global Networks (Oxford)*, 16(2): 133–44.

Baldassar, L., Ferrero, L., and Portis, L. (2017) ' "More like a daughter than an employee": the kinning process between migrant care workers, elderly care receivers and their extended families', *Identities: Global Studies in Culture and Power*, 24(5): 524–41.

Baldassar, L. and Wilding, R. (2020) 'Migration, aging, and digital kinning: the role of distant care support networks in experiences of aging well', *The Gerontologist*, 60(2): 313–21.

Baltar, F. and Brunet, I. (2012) 'Social research 2.0: virtual snowball sampling method using Facebook', *Internet Research*, 22(1): 57–74.

Bellah, R., Madsen, R., Sullivan, W., Swidler, A., and Tipton, S. (1985) *Habits of the Heart: Individualism and Commitment in American Life*, Berkeley, CA: University of California Press.

Brinkmann, S. (2007) 'Could interviews be epistemic?: An alternative to qualitative opinion polling', *Qualitative Inquiry*, 13(8): 1116–38.

Bryceson, D. and Vuorela, V. (2002) *The Transnational Family: New European Frontiers and Global Networks*, New York: Berg.

Carsten, J. (2020) 'Imagining and living new worlds: the dynamics of kinship in contexts of mobility and migration', *Ethnography*, 21(3): 319–34.

CWM (2020) 'Australia's most popular social media sites 2020', retrieved from: https://www.civicwebmedia.com.au/australias-most-popular-social-media-sites-2020/

DeGennaro, T. (2020) '10 most popular social media sites in China (2020 updated)', retrieved from: https://www.dragonsocial.net/blog/social-media-in-china/

Eynon, R., Fry, J., and Schroeder, R. (2011) 'The ethics of Internet research', in N. Fielding, R. Lee, and G. Blank (eds) *The SAGE Handbook of Online Research Methods*, London: Sage, pp 22–41.

Hagel, P. (2015) *Towards an Understanding of 'Digital Literacy(ies)'*, Geelong: Deakin University Library.

Holland, M. (2012) *Social Bonding and Nurture Kinship: Compatibility Between Cultural and Biological Approaches*, London: Createspace Independent Publishing.

Howell, S. (2003) 'Kinning: The creation of life trajectories in transnational adoptive families', *Journal of the Royal Anthropological Institute*, 9(3): 465–84.

Kozinets, R. (2012) 'The method of netnography', in J. Hughes (ed) *SAGE Internet Research Methods* (Vol 2012), London: Sage, pp. 58–73.

Mannay, D. (2016) *Visual, Narrative and Creative Research Methods: Application, Reflection and Ethics*, London: Routledge.

Mouzon, D. (2014) 'Relationships of choice: can friendships or fictive kinships explain the race paradox in mental health?', *Social Science Research*, 44: 32–43.

PRC (2019) 'Social media fact sheet', retrieved from: https://www.pewresearch.org/internet/fact-sheet/social-media/

Sahlins, M. (2011) 'What kinship is (part one)', *Journal of the Royal Anthropological Institute*, 17(1): 2–19.

Souralová, A. (2015) 'Paid caregiving in the gendered life course: a study of Czech nannies in Vietnamese immigrant families', *Czech Sociological Review*, 51(6): 959–91.

Souralová, A. (2020) 'Grandparents, kinship ties, and belonging after migration: the perspective of second-generation grandchildren', *Global Networks*, 20(2): 362–79.

Statcounter (2020) 'Social media stats Viet Nam', retrieved from: https://gs.statcounter.com/social-media-stats/all/viet-nam

Tran, G. (2018) 'Sharing culture values across generations in Vietnamese Australian families', [doctorate], Swinburne, Victoria, retrieved from: https://researchbank.swinburne.edu.au/file/da7644a1-d43a-4d07-89f7-eeda2aa40ea5/1/thi_thanh_tran_thesis.pdf

Vildaite, D. (2019) 'Transnational grandmother–grandchild relationships in the context of migration from Lithuania to Ireland', in V. Timonen (ed) *Grandparenting Practices around the World* (1st edn), Bristol: Bristol University Press, pp 131–48.

Wang, Q., Myers, M., and Sundaram, D. (2013) 'Digital natives and digital immigrants: towards a model of digital fluency', *Business and information Systems Engineering*, 5(6): 409–19.

PART IV

Recurring and longer-term crises

12

A timed crisis: Australian education, migrant Asian teachers, and critical autoethnography

Aaron Teo

Once, at an informal gathering with other young married couples who would later become close friends, the discussion of undergraduate experiences came up. This gathering was held in the living room of one of the couple's houses and was packed to the rafters with all six couples and two toddlers. I was perched on the edge of a foldable black chair, sandwiched between my wife and Sterling, father to one of the girls gently assisting a toy horse navigate the perilous landscape that was the living room floor.

As the extroverts in the group vied for speaking time, I retreated into myself for a moment, taking the opportunity to reflect on *my* experience at university. Suddenly – to my mind at least – I heard someone snarl, "Those Ayy-shhiann students". As the only ethnic minority in the group, my ears immediately pricked up as I noted that the source of this rant was from Liesl, mother to the more rambunctious of the two little girls. Liesl continued her story, voice animated and arms gesticulating wildly. Apparently, Liesl's undergraduate experience had not been quite as pleasant as others in the group. She continued, lamenting how completing projects with Asian international students was one of her worst nightmares – alas, she explained their reticence in class and inability to communicate clearly meant that she was *always* in charge of the group; that she was in charge of getting *all* the work done.

I sat there listening, completely aghast. As I felt the physical discomfort of my sitting position metamorphose into equal parts psychological and emotional discomfort, I shuffled awkwardly in my seat. Liesl, however, did not seem to notice this. Did she not realise *what* she was saying, and to *whom* she was saying it? Did she not realise that I was once one of *those* international students?

As she persisted with her tale, I felt a sense of rage and indignation bubbling under the surface. How could I respond? Would I address the racialised undertones of her essentialising comment? Would I suffer from momentary deafness and ignore the comment entirely? Would I pull Liesl up and in so doing, unsettle the jovial atmosphere that evening? Was there really a compromise between any of these extremes? I had mere milliseconds to decide before the moment passed.

★★★★★

Racism is a lot like Liesl's animated story-telling that day – it often goes unnoticed to those with some sort of power telling the story, but eats away at the hearts, minds, and bodies of less powerful 'others'. Racism, like Liesl's story, also calls for an immediate response and to be dealt with as a matter of urgency, which was, regrettably, more than I could bring myself to do at that moment in time. What makes this parable even more poignant – I believe – is that ironically, despite my best efforts to ignore the comment, this incident, along with numerous other run-ins with racism, continued eating away at me for the longest time, slowly but surely forcing me towards a crisis point.

★★★★★

One of my fondest childhood memories revolves around the time spent in amusement arcades. In an era where the very first PlayStation had only *just* been released and where it wasn't yet the norm to own a gaming console, the arcade was – whenever I could persuade my parents that is – my preferred choice of entertainment. Like most of my primary school–aged peers, I was intoxicated by the motley of bright lights and cacophony of sounds; besotted with the room full of machines crammed together in a cluttered but organised mess that purred and whirred for your attention. While there were always a few favourite machines that I indulged, *Time Crisis* – a first-person light gun shooter game that required players to eliminate all on-screen enemies within a specified time limit across different levels – was, without doubt, the apple of my eye.

What was it about the game that exhilarated me most? Perhaps it was the ability to right the wrongs perpetrated by the game's villains; perhaps it was the high-risk situations players had to navigate; perhaps it was the fact that these things had to happen both surely *and* swiftly, since a loss of time equated to loss of in-game life. Concomitantly, it was also the sheer challenge of *Time Crisis* that often reduced me to a paroxysm of frustrated tears – paired with my fond memories is the image on screen of 10 seconds counting down and two options: one to end the game where I had failed; the other to reinsert a token and try again.

★★★★★

As I stare at my laptop screen, attempting to disentangle all the information I had been reading on methodology, I am distracted by the incident with Liesl, which involuntarily replays in my head for the umpteenth time. I let out a defeated sigh, wishing I could just stay focused on the task and keep the niggling pain from the memory away.

Just then, as I retreat into myself again and leverage my capacity for self-reflection (Francis and Hester, 2012: 35), I feel Carolyn Ellis' (2004) gentle tap on my shoulder.

"You know, personal experience, subjectivity, emotion and your influence as the researcher can't – shouldn't – be kept separate from your research. You see, the thing is, I don't know that we can ever *truly* be separated from our social milieu (Wall, 2008). Considering the myriad ways personal experience impacts the research process, I think it's a bit of a fool's game to assume that we can research from a neutral and impersonal perspective (Denzin and Lincoln, 2000). There actually *is* a way of examining how the private troubles of individuals are connected to broader public issues (Denzin, 2014) – a form of research (and writing) that can simultaneously recount and analyse personal experience to interpret larger cultural contexts (Ellis and Bochner, 2000) – a method where personal experience is a valid starting point for researching deeper sociological understandings (Wall, 2008)."

I briefly ponder Carolyn's reminder before responding.

"You mean autoethnography, where I'd be making *myself* the experimental subject and treating these experiences as primary data (Jackson, 1989) – using my own sense making as broader *ethnographic* data (Atkinson et al, 2003)? Hmmm ..."

"Well, yes. What merit is there in perpetuating the insider versus outsider/ objective observer versus participant/individual versus culture dichotomy when we only ever sit at the intersection of these perspectives (Ellis et al, 2011)? What's the merit of keeping within these 'tidy binaries' (Lather, 2006: 36) and not acknowledging our ever-present doubleness (Mackinlay, 2019)? As Dwyer (1979) reminds us, examining culture necessitates embracing the relationship between Subject and Object (or Self and Other), and consequently, presupposes an ongoing impetus to pursue the Self even as we pursue the Other."

"I suppose ... but looking at the self – *my-self* – feels like I'm placing it in jeopardy. It feels like a *huge* gamble (Dwyer, 1979)!"

"But of course – exploring the Self and recognising the Self as different is *always* an act of vulnerability (Jang, 2017), especially when 'feelings are a significant part of the research process' (Ellis, 1993: 724). Nevertheless, foregrounding the personal when investigating the social is 'invaluable when researching and writing about such subjective and emotionally significant experiences' (Brennan and Letherby, 2017: 164), with autoethnography functioning as a handy means of approaching painful subjects (Matthews, 2019)."

"Ha! Feelings … Pain – how'd you guess? I'm just desperate to know why all this has happened and *continues* to happen to me – better yet, find *some* way to make this pain go away (hooks, 1994)!"

"Well, then I guess the only thing left to do is to write, no? I suppose vulnerable writing isn't for *everyone* (Behar, 1996), but when we write, we do so to find the truth of our experiences (Ellis, 2004). We write to investigate our constructions of ourselves, the world and others (Richardson, 2000) – to 'find something out … [and] learn [what we] did not know before [we] wrote it' (Richardson, 2001: 35). Indeed, we write with curiosity to respond to an existential crisis (Bochner, 2013), and with urgency 'from a place of personal–political–pedagogical–philosophical crisis where writing about [our] crisis bec[omes] critical' (Mackinlay, 2019: 203)."

I let the impassioned words about autoethnography slowly sink in, knowing with each mental recapitulation that *this* had to be the turning point in my crisis (Denzin, 1989).

★★★★★

10, 9, 8 … He silently screeches in frustration.

7, 6, 5 … His adrenaline spikes as he fumbles through his pocket for another token.

4, 3, 2 … He catches his breath as he slams the token into the *Time Crisis* coin slot and fires at the option to continue – he was determined to do better this time.

★★★★★

I let out a mixture of a disheartened sigh and disgusted grunt as I click on the article in my Facebook feed titled 'After Covid-19, Australia has an anti-Asian racism outbreak to deal with'.

I scroll down and read about the rise in racial abuse linked to the global pandemic; about being spat on and called 'Asian dogs' and 'Asian sluts'; about the threats, intimidation, and being told to 'eat a bat' or 'go back to where you came from'. I feel my blood start to boil as I read about the gaps in human rights legislation and the impact on physical well-being and mental health (Tan, 2020).

I click on a related report that tells me about a collective Asian Australian memory of racial trauma, and another that reminds me of the parallels in North America following the use of the term, 'Chinese virus' (Asian Australian Alliance et al, 2020).

I slam my laptop shut as my rage bubbles to the surface. As I drag my fingers repeatedly through my hair, I wonder what the point of my research is, and what more I can do.

★★★★★

"Sorry, Carolyn, what's the *point* of all this writing if all I'm doing is exploring a personal crisis? I know we talked about autoethnography as a way of gaining deeper sociological understandings (Wall, 2008) as we investigate ourselves, the world, and others (Richardson, 2000). I mean, we can both agree that even though it's not traditional social science, it's still sociologically useful (Ellis, 1997)… but what good is it if it's not *meaningful* work (Bochner, 2013), especially in this climate of COVID-19 racism against individuals from Asian backgrounds (Monzon and Bapuji, 2020). Is *this* not a more pressing crisis, especially considering it extends beyond the pandemic itself (Devakumar et al, 2020)?"

"Ah, Aaron, I'm all too familiar with the desire for our work and lives to do and be something meaningful (Bochner, 2013). Autoethnography really *is* germane in this regard – it's more than just sociological research and personal therapy (Ellis 1993), you know – what we're talking about here is using the self-as-event (Ellis, 2004) to write story as research that is inherently political. It compels us to adopt a political stance towards reality (Freire, 1996) – when we write autoethnography, we 'sensitise readers to issues of identity politics, to experiences shrouded in silence, and to forms of representation that deepen our capacity to empathise with people who are different from us' (Ellis et al, 2011)."

Carolyn somehow intuitively knows that I've started making links to anti-Asian racism and uses this as an opportunity to press on.

"As for what you're concerned with, a number of colleagues have written about critical autoethnography in particular, which connects deeply personal experiences like race, gender, culture, language, sexuality, and other aspects of marginalisation and privilege to broader educational and societal contexts to address how power and privilege play out (Marx et al, 2017). In that regard, critical autoethnography is particularly useful because it legitimates first-person accounts of discrimination and difference as a means of critiquing colonialism, racism, sexism, nationalism, regionalism, and ethnocentrism (Boylorn and Orbe, 2014). Indeed, critical autoethnography allows us to showcase 'the lived experiences of real people in context, examine social conditions and uncover oppressive power arrangements, and … fuse theory and action to challenge processes of domination' (Boylorn and Orbe, 2014: 20), making it the perfect tool for speaking back to larger structural inequities."

"Okay, I'm starting to *see* autoethnography's political nature, and how (critical) autoethnography aims to catalyse emancipatory personal *and* social change (Ellis et al, 2011). Won't it only appeal to a rather niche market though?"

"Oh, Aaron, what would the point of it *be* then? We share our personal stories to allow readers to empathise and actively participate in our experiences (Ellis and Bochner, 2000) to co-create meaning (Ai, 2017).

In writing these personal stories, which, as we already discussed, exposes a 'vulnerable self' (Ellis, 2004: 37), we share private details and emotions to ensure that a wide range of traditional and non-traditional audiences (Ellis et al, 2011) are able to 'engage in dialogue regarding the social and moral implications of the different ... standpoints encountered' (Ellis and Bochner, 2000: 748)."

"Right, so by writing stories like mine which 'are not often told', I'm also 'exposing, analysing, and challenging the majoritarian stories of racial privilege' (Solórzano and Yosso, 2002: 32) and broader structures of racism?"

"Well of course! What we write – the language we use – is more than just a 'mere selection of words – it is inherently a political choice' (Collins, 1998: xxi). As our learned friend Stacy Holman Jones says, autoethnography allows us to 'enmesh the personal within the political and the political within the personal in ways that can, do and must matter' (Holman Jones, 2005: 774) – when we write autoethnography, we engage in a 'radical democratic politics committed to creating space for dialogue and debate that instigates and shapes social change' (Holman Jones, 2005: 763)".

I let the impassioned words sink in again as Carolyn smiles and gracefully bids me farewell for now.

★★★★★

I quickly reholster the plastic arcade gun in the *Time Crisis* gun holder and wipe my clammy right hand against the side of my pants. I had just – barely – made it past level two. I feel my heart racing and the drops of perspiration trickling down the nape of my neck – perhaps it was the formidable intruding humidity that could never quite be vanquished by the arcade's air-conditioning; perhaps it was the adrenaline from being shot at under timed pressure, or the fact that I had only one of my three lives left to complete the final level.

As my performance statistics for level two flash across the screen, I take a deep breath and attempt to steady myself as level three commences.

★★★★★

NOTIFICATION OF APPROVAL (26 March 2020) – #032620454
    Dear Aaron
I am pleased to advise that your project #032620454 has been approved and your Approval Form is attached. Approval is subject to the conditions listed on the Approval Form and the Additional Notes document which is also attached. Please print out both documents for your record.

If you have any questions or concerns, please do not hesitate to contact the Human Ethics Office. For any future amendments to existing approvals, please visit our website to download the latest version of the amendment form.

Yours sincerely
Jane Doe
Human Ethics Administrative Assistant

★★★★★

The email announcing the new milestone in my doctoral journey is received with mixed emotions. A week prior, the university temporarily pauses all in-person and online lectures after three students test positive for COVID-19. Soon after, the Australian government bans all arrivals by non-citizens and non-residents and announces the closure of non-essential indoor venues. A couple of days before the email, the daily rise in new COVID-19 cases hits an unprecedented high in Queensland and all non-essential services are shut down (ABC News, 2020).

The email is sent within the same six hours that Queensland closes its borders and declares all schools closed to students (ABC News, 2020) – my excitement at the prospect of collecting data is quickly stymied by a sense of impending anxiety and dread about what would happen next.

Indeed, with circumstances changing so extremely and so rapidly, what *would* happen to my grand plan of supplementing critical autoethnography with the voices of my co-researchers (Ellis et al, 2011) – other recently migrated Asian teachers – through in-person interactive (Ellis, 2004) in-depth semi-structured interviews (Cohen et al, 2018)? What *would* become of the plan to draw on multiple forms of qualitative data (Creswell, 2018) to explore personal biographies and experiences, obtain information on attitudes, emotions, and personal positions on particular issues (Newby, 2010) as a way of foregrounding collective political voice (Museus and Iftikar, 2013)? Alas, I had considered the ethics of occupying a simultaneous position of power and subjugation (Dwyer and Buckle, 2009) as well as potential issues around informed consent, confidentiality, beneficence, do no harm (Cohen et al, 2018), and imposition of personal views (Wall, 2008) – would that now all be for nought?

I am reminded of Robert Burns' poem about the best-laid plans and wonder to myself what Carolyn would say as I hesitantly search for a way out of this *new* crisis.

★★★★★

I charge up the stairs into my study after a tedious drive home from school. After nearly two months of learning from home, students had finally been allowed to gradually return to school campuses. As a high school teacher, it was a strange existence, with school life teetering precariously on the edge of what used to be normal.

As I juggle powering up my laptop, activating the iPad recording application, and ensuring the respective chargers are plugged in, I wonder if the other teacher I am about to interview feels the same about school life during COVID-19. I wonder as well, in between hurriedly ensuring that the digital versions of the participant information sheet and consent form are open *and* that my physical notepad is on hand, how this first of many Zoom interviews will go. While I count myself lucky that the main change to data collection is merely to move interviews online, I am also deeply nervous.

On one hand, using Zoom had already allowed me to move beyond the usual restrictions of time and space (Burkitt, 2004) to engage with individuals around the country who were likely to represent a 'variety of positions ... [with] differences in experience' (King and Horrocks, 2010: 29). On the other, I had a feeling that, compared with face-to-face interviews, what I was doing would not offer the same opportunity to develop the 'rapport ... [which would] enabl[e] ... participant[s] to feel comfortable in opening up' (King and Horrocks, 2010: 48) to me; I was wary of the potential difficulty of interviewees discussing sensitive topics like racism with an unknown researcher over an online platform (Seitz, 2015). I am concerned that I have lost out on the nuances of eye contact (Seitz, 2015) and the 'full range of postural, gestural, and expressive movement that the body conveys, as well as the intentionality that is carried and expressed in that movement' (Bayles, 2012: 578). I am also concerned about technical glitches in sound and video quality (King and Horrocks, 2010), and whether I had done enough ethically around the 'access to data ... and protection of privacy and confidentiality' (Garcia et al, 2009: 53).

Nevertheless, the time is upon me, and I click on the 'start meeting' button. After the obligatory introductions and small talk, I move on to a quick verbal review of the participant information sheet.

I rattle on about how the project aims to explore how notions of 'Asianness' are understood and performed by recently migrated pre-service and early career teachers from 'Asian' backgrounds in the Australian education context, and explain that I am particularly interested in their unique stories as educators and the intersection with individual notions and performances of race. In line with autoethnography's 'capacity to forge and maintain [a] model of solidarity [and] open dialogue' (Bochner and Ellis, 2016: 215), I confess my hopes for the project to function as a form of community-building and reiterate that participation is entirely voluntary. I then outline the corresponding time requirements as well as the potential risks and benefits of participation.

Finally, I point out that all interview data will be presented through autoethnography and step through the associated ethical considerations. I elucidate that because writing about personal experience in autoethnography implicates the author as well as significant others (Trahar, 2009), there is a foremost responsibility to consider those who are either unable to speak for themselves, or unable to purposefully consent to their representations in the writing (Wall, 2008). I specify that as an autoethnographer, I have to be keenly aware of these 'relational concerns' from the start of my inquiry and throughout the writing process (Ellis, 2004), meaning that I am committed to allowing anyone implicated in my writing the liberty of perusing and responding to how they have been represented (Wall, 2008).

I also explain that because I do not wish to abuse the emphatic power imbalance favouring the writer (Lovell, 2005), my ultimate aim is for the autoethnography's contribution in catalysing change (Ellis et al, 2011) to outweigh all plausible discomfort and ethical quandaries for the author, characters, and readers (Ellis and Bochner, 2000).

Once I have given the option of using a pseudonym to retain anonymity and guard against any unwelcome 'peeking in on damaged selves' (Ellis and Bochner, 2000: 749), I click on the 'record' button and proceed with bated breath.

★★★★★

As he reholsters the plastic arcade gun for the final time, he breathes a heavy sigh of relief as the end credits start scrolling by on the screen in front of him. He jingles the coins in his pocket while waiting for the concluding scoreboard to appear and realises that the pocket is significantly lighter; nevertheless, he celebrates his efforts at completing the game *this* time. The final scores start to emerge on screen, prompting him to ponder what he would do differently to improve *next* time – perhaps he could achieve a higher score; perhaps he would eventually be able to finish the game on a single token. As he is about to insert another coin to test his hypothesis, he hears his mother reminding him that it is time to go for now.

★★★★★

"So, Aaron, what do you think about your crisis *now*?"

I am deep in thought writing my latest diary entry about yet another run-in with racism, and so Carolyn's question catches me by surprise.

"Geez – you scared me there … Brilliant to see you again though! Hmm, good question. You know how I like my checklists and wrapping things up in an organised fashion? Yeah … no luck with that here. I wish I could tell you that I had managed to resolve it; that there was at least a 'neat ending' (Mackinlay, 2019: 183) of sorts, but the thing is … as I continue to write autoethnography, I'm no longer sure if this crisis 'end[s] at the beginning, or perhaps, beg[ins] at the ending' (Mackinlay, 2019: 13). It's almost like they've 'fold[ed] into one another' (Mackinlay, 2019: 46). What I *can* say though, is that writing through a 'fragmented self' (Mackinlay, 2019: 17) about my experiences and insights concerning specific moments in time in different ways has allowed me to 'discover new aspects of [my] topic and [my] relationship to it' (Richardson, 1994: 516), all the while speaking back to inequitable racialised systems and situations (Boylorn and Orbe, 2014) with urgency. I'm also starting to enjoy that autoethnography is about fluid, flexible, and open-ended possibilities rather than finite, categorical conclusions (Adams and Holman Jones, 2008), which makes me realise that this 'crisis is not where I *want* to end writing critical autoethnography' (Mackinlay, 2019: 204) – I mean, in this ongoing climate of anti-Asian racism, this surely *cannot* be where I 'end'. I'm so sorry, I've rambled on – does that answer your question? I don't know, what do *you* think?"

References

ABC News (2020) 'Queensland's coronavirus timeline: how COVID-19 cases spread around the state', *ABC News*, [online], 25 September, available from: https://www.abc.net.au/news/2020-03-28/coronavirus-timeline-queensland-tracking-spread/12077602?nw=0 [accessed 16 October 2020].

Adams, T. and Holman Jones, S. (2008) 'Autoethnography is queer', in N. Denzin, Y. Lincoln, and L. Smith (eds) *Handbook of Critical and Indigenous Methodologies*, Los Angeles, CA: Sage, pp 373–90.

Ai, B. (2017) 'Constructing an academic identity in Australia: an autoethnographic narrative', *Higher Education Research & Development*, 36(6): 1095–1107.

Asian Australian Alliance, Chiu, O. and Chuang, P. (2020) *COVID-19 Coronavirus Racism Incident Report*, Asian Australian Alliance, New South Wales.

Atkinson, P., Coffey, A., and Delamont, S. (eds) (2003) *Key Themes in Qualitative Research: Continuities and Changes*, Walnut Creek, CA: AltaMira Press.

Bayles, M. (2012) 'Is physical proximity essential to the psychoanalytic process? An exploration through the lens of Skype', *Psychoanalytic Dialogues*, 22(5): 569–85.

Behar, R. (ed) (1996) *The Vulnerable Observer: Anthropology that Breaks Your Heart*, Boston, MA: Beacon Press.

Bochner, A. (2013) 'Putting meanings into motion: autoethnography's existential calling', in S. Holman Jones, T. Adams, and C. Ellis (eds) *Handbook of Autoethnography*, Walnut Creek, CA: Left Coast Press, pp 50–6.

Bochner, A. and Ellis, C. (2016) 'The ICQI and the rise of autoethnography: solidarity through community', *International Review of Qualitative Research*, 9(2): 208–17.

Boylorn, R. and Orbe, M. (eds) (2014) *Critical Autoethnography: Intersecting Cultural Identities in Everyday Life*, Walnut Creek: Left Coast Press.

Brennan, M. and Letherby, G. (2017) 'Auto/biographical approaches to researching death and bereavement: connections, continuums, contrasts', *Mortality*, 22(2): 155–69.

Burkitt, I. (2004) 'The time and space of everyday life', *Cultural Studies*, 18(2): 211–27.

Cohen, L., Manion, L., and Morrison, K. (eds) (2018) *Research Methods in Education* (8th edn), London, New York: Routledge.

Collins, P. (1998) 'It's all in the family: intersections of gender, race, and nation', *Hypatia*, 13(3): 62–82.

Creswell, J. (2018) 'Chapter 9: Qualitative Methods', in J. Creswell and J. Creswell (eds), *Research Design: Qualitative, Quantitative, and Mixed Methods Approaches* (5th edn), Los Angeles, CA: Sage, pp 179–211.

Denzin, N. (ed) (1989) *Interpretive Interactionism*, Newbury Park, CA: Sage.

Denzin, N. (ed) (2014) *Interpretive Autoethnography* (2nd edn), Thousand Oaks, CA: Sage.

Denzin, N. and Lincoln, Y. (2000) *Handbook of Qualitative Research* (2nd edn), Thousand Oaks, CA: Sage.

Devakumar et al (2020) 'Racism, the public health crisis we can no longer ignore', *The Lancet*, 395: 112–13.

Dwyer, K. (1979) 'The dialogic of ethnology', *Dialectical Anthropology*, 4(3): 205–24.

Dwyer, S. and Buckle, J. (2009) 'The space between: on being an insider-outsider in qualitative research', *International Journal of Qualitative Methods*, 8(1): 54–63.

Ellis, C. (1993) 'There are survivors: telling a story of sudden death', *The Sociological Quarterly*, 34(4): 711–730.

Ellis, C. (ed) (2004) *The Ethnographic I: A Methodological Novel about Autoethnography*, Walnut Creek, CA: AltaMira Press.

Ellis, C. and Bochner, A. (2000) 'Autoethnography, personal narrative, reflexivity', in N. Denzin and Y. Lincoln (eds) *Handbook of Qualitative Research* (2nd edn), Thousand Oaks, CA: Sage, pp 733–68.

Ellis, C., Adams, T., and Bochner, A. (2011) 'Autoethnography: an overview', *Historical Social Research / Historische Sozialforschung*, 36(4(138)): 273–90.

Francis, D. and Hester S. (2012) *An Invitation to Ethnomethodology: Language, Society and Social Interaction*, Thousand Oaks, CA: Sage.

Freire, P. (ed) (1996) *Pedagogy of the Oppressed* (new revised edn), London: Penguin.

Garcia, A., Standlee, A., Bechkoff, J., and Yan, C. (2009) 'Ethnographic approaches to the Internet and computer-mediated communication', *Journal of Contemporary Ethnography*, 38(1): 52–84.

Holman Jones, S. (2005) 'Auto ethnography: making the personal political', in N. Denzin and Y. Lincoln (eds) *Handbook of Qualitative Research*, Thousand Oaks: Sage, pp 763–91.

hooks, b. (ed) (1994) *Teaching to Transgress: Education as the Practice of Freedom*, New York: Routledge.

Jackson, M. (ed) (1989) *Paths Toward a Clearing: Radical Empiricism and Ethnographic Inquiry*, Bloomington, IN: Indiana University Press.

Jang, B. (2017) 'Am I a qualified literacy researcher and educator? A counter-story of a professional journey of one Asian male literacy scholar in the United States', *Journal of Literacy Research*, 49(4): 559–81.

King, N. and Horrocks, C. (eds) (2010) *Interviews in Qualitative Research* (1st edn), Thousand Oaks, CA: Sage.

Lather, P. (2006) 'Paradigm proliferation as a good thing to think with: teaching research in education as a wild profusion', *International Journal of Qualitative Studies in Education*, 19(1): 35–57.

Lovell, S. (2005) 'Seductive whisperings: memory, desire, and agency in auto/biography', *Thirdspace*, 4(2): 32–44.

Mackinlay, E. (ed) (2019) *Critical Writing for Embodied Approaches*, Cham: Springer.

Marx, S., Pennington, J., and Chang, H. (2017) 'Critical autoethnography in pursuit of educational equity: introduction to the IJME special issue', *International Journal of Multicultural Education*, 19(1): 1–6.

Monzon, V. and Bapuji, H. (2020) 'The toxic spread of COVID-19 racism', *Pursuit*, [online], 27 April, available from: https://pursuit.unimelb.edu.au/articles/the-toxic-spread-of-covid-19-racism [accessed 16 October 2020].

Museus, S. and Ifitikar, J. (2013) 'Asian critical theory (AsianCrit)', in M. Danico (ed) *Asian American Society*, Thousand Oaks, CA: Sage, pp 18–29.

Newby, P. (ed) (2010) *Research Methods for Education*, London: Taylor & Francis.

Richardson, L. (1994) 'Writing: a method of inquiry', in N. Denzin and Y. Lincoln (eds) *Handbook of Qualitative Research*, Thousand Oaks: Sage, pp 516–29.

Richardson, L. (2000) 'Evaluating ethnography', *Qualitative Inquiry*, 6(2): 253–5.

Richardson, L. (2001) 'Getting personal: writing-stories', *International Journal of Qualitative Studies in Education*, 14(1): 33–8.

Seitz, S. (2015) 'Pixilated partnership, overcoming obstacles in qualitative interviews via Skype: a research note', *Qualitative Research,* 16(2): 229–35.

Solórzano, D. and Yosso, T. (2002) 'Critical race methodology: counter-storytelling as an analytical framework for education research', *Qualitative Inquiry*, 6(1): 23–44.

Tan, S-L. (2020), 'You Chinese virus spreader: after Coronavirus, Australia has an anti-Asian racism outbreak to deal with', *South China Morning Post*, [online], 30 May, available from: https://www.scmp.com/week-asia/people/article/3086768/you-chinese-virus-spreader-after-coronavirus-australia-has-anti [accessed 10 October 2020].

Trahar, S. (2009) 'Beyond the story itself: narrative inquiry and autoethnography in intercultural research in higher education', *Forum Qualitative Sozialforschung / Forum: Qualitative Social Research*, 10(1): Art.30.

Wall, S. (2008) 'Easier said than done: writing an autoethnography', *International Journal of Qualitative Methods*, 7(1): 38–53.

13

Building relationships and praxis despite persistent obstacles

Maria Grazia Imperiale

Introduction

This chapter discusses how *participatory methodologies* were developed for use in what became an entirely online study researching critical English language education in a context of protracted crisis; that is, the Gaza Strip (Palestine). The project on which this chapter is based was developed between 2014 and 2017; however, this chapter was written in summer 2020 when people in most countries of the world were self-isolating, due to the COVID-19 pandemic. Contexts of protracted crisis as in the Gaza Strip, as well as more generally contexts in the Global South in which different forms of knowledges and multiple ways of working coexist, are well positioned to illuminate the research landscape and methodological adaptations that these times of uncertainties require.

The Gaza Strip has been under blockade since 2007, and this impedes free movement and the flows of people and goods into and out of the Strip. The condition of forced immobility has consequences for the mental and physical well-being of Gazan inhabitants. In the context of academia, the blockade affects the mobility of staff, who, hence, cannot attend international conferences and events, making it challenging to create networks and long-lasting, collaborative partnerships. In addition, the flow of knowledge into and out of the Strip is affected not just metaphorically, as books and any other materials published outside the Strip cannot easily be posted and reach colleagues inside the Strip. The study on which this chapter is based aimed at co-constructing critical, creative, and localised pedagogies for English language education in secondary schools in the Gaza Strip (Imperiale, 2017; Imperiale et al, 2017; Imperiale, 2018; Imperiale, 2021). Through a series of workshops, that were held entirely online, the researcher – based in the UK – and the participants, 13 pre-service English teachers based in the Gaza Strip, analysed and developed teaching materials and lesson plans for teaching English adopting creative and critical methodologies. Some of the teaching materials were then trialled and evaluated based on participants' use of them in their classrooms. The study was grounded in participatory methodologies, and consisted of a cycle of critical participatory action research (CPAR), which included the phases of planning, action, observation, and reflection.

This chapter is structured as follows: in the next section I present the research context, important to understand the research design and methodological considerations; then I focus on the chosen methodology, the research design, and on how methods were used. I then describe the main challenges and I reflect on ethical considerations of the study. In the conclusions, I point out the implications of this study and my personal insights into doing research in times and contexts of crisis.

Researching in a context of protracted crisis: the Gaza Strip

The Gaza Strip, with the West Bank and East Jerusalem, constitute the Occupied Palestinian Territories. The Gaza Strip is one of the most densely populated areas on the planet, inhabited by almost two million Palestinians living in a very small piece of land, measuring about 40 km in length and between 14 and 16 km in width. Tawil Souri and Matar (2016) present some of the statistics of the Gaza Strip, which are worth citing in full as these offer an insight into Gaza's astonishing reality and its numbers:

> More than two thirds of the population is made up of refugees; 70% live in poverty; 20% live in 'deep poverty'; just about everybody has to survive on humanitarian hand-outs; adult unemployment hovers around 50% give or take a few percentage points; 60% of the population is under the age of 18. This is the Gaza where on a good day there is no electricity 'only' 20 hours a day; where before the latest Israeli military operation, in summer 2014, there was already a shortage of 70,000 homes; where 95% of piped water is below international quality standards; where every child aged 8 or younger has already witnessed three massive wars. (Tawil Souri and Matar, 2016: 3)

People in the Gaza Strip live in a condition of 'forced immobility' (Stock, 2016) which is detrimental to transnational social relationships and to individuals' development, their autonomy, and self-determination, and individuals' mental and physical well-being (Smith, 2015; Fassetta et al, 2017; Imperiale, 2018). Movements into and out of the Strip are virtually impossible as both the Eretz crossing (at the border with Israel) and the Rafah crossing (at the border with Egypt) are usually sealed, with just some rare exceptions (Winter, 2015; Tawil-Matar, 2016). In addition, three military operations were carried out by the Israeli government respectively in 2008, 2012, and 2014, which devastated the living conditions of people in the Strip (Fassetta et al, 2020).

One way for the Gazan inhabitants to tackle, and perhaps even survive, forced immobility has been the increasing reliance on an Internet connection, which may potentially enhance the chances of online employment and reduce isolation (Fassetta et al, 2017; Imperiale et al, 2017). However, it must also be noted that, first, as Aouragh puts it, no technological medium can 'transcend economic gaps' (Aouragh, 2011: 52), neither can it be a replacement of human freedom and of human development (Imperiale, 2018).

Nevertheless, several cross-border academic research projects have been conducted in the last decade through online international collaborations. In a recent edited book entitled *Multilingual Online Academic Collaborations as Resistance* (Fassetta et al, 2020), authors describe a series of online academic collaborations between higher education institutions in the UK and US and the Islamic University of Gaza. The contributions in the book tell the story of the challenges and of the gratifications of collaborating online, when intercultural encounters are affected by the lack of physical proximity. Those efforts are described as 'a form of defiance and resistance to the physical confinement experienced by Gaza's academics, students and the general population' (Fassetta et al, 2020: 1).

Methodology: critical participatory action research for a social-justice-through-education agenda

As the research project was framed by an intrinsic commitment towards social justice through education, the research process reflected this social endeavour: the chosen methodology was a cycle of critical participatory action research (CPAR). This CPAR consisted of a series of workshops that were designed, developed, and delivered, analysed and evaluated, responding to the needs of the participants: at its heart was a practice-based approach which makes participation and knowledge co-construction prominent.

While CPAR is considered as a research methodology, it is important to acknowledge that the scholars who developed and adopted CPAR describe it as 'a worldview', a 'philosophy of life', and 'a social practice' (respectively in Reason and Bradbury, 2001; Fals Borda, 2001; Kemmis et al, 2014). These scholars agree that participatory research should be considered as something more than a methodology, as not limited to the use of instrumental techniques for collecting research data. *Critical* PAR is conceived to be a 'practice-changing-practice' that aims to change both discourse and individuals' practices in the public spheres (Kemmis et al, 2014: 28). It is therefore grounded in *praxis*, combining pragmatic approaches and knowledge co-construction (Freire, 1996).

Participation is a core tenet of CPAR, which is based on the theory of communicative action (Habermas, 1984) and on the opening of public spheres as safe places where the participants engage in conversation and in democratic participation. Following the tradition of Habermas, participants commit to genuine conversations based on comprehensibility, truth (in the sense of accuracy), and sincerity. Establishing a public sphere means establishing a set of relationships, wherein individuals relate to one another freely, respectfully, openly, and purposefully (Habermas, 1984). This relationship and the commitment to these kinds of conversations aim to involve the participants and the researcher equally in research (Kemmis et al, 2014). This approach, therefore, seeks to avoid the imposition of the research agenda on to participants, trying ultimately to develop research that is beneficial for the participants who take part in it.

CPAR as part of emancipatory praxis in difficult circumstances

The methodology of CPAR was chosen for this project based on the following rationales, which will be further unpacked in the following pages:

- educational research *with* people living in precarious and difficult circumstances requires ethical approaches which avoid extractive ways of conducting research and are rather grounded in participation; participants were recognised as experts, and therefore knowledge was co-constructed rather than extracted;
- in contexts of crisis, the relationship between knowledge and power is intertwined and embedded in praxis, and CPAR is underpinned by emancipatory aims which challenge power imbalances;
- the methodology was initially designed for face-to-face research. When the study was conceived it seemed possible to travel to the Gaza Strip; however, when access was denied, the methodology was adapted for use online.

Research in vulnerable settings requires strong ethical principles, which underpin CPAR and its focus on participation and emancipation. Much has been written about participation in research, and the ethical necessity of conducting research with participants, and not on research subjects, or worse, on 'objects of investigation' (Freire, 1996: 87). The work of Freire and Fals Borda is relevant in this regard: the authors emphasise the ethical dimension of participation in pedagogical and political action aiming at emancipatory objectives. Freire highlights that through participation, critical awareness of reality and self-awareness are deepened: participation is a starting point for developing 'cultural action of a liberating character' (Freire, 1996: 87). Equally important, in this study participants did not only have an active role in participating in knowledge co-construction, but were also considered the experts on their own context. Melanie Walker (2019), based on Miranda Fricker's (2007) work and on the work of Amartya Sen (2009), writes that students within higher education need opportunities to make their 'epistemic contribution capability' flourish – that is, to be able to receive and interpret knowledge in the ways they value. In this research project, by acknowledging who the experts were, I provided a space for participants to exercise their epistemic agency.

Also in the literature on participatory action research, the intertwined relationship between knowledge and power is often explored. Gaventa and Cornwall posit that:

> We can also more clearly situate knowledge as one resource in the power field. Knowledge, as much as any resource, determines definitions of what is conceived as important, as possible, for and by whom. Through access to knowledge and participation in its production, use and dissemination, actors can affect the boundaries and indeed the conceptualization of the possible. (Gaventa and Cornwall, 2001: 72)

Research, therefore, can be empowering, aiming at social transformation, not only communicating unheard participants' voices, but also acknowledging their power to build knowledge and to contribute to transformative actions. In this study, knowledge, reflection, and power were produced, explored, and countered in *praxis*. Regarding the power imbalances between the researcher and the participants in this study – and acknowledging that those power imbalances can only be reduced to a certain extent – we used the power of languages and multilingualism: the research was conducted mostly in English, with also a partial use of Palestinian Arabic. The researcher, who has only a limited knowledge of Arabic and of Palestinian Arabic, was at times *incompetent* and at times needed participants' translations (for more on the multilingual dynamics of this research, see Imperiale, 2018; Imperiale, 2021). Languages and language choices helped us navigate (linguistic) power dynamics and relationship building.

Finally, the research was initially designed for face-to-face work. CPAR was chosen for its attention and focus on *localised* practices, as, being ecologically sensitive to the sites in which research is carried out, it aims to ameliorate local educational or social issues (Kemmis et al, 2014). In addition to the local focus of CPAR, it must be added that Noffke (2009) highlighted the global dimension of CPAR: the local intersects with a broader overarching political aim devoted to human flourishing and social justice, which prefigures research as embedded in a global context. The attention to both the local and global dimension made CPAR a good fit with the educational project's local-global scope, and a robust methodology for this specific research project. However, when in-person physical access to the Gaza Strip was denied (see Imperiale, 2018), considerations were made about other possible ways of achieving the same research purposes or re-profiling the whole work. However, the choice that seemed most appropriate was to

Figure 13.1: The critical participatory action research cycle

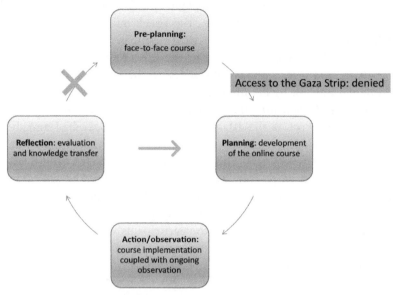

adapt CPAR to the online environment, rather than to adapt the principles and the vision of the research project.

How methods were used

Based on Kemmis et al's critical participatory action research planner (2014), the research design was structured by adapting the phases of CPAR – namely planning, action, observation, and evaluation – to serve the needs of the project. The cycle of CPAR, illustrated in Figure 13.1, involved four phases: (1) a first *planning phase*, during which access to the Gaza Strip was sought, participants were recruited and the series of workshop was planned, informed by participants' initial doings-sayings-relatings; (2) a *(re)planning phase*, after access to the Gaza Strip was denied, in which the course was amended to suit online delivery; (3) the merged *action–observation phase*, in which the workshop series was implemented and observed in a continuous process; and finally, (4) the *reflection phase*, in which data analysis and the evaluation of the research project was conducted.

The planning phases: seeking access, workshops' planning, and participant recruitment

During the planning phases, in addition to the development of the workshop series, access to the Gaza Strip was sought – unsuccessfully – and participants were recruited. In order to attempt to get access to the Gaza Strip, several actors were contacted: the Italian Consulate in Israel, the British Consulate in Israel, the Israeli Embassy in the UK, the Israeli information centre in Scotland, the Israeli Ministry of Defence, the Palestinian Authority Embassy in the UK, and the Egyptian Embassy in the UK. After extensive email correspondence and several phone calls, access to the Strip was denied.

Access denial was not totally unexpected, due to the blockade imposed on the Gaza Strip. Anticipating this option, the researcher and the partners involved in the project at the Islamic University of Gaza had already developed 'a Plan B'. It was already agreed that should it not be possible to travel to Gaza, the series of workshops would be conducted online, via Skype or by using other video-conference software. Therefore, the workshop series was promptly redesigned, considering the online practice architectures and the technological constraints. This proved challenging, frustrating, and discouraging, and it was only thanks to the participants' enthusiasm towards the research project that it was possible to continue the research endeavour – as will be further described later.

While seeking access, participants were also recruited. Identifying and recruiting participants was done in cooperation with the partner university, the Islamic University of Gaza (IUG). In cooperation with Prof Nazmi al-Masri who, as local academic partner, is the expert on the IUG institutional procedures, selection criteria were developed, and the workshop series was announced on the IUG website. Out of a cohort of 29 applicants, 13 participants were selected according to their academic attainment, their motivations, their teaching experiences, and the content and quality of their application form. Participants were all young women: the sample composition was representative of the student population in the English department at IUG, which consists mostly of females. In addition, as the project was developed in partnership, such an all-women group of participants allowed the researcher not to interfere with the IUG rules: in the institution male and female students are allocated different classes, they attend their courses in different buildings, and female teachers cannot teach male students. Having only female participants, therefore, was considered appropriate to the context.

The action/observation/evaluation phase: the workshop series in a snapshot

The series of workshops involved exploring the use of political cartoons, comics, drama, and films for English-language teaching. All the activities were embedded in the Gaza Strip context: we referred to *English for Palestine*, which is the textbook adopted in schools in Palestine and in the Gaza Strip, and dealt with authentic material relevant to the Palestinian context. For example, we integrated the *English for Palestine* textbook with the political comic books *Palestine* and *Footnotes in Gaza* by Joe Sacco; the website 'Palestine Remix', YouTube videos, poems, and extracts from books written by Mahmoud Darwish and Ghassan Kanafani, two of the main Palestinian writers.

The format of the online workshops was highly interactive, consisting of a combination of input sessions, group work, interactive activities, discussions, peer learning, peer observation, lesson planning, and teaching practices in which the trainees planned, developed and delivered simulated English lessons by teaching to their peers. At the end of the course, participants received a Certificate of Attendance.

After the workshops, participants were involved in filling in a feedback form, they took part in interviews and focus groups, and they wrote a final reflection on a topic of their choice – this data was gathered to conduct the evaluation of the project. Without being asked to do so, however, several participants continued to communicate with the researcher as they moved into new jobs and new positions: sometimes they asked for advice on how to apply to a foreign university, other times they wanted to share their teaching practices and ideas. As such, relationships extended beyond the CPAR cycle and the research project itself: participants nurtured friendships and some of them are still in contact with each other. Some of the participants were involved in subsequent research projects co-designed by the researcher and the IUG Co-I Prof Al-Masri, ensuring long-term collaborations.

Challenges and how those were addressed

The challenges encountered were identified and categorised on two levels: first, those related to the frustration of being *always* and *only* online which were mostly challenges the researcher faced since the participants attended the workshop series together from a class at the IUG; and second, the challenges related to technological issues, which affected everyone.

The process of conducting the whole research online, without having the opportunity to meet participants face to face, proved extremely challenging, tiring, and frustrating. Despite all the gratifications that came with the project, the lack of physical proximity, of sharing the same classrooms, of sitting next to each other was difficult to deal with. At the time of writing, after summer 2020, the majority of the world has experienced the issues and frustrations that come with working at a distance. During the pandemic, educators have been forced to reflect on the tension between teaching and learning as a fundamentally human and interpersonal activity with many different values and outcomes, and the technological deterministic idea that technology could replace the relational, interpersonal element of the teaching and learning process. However, when the project was conducted (in

2015–16), not many participatory researchers had experienced the challenges of developing participation and of building relationships entirely online – and therefore there were not many resources that might have helped deal with the emotional burden and with participants' and researchers' well-being in those specific circumstances.

How was this addressed? In hindsight, and as written more exhaustively in other articles (Imperiale, 2018, 2021), it was important to be flexible and open to the possibilities and the *constraints* that were part of the nature of the project. During the project, participants were an inspiration thanks to their resilience, how they dealt with the difficult conditions, their persistence and steadfastness: with the clear aim of completing the research project, and thanks to participants' enthusiasm and guidance, there was no choice but to put frustration aside, and enjoy the relationships as these unfolded. This required the ability to let things go, without being in control at all times.

The technical challenges, to list a few, consisted in poor audio- and video-quality, interruptions and disruptions due to poor Internet connection, frequent power-cuts in Gaza, etc. In an article (Imperiale et al, 2021) those are addressed in detail: for example, what it means to work when you spend half of your time not hearing properly, not being able to see the person at the other end of the screen, when connection drops and calls fail, when you rely on blurred images of participants and on the colour of their hijab and the sound of their voices in order to be able to identify them, and the list could continue. Not being able to see our research partners, on one hand, reminds us that we cannot take partnerships for granted; on the other hand, when partnerships are built entirely online, it also tells us about the determination and willingness to connect, despite the challenges. If, on one hand, we still may miss something; on the other hand, it is important to explore what connects us. Finally, it must also be acknowledged that challenges often can also represent opportunities.

These challenges were addressed by adopting an open and flexible attitude which allowed us to work *within* those disruptions rather than *against* them, having a series of plan Bs and Cs ready to be put into place (for example, use of other mobile software; a plan for working in asynchronous modality; a participant ready to become a researcher when connection failed – for example, taking notes and pictures during the workshops). Because the participants were the main agents of adaptation, power shifted from the researcher to the participants, who, in their words, 'felt the responsibility' to make this project happen (Imperiale, 2018). At the heart of the whole research project, therefore, there were relationships and an 'immanent ethics of responsibility' (MacDonald and O'Regan, 2012).

Ethical considerations

Careful attention was given to ethics throughout the research process. Ethics was therefore considered as a continuous process that lasted from its inception to its evaluation and dissemination. The research study was underpinned by what has been described as an 'immanent ethics of responsibility', ethics arising from 'the immanence of the relationship with the other rather than through a Kantian appeal to a transcendental moral signified' (MacDonald and O'Regan, 2012: 10). This study worked on the basis that ethics is situated in praxis and in relationships building. It therefore acknowledged the precariousness of the encounters and the immanency of relationships. Important to the study was what Judith Butler in *Giving an Account of Oneself* (2005) has written about how we encounter others and how we establish relationships with, in this case, participants:

> The ethical valence of the situation is thus not restricted to the question whether or not my account of myself is adequate, but rather concerns whether, in giving the account I establish a relationship to the one to whom my account is addressed and whether both parties to the interlocution are sustained and altered by the scene of address. (Butler, 2005: 50)

The idea of relationships of accountability and giving an account to each other takes ethics beyond the procedural and practical issues listed in the ethics forms that researchers need to fill in. This study involved participants who might be othered as 'vulnerable' by institutional ethics committees as some of them were refugees, young women living in a post-conflict context, in a context of protracted crisis. What was considered to be an ethical process of conducting research with people living in difficult circumstances was therefore *not* underpinned by universal moral principles and by institutionalised 'box-ticking' codes of ethical practices, but rather consisted of exploring and developing a safe public sphere in which relationships of trust were built, and where research has a clear purpose of benefitting participants in the first place. Rooting research in participation and engaging with the messiness of intercultural relationships allowed the opening up of a safe space for the exploration and the development of language pedagogies and of research methodologies for well-being.

The development of researcher–participants relationships also allowed to protect researcher's and participants' safety and well-being, that is key to conduct research in challenging circumstances. Equally important, at the time of the project, I was the co-convenor of GRAMNet (Glasgow Refugee Asylum Migration Network) which was a peer-to-peer support network in which researchers working on difficult topics, shared theories, findings, social events, writing retreats, book clubs, workshops, and other useful events around our research. Establishing a support network for researchers working in similar areas could be included as a way to mitigate researchers' risks, which might involve vicarious trauma, issues of transference, and others that affect mental well-being.

Concerning the institutionalised ethical procedures, before undertaking the research project, ethical approval was obtained from the University of Glasgow Ethics Committee of the College of Social Sciences, for dealing with *human subjects*. Interestingly, in the formula used by the Ethics Committee, participants are labelled as 'human subjects', merely as a category to be subjected to research. This seems to be in contradiction with the understanding of ethics as a process of relationship building in the research encounter. In addition, although the ethical approval form does not consider the role of languages in research, languages were important. The participant information sheet and the consent form were provided both in English *and* in Arabic. The forms included an outline of the purposes of the research project, the consequences for participants should they decided to take part in it, the reasons why they had been selected, their power to withdraw at any point during the research, and issues of anonymity and confidentiality.

All the participants spoke fluent English; hence, the Arabic translation was not needed. However, the rationale for providing both versions was twofold: the first point was related to the English-language proficiency of the participants; that is, the form in Arabic was provided in case participants might have preferred to sign a document in their native tongue rather than in a foreign one; the second argument instead carries a symbolic value. By showing the participants respect for their own native language and presenting them with the possibility to work both in English and in Arabic, was important to comply with the understanding of ethics as relationship building and, hence, encompassing linguistic hospitality (Ricoeur, 2004). These considerations related to researching multilingually are often overlooked and underestimated in research processes, research dissemination, and also in research ethics, but are crucial to the research outcomes (Holmes et al, 2013). Whereas English is usually the language of research and publications, researching in languages other than English allow us to reflect on decolonising dynamics and on problematising the role that English – as a colonial language – carries (Phipps, 2019).

Conclusion

This chapter discusses participatory methodologies for education research in a context of protracted crisis. It is hoped to be relevant to those researchers who are working in a situation of crisis, and to those who are shifting and adapting methodologies in order to carry out research despite travel restrictions and the impossibility of physical proximity. Specifically, by sharing the methodological considerations of this research project, I hoped to offer educational practitioners, teacher trainers, and language educators more broadly a tool to enhance their reflections and to encourage them in pursuing their challenging work amid even more challenging circumstances.

To conclude, reflecting on my learning and trying to summarise it, I would like to draw attention to:

(a) *The potential of the unexpected, of the accidental and the importance of learning to embrace what is unpredictable.* In every research project, issues and challenges emerge. In these times of particular challenges and uncertainties, it is crucial that researchers embrace what Linda Tuhiwai Smith, in *Decolonizing Methodologies*, described as 'strategic positioning':
    'The end result cannot be predetermined. The means to the end involves human agency in ways which are complex and contradictory. The notion of strategic positioning as a deliberate practice is partially an attempt to contain the unevenness and unpredictability, under stress, of people engaged in emancipatory struggles' (Tuhiwai Smith, 2006: 186).

(b) *The acknowledgment of the digital in shaping our projects.* It is necessary that – as researchers involved in social research – we understand how technology and 'non-human' actants shape our interaction. Actor–Network Theory and new materialist scholars are well positioned to help us guide our understanding of how relationships evolve and how they are affected by objects and things.

(c) *Ethics and relationships should be foregrounded in every research project.* The recognition of ethics as an ongoing process, built in immanent relationships, may help foreground ethical considerations. To guide our research from an ethical point of view, we find that formula and tick-box exercises are sometimes not exhaustive. I therefore invite researchers to consider how relationships are built, how they evolve, and what's the legacy of each research project in terms of sustainability and long-term impact.

This chapter provides reflections that might be useful for researchers that are trying to work in precarious conditions, adopting participatory and decolonising methodologies that recognise and value the primacy of knowledge that comes out of such difficult contexts. The chapter does not aim to be a how-to guide to conduct research in times and contexts of crisis, as each research is contextually grounded, but it hopes to provide stimuli for reflections, learning from those contexts which know better how to deal with crisis and emergencies.

Acknowledgements

I am especially thankful to Prof Elizabeth Erling for her feedback and advice when writing this chapter. I also would like to thank the editors and the anonymous reviewers for their insights and useful comments.

References

Aouragh, M. (2011) *Palestine Online: Transnationalism, the Internet and the Construction of Identity*, London: Tauris Academic Studies.

Butler, J. (2005) *Giving an Account of Oneself*, New York: Fordham University Press.

Fals Borda, O (2001) 'Participatory (action) research in social theory: origins and challenges', in *Handbook of Action Research*, London: Sage, pp 27–37.

Fassetta, G., Al-Masri, N., and Phipps, A. (eds) (2020) *Multilingual Online Academic Collaborations as Resistance: Crossing Impassable Borders*, Multilingual Matters.

Fassetta, G., Imperiale, M., Frimberger, K., Attia, M., and Al-Masri N. (2017) 'Online teacher training in a context of forced immobility: the case of the Gaza Strip', *European Education*, 49(2–3): 133–50.

Freire, P. (1996) (first published in 1970) *Pedagogy of the Oppressed*, London: Penguin.

Fricker, M. (2007) *Epistemic Injustice: Power and the Ethics of Knowing*, Oxford: Oxford University Press.

Gaventa, J. and Cornwall, A. (2001) 'Power and knowledge', in *Handbook of Action Research*, London: Sage, pp 70–80.

Habermas, J. (1984) *Theory of Communicative Action, Volume One: Reason and the Rationalization of Society*, trans. T.McCarthy, Boston: Beacon.

Holmes, P., Fay, R., Andrews, J., and Attia, M. (2013) 'Researching multilingually: new theoretical and methodological directions', *International Journal of Applied Linguistics*, 23(3): 285–99.

Imperiale, M. (2017) 'A capability approach to language education in the Gaza Strip: "To plant hope in a land of despair"', *Critical Multilingualism Studies*, 5(1): 37–58.

Imperiale, M. (2018) *Developing Language Education in the Gaza Strip: Pedagogies of Capability and Resistance*, Unpublished PhD thesis (University of Glasgow).

Imperiale, M. (2021) 'Intercultural education in times of restricted travels: lessons from the Gaza Strip', *Intercultural Communication Education*, 4(1): 22–38.

Imperiale, M., Phipps, A., Al-Masri, N., and Fassetta, G. (2017) 'Pedagogies of hope and resistance: English language education in the context of the Gaza Strip, Palestine', in E. Erling (ed) *English across the Fracture Lines*, London: British Council, pp 31–8.

Imperiale, M., Phipps, A., and Fassetta, G. (2021) 'On online practices of hospitality in higher education', *Studies in Philosophy and Education*, early online publication. doi: 10.1007/s11217-021-09770-z.

Kemmis, S., McTaggart, R., and Nixon, R. (2014) *The Action Research Planner: Doing Critical Participatory Action Research*, London: Springer.

MacDonald, M. and O'Regan, J. (2012) 'The ethics of intercultural communication', *Education Philosophy and Theory*, 45(10).

Noffke, S. (2009) 'Revisiting the professional, personal, and political dimensions of action research', in *The SAGE Handbook of Educational Action Research*, London: Sage, pp 6–23.

Phipps, A. (2019) *Decolonising Multilingualism: Struggles to Decreate. Series: Writing without Borders*, Multilingual Matters.

Reason, P. and Bradbury, H. (2001) 'Introduction: inquiry and participation in search of a world worthy of human aspiration', in *Handbook of Action Research*, London: Sage, pp 1–15.

Ricoeur, P. (2004) *Sur la Traduction*, Paris: Bayard.

Sen, A. (2009) *The Idea of Justice*, London: Allen Lane.

Smith, R. (2015) 'Healthcare under siege: geopolitics of medical service provision in the Gaza Strip', *Social Science and Medicine*, 146: 332–40.

Stock, I. (2016) 'Transnational social fields in forced immobility: relations of young Sub-Saharan African migrants in Morocco with their families and friends', *Identities. Global Studies in Culture and Power*, 23(4): 407–21.

Tawil-Souri, H. and Matar, D. (2016) *Gaza as Metaphor*, London: Hurst.

Tuhiwai Smith, L. (2006) (first published in 1999) *Decolonizing Methodologies*, Dunedin: The University of Otago Press.

Walker, M. (2019) 'Defending the need for a foundational epistemic capability in education', *Journal of Human Development and Capabilities*, 20(2): 218–32.

Winter, Y. (2015) 'The siege of Gaza: spatial violence, humanitarian strategies, and the biopolitics of punishment', *Constellations*, 23(2): 308–19.

14

Managing ethical tensions when conducting research in fragile and conflict-affected contexts

Gbenga Akinlolu Shadare

Introduction

Most researchers understand that working with human participants not only enriches and validates their research but also imposes a duty of care and due diligence which comes with appreciating what Guillemin and Gilliam described as 'ethical tensions' (2004: 271). Actually, the starting point of any research should be the awareness and recognition of the ethical tensions and dilemmas that might arise in a given research situation. However, while it is helpful for researchers to have clarity about ethical tensions and dilemmas, it is often difficult in practice to maintain and keep a balanced focus between critical reflection on researcher positionality and ethical responsibility for participants' welfare. In essence, researchers must understand the 'ethically important environments' in which prime consideration is devoted to the 'welfare and integrity of the individual participants involved in the research' (Guillemin and Gilliam, 2004: 271). Thus, researchers require not just a 'common sense' understanding that draws on their experiences and knowledge but must also exhibit a comprehensive ethical and methodological reflection, when undertaking challenging research. Nonetheless, nothing compares to the peculiar uncertainties and difficulties that arise when conducting research in fragile or conflict-affected environments where managing ethical tensions and ethical moments requires flexibility and adaptability.

This chapter is based on my experience while undertaking doctoral research in the northern region of Nigeria where persistent conflicts occasioned by the brutal terrorist attacks perpetrated by Boko Haram insurgents massively destroyed the regional economy, disrupted livelihoods, and created pervasive insecurity. Boko Haram are a notorious Islamic state-sponsored, Jihadist terrorist group operating in the predominantly Muslim north of Nigeria (also parts of Chad, Niger, and Cameroon republics) for over a decade. They kidnapped, in April 2014, the Chibok schoolgirls.

'*Boko Haram*' in Hausa language means: 'Western education is sinful'. The lessons and insights garnered from the experience of undertaking research in that context constitute the focus of this chapter. The experience of undertaking fieldwork in an unstable and fragile context is not novel to me. However, the peculiar insights gleaned from the unorthodox practices and unconventional norms that characterised the research endeavour is what this chapter contributes to the burgeoning literature of researching in uncertain times and in difficult regions where the work is challenged by many risks that could impede success.

This chapter is structured as follows: the first section provides the background of the research undertaken in Nigeria, followed by definitions of the operative terms to give some clarity to the research context. A discussion of the challenges encountered during fieldwork and how the challenges were overcome or mitigated is presented. The chapter closes with useful tips and lessons for researchers navigating and undertaking research in unfamiliar/unconventional terrains.

Research background

Generally, in over two and half decades, social protection (SP) has appreciably transformed Global South countries largely due to the commitments of governments in Latin America, Africa, and Asia to the transformation of their welfare regimes to incorporate SP for previously excluded families and social groups. Direct financial help for individuals, families, and households (known as cash transfer programmes) is at the centre of this transformation. National governments are therefore implementing pro-poor policies to ameliorate and safeguard the living conditions of their populations under the UN's 17 Sustainable Development Goals. Increasingly, low-and-middle-income countries like Nigeria are placing their citizens at the centre of core policies and developmental programmes.

Thus, my research was motivated by the desire to uncover support for redistribution and come up with a way to characterise the evolving 'Nigerian welfare regime'. The other principal research question was understanding how SP programming impacted communities and livelihoods. Admittedly, tackling that question is problematic in itself, and requires more than a limited PhD research project to resolve. However, examining the factors of underdevelopment and the actions of national governments in developing countries is critical. My doctoral research investigated the lived experiences of beneficiaries of Nigerian cash transfers to gain an understanding of their unique perspectives. Nigeria is important particularly because it is on the cusp of SP transformation (Shadare, 2019), and because the country is a 'slow-starter' and 'late-comer' to SP, which had operated for several decades in other countries in Africa, Latin America, and Asia. Consequently, because SP has just operated for barely a decade in Nigeria, very limited research existed on the Nigerian case and in other fragile settings in Africa (Shadare, 2020).

Therefore, it was critical to understand how SP programmes operated in the country; and more importantly, how beneficiaries perceived SP impacts on their livelihoods. In so doing, my research contributed to the expanding literature on SP programmes in Nigeria in particular and in fragile contexts in general. Beneficiaries' perspectives and attitudes towards SP programmes, in any contexts, are shaped by context-specific factors. Hence, studying variations are crucial if SP programmes are to be appropriately and efficiently delivered. Incorporating the voices, perspectives, and lived experiences of beneficiaries into any study of SP is consequently highly significant. My qualitative research investigated SP programming through the lens of citizens as beneficiaries, users, and influencers of policies and through the views of policymakers, programme administrators, politicians, and elites, and yielded useful insights about the nuanced and contextual nature of social policy programmes in Nigeria.

Prior preparations before fieldwork

I am a British citizen of Nigerian descent and I was keenly aware of the challenges of conducting research in Nigeria. It was essential to be fully prepared for any emergencies or difficulties that might arise. Consequently, I contacted knowledgeable and reasonably well-informed people in Nigeria ahead of my fieldwork to assist with on-the-ground preparations. This anticipatory groundwork turned out to be beneficial for the research. It was very helpful to work closely with programme executives and coordinators at both national and sub-national levels in Nigeria. Importantly, because of the tense security situation in research locations, security personnel and the police were engaged and paid to provide security during travels to locations. This move had ethical implications, which are discussed later in the chapter.

Research integrity and procedural ethics

Normatively, every research project should be conducted ethically. Therefore, most research is underpinned by certain fundamental principles and required by design to include procedural ethics that must be rigorously followed. Procedural ethics, according to Chiumento et al (2020), encompasses the different processes of ethics approval that precede fieldwork; namely, development of research protocols, participant information sheets, informed consent forms, and procedural documentation that support the research. This process involves 'ethical thinking' and 'rational decision making' which both provide a framework for the research and helps to minimise harm or risk to participants and enhances data management practices (Biros et al, 2010; Pollock, 2012). However, distinction must be made between procedural ethics (the protocols that inform ethical approvals for a research) and process or situational ethics (the realities arising during the conduct of research) to guarantee research integrity. Researchers, especially qualitative researchers, are keenly aware of the necessity of assuring ethical conduct in their research especially when these practicalities are challenged by differing cultural and ethical values. This chapter argues that the application of *Western* procedural ethics is potentially inappropriate and calls for a re-evaluation and re-adjustment of ethical standards and procedures to fit with the cultural settings of non-Western societies. Mugumbate and Chereni (2019) suggested that research in African countries should employ the culturally appropriate ethical principle of Ubuntu instead of imported Euro-Western ethical frameworks. According to Ifejika (2006), Ubuntu simply means: 'I am, because you are', and is rooted in humanist African philosophy which views the community as one of the building blocks of society, incorporating the concepts of common humanity and oneness. Chilisa (2012) similarly stressed the need for researchers to be respectful to the researched communities. Therefore, applying procedural ethics designed for undertaking research in Western contexts to traditional, multicultural, and diverse settings of Africa, for example, requires applying methodologies that are respectful and inclusive of all knowledge systems and indigenous epistemologies (Kovach, 2009; Gone, 2019). So, as a doctoral researcher, I was conscious of my 'indigenist' ideological stance and the importance of reflecting this in my research which will also honour my ethnic roots. Churchill (1996) considers the indigenist stance as a situation where a researcher actively strives to hold the rights of indigenous people as his/her primary political goal, while also incorporating their own traditions in their work. Researchers undertaking research with this 'mindset' are able to weave into their research elements that are respectful of, and beneficial to, the researched community. Before returning later to this matter, I provide important definitions in the next section in order to set the context.

What are ethical tensions and ethically important moments?

Simply put, ethical tensions are 'the difficult, often subtle, and usually unpredictable situations that arise in the practice of doing research' (Guillemin and Gillam, 2004: 262). These are also described as 'ethically important moments'; which, collectively, are events that raise morally troubling concerns involving uncertainty, distress, or dilemma (Bushby et al, 2015). Ethical tensions manifest in three ways: ethical uncertainty, ethical distress, and ethical dilemmas.

Ethical uncertainty occurs when a researcher is uncertain about which moral principles to apply in a given situation or whether a situation is indeed a moral problem. Ethical distress on the other hand is when the researcher knows the right course of action but feels constrained to act otherwise because of institutional and organisational rules. Ethical dilemmas arise when the researcher is confronted with two or more equally pleasant or unpleasant situations that are mutually exclusive. Ethical tensions are experienced by every researcher. How these tensions are managed has serious implications for the particular research endeavour.

Defining fragile, weak, and conflict-affected states

'Fragile' or 'Weak' States (FWSs) are countries where the government has limited capacity or is incapable of providing basic services and security to its citizens. They are characterised by pervasive insecurity, unstable and tenuous state–citizen relationship, or weak institutions that are incapable of resolving conflicts. Conflict-affected countries (CACs), on the other hand, are experiencing prolonged episodes of extreme violence, conflicts, or persistent situations of latent violence. Often, in these countries basic public goods are non-existent with serious threats to lives and properties (Khan-Mohmand et al, 2017).

It is estimated that over 2 billion people live in these countries and the recurring elements are: weak governance, weak institutions, and weak capacities to govern or uphold peace (World Bank, 2020). Also, about half of the world's poor reside in these countries presently, with over 60 per cent of the world's poor projected to live in them by 2030 (OECD, 2018). Gaining legitimacy with citizens is a challenge in these states although some have fairly stable government albeit with extractive and authoritarian political systems, often contested at margins, sometimes violently (Acemoglu and Robinson, 2012; North et al, 2013). Using data from OECD (2018), a typology is provided in Table 14.1.

Table 14.1: Typology of fragile, weak, and conflict-affected states

Conflict-affected countries

Afghanistan, Democratic Republic of Congo (DRC), Somalia, Yemen, South Sudan, Mali, Haiti, and Central African Republic

Fragile or weak states

Pakistan, Mozambique, Nigeria, Angola, Liberia, Sierra Leone, Venezuela, Zimbabwe, Kenya

The Nigerian context

Based on Khan-Mohmand et al (2017), Nigeria presents the classic features of a 'borderline fragile state', due in large part to the crises of insecurity and instability exacerbated by Boko Haram, particularly in the north-eastern region of the country where several terrorist acts were perpetrated over the past decade. Nigeria enjoys relative stability at the centre with state legitimacy, authority, and capacity intact. Abuja (the federal capital) and the southern regions are also mostly peaceful. However, since gaining independence from Britain in 1960, Nigeria has struggled with the challenges of nation building (Achebe, 1984). As a federation, Nigeria experienced several military regimes (1966–79 and 1984–99) and a 30-month civil war (1967–70). In 1999, Nigeria returned to civilian democracy and has operated a three-tier government with a Federal Capital Territory in Abuja and 36 states, subdivided into 774 local governments. Nigeria is also uniquely diverse culturally and socially, making for complex geopolitics. Contentions for political power and influence by the elites and the interest groups supported by tribal and ethnic leaders are rampant, resulting in prebendalism, a situation that exacerbates corruption among rent-seeking politicians and their cronies (Joseph, 1987, 1996; Akinsanya and Ayoade, 2013). These interpretations are not contradictory, but consistent, explaining rent-seeking as a function of the complex divide and rule structures that originated in colonialism and continued in the complex power-sharing politics of post-independence federalism in Nigeria (Joseph, 1996; Mamdani, 2012, 2020). Hence, the federal system was supposedly crafted to manage the complexities of governance in a multi-ethnic, multi-tribal country of about 250 ethnic groups with the dominant tribes (Igbo, Yoruba, and Hausa) always jostling for hegemony (Gboyega et al, 2011). Adewale (2011) described Nigeria as a complex conglomeration of diversities with multifarious identities and interpretations.

Indeed, the complexity of Nigeria's geopolitical structure is befuddling to many observers. Paden (2008) argues this complexity makes Nigeria a globally unique nation having a strong political resilience as a mechanism for resolving her complex ethno-linguistic and religious diversity. With a near parity of Muslim and Christian populations, Nigeria is potentially a unique model for interreligious political accommodation and a bridging actor in global politics between the West and the Islamic world (Paden, 2008). In theory, Nigeria's geopolitical duality and religious bipolarity could make her a distinctively dynamic cultural and socially diverse polity, but its heterogeneity has provoked competition and/or conflict rather than unity, inflamed inter-social, inter-ethnic, and inter-cultural tensions, and continuously precipitated domestic conflagrations (Adewale, 2011). Nigeria has abundant natural resources but low levels of human development, low capital investment, and a complex geopolitical environment. Persistently deep issues of poverty, inequality, extreme deprivation, class divisions, and political uncertainties have undermined growth and development; many observers refer to them as 'the bane of Nigeria's economic progress' (Shadare, 2020).

Challenges of conducting research in Nigeria

Procedural ethics informing data collection in fragile settings are the same as in other settings. What, however, makes data collection in fragile settings a difficult endeavour is the application or readjustment of situational ethics. Conducting research in a fragile and conflict-afflicted country like Nigeria comes with its peculiar challenges, particularly for a doctoral researcher seeking to investigate the effects of social policy and societal transformation. In the north-eastern region, for example, the consequences of Boko Haram's operations turned the region into a displacement zone where hazards, uncertainties, and issues like food insecurity contributed to the escalation of violence. The cumulative effects of prolonged terrorists' activities transformed the landscape into a war zone; in many communities, villages, and towns, people experienced precarious existences: their lives were exposed to greater risks of deprivation, starvation, and hunger. This situation was so severe in certain communities that specific government SP programmes were delivered to beneficiaries by non-state actors (including civil society organisations, aid donors, and non-governmental organisations, and so on) and sometimes through operators working in neighbouring states. Economic activities were paralysed in many parts of this region. Although fieldwork was not carried out in the most affected areas of the region, due to heightened risks of insecurity and potential threats to my life; it was still impossible to ignore the effects of the activities of Boko Haram in Kano and Jigawa states which share borders with the north-eastern region (Borno, Yobe, Bauchi, Gombe, Taraba, and Adamawa states are the six states constituting the region) where most of the terrorist activities occurred.

The research challenges were not necessarily the result of violence, fragility, or conflict per se, which are formidable, but emanated essentially from the general context of insecurity and restricted flow of information within Nigeria. For instance, key actors, contacts, and research participants were difficult to identify and recruit. When information could be found, other vital elements of the bigger picture were often missing or unavailable. So, for researchers conducting research in fragile or conflict-affected contexts, careful consideration must be given to the choice of methods for eliciting information and collecting data. This is what situational ethics entails. Khan Mohmand et al (2017) suggested that empirical research approaches and methodologies need to be carefully matched to the configuration of fragility and conflict in each country being investigated. Borrowing from the typology developed by Khan-Mohmand et al (2017), Nigeria is a 'borderline' fragile state which implied taking hard decisions with regard to the north-east region where conflict was mostly confined. Therefore, a major challenge was determining how to be creative and adaptive in my methodological approach in order to effectively undertake my fieldwork in Nigeria.

Key ethical considerations that informed research preparation prior to and during fieldwork

Berg (2009) and Guillemin and Gillam (2004) defined 'ethics' in research as keeping within the guidelines of acceptable and unacceptable conduct, including matters of privacy, safety, and the confidentiality of data and research participants. Besides, maintaining participants' confidentiality after obtaining informed consent was deemed critical. Researchers have the responsibility of being professional and respecting relationships and materials at all times. They do this best by maintaining transparent communication throughout the research period. Implementing the transparency principle was different, however, owing to different cultural practices and norms. For example, informed consent could not be given by female participants unless they had the permission of their husbands.

Re-educating and reassuring participants – a critical phase

Participants were informed about the purpose of the research, which was not a government-funded work, but a self-funded research meant purely for educational and research purposes. Their scepticism was not surprising as governments in fragile states struggle for legitimacy in the eyes of their citizens. As it turned out, there is a low level of trust for government and institutions among citizens in Nigeria. Thus, potential research participants can perceive 'educated' natives and Western researchers as intruders and predators (Sinclair, 2003). Also, because a great deal of research in fragile settings assumes a perspective of deficiency whereby only debilitating problems have been the focus, and where the ways of life, and perspectives of the indigenous people have been pathologised, potential research participants can be unwilling to participate in any research that will only present skewed representations of their realities and lived experiences (Poupart, Baker, and Horse, 2009). However, as Denzin and Lincoln (2005) suggested, many researchers are now emphasising inclusivity of 'voice', worldview, and culture which takes a serious look at issues of representation of the 'other' and other 'ways of knowing'. Participants' agency is thus critical, although participation may be subject to gatekeepers of one kind or another. Therefore, it is important to get ethical principles right. A few considerations that applied during fieldwork and which helped to overcome these ethical problems included being innovative and thoughtful, and thinking outside the box. Hence, it was important for me to operate with the following principles which were central to the direction of the research. The first was cultural sensitivity and empathy that addressed the specific needs of research participants. The second related to privacy and informed consent where participants had to be assured that their interests were protected and that there would not be consequences. This might have been due to previous cases where citizens were accused of 'exposing secrets' which resulted in some of them being unfairly ostracised by their communities. Also, some participants were afraid that they were being surreptitiously targeted by government for some reasons. This is why informed consent was critical. Informed consent was obtained in writing or, to overcome language and/ or literacy barriers, by audio recording of participants' verbal consent. Assurances sought by participants for protection, based on their expressed apprehensions, were firmly granted. Those not satisfied with the assurances opted out of the process. The 'do no harm' principle was applied throughout the research process.

Peculiar challenges experienced during fieldwork

Typically, researchers experience a plethora of challenges when conducting research in fragile states. Limited resources, especially funding, can affect research. In my case this was mitigated by having funding set aside to address any difficulty that might suddenly arise during research operations. Anecdotally, limited funding does not support meaningful research activities in fragile contexts because of the uncertainties and difficulties in the operating environments. Also, poor infrastructure, facilities, and Internet connectivity/ access issues impact research operations. This was not different for me. Poor or bad roads affected commuting and given that my safety was critical, route or travel re-planning was frequent. Cases of kidnapping are rife and rampant in Nigeria, especially for returnee *diasporans*, perceived as having an 'economic advantage' and so easy targets for kidnappers. Thus, plans for travelling between research locations in northern Nigeria were constantly reviewed and altered; and journeys were sometimes made at awkward times and days in line with protective and safety assurances from local contacts familiar with the terrain. My safety and security, including threat to life and theft of research materials, were palpable fears. Local researchers are not as well resourced as their diaspora counterparts for obvious reasons. Therefore, I took extra precautionary measures for protection. This increased the challenge and added complexity that arises for a *diasporan* like me aiming to conduct high-quality ethical research using unskilled local staff.

Given the peculiar nature of Nigeria, cultural barriers such as language problems, unorthodox norms and beliefs, and religious practices seriously impacted the research. These were mostly Islamic practices as this is the predominant religion in northern Nigeria leading to more restrictive norms and rules. Nigeria's official language is English but with over 250 local dialects and languages, there are fewer proficient speakers. Nonetheless, Pidgin English, the nation's unofficial lingua franca, is widely spoken. Semi-structured interviews and focus group discussions were also conducted in local languages: Hausa, Fulani, Igbo, and Yoruba, which was possible with the help of interpreters in some cases, although I speak Yoruba fluently and understand a little Hausa and Igbo. Engaging the services of interpreters in qualitative research is often generally regarded as fraught with methodological difficulties such as the perception of their roles as 'invisible' and the 'minimisation of their functions' which can reinforce inequalities in research and negatively impact upon the research process (Edwards, 1998). However, interpreters can function as active agents in a triadic relationship premised on egalitarian and transparent principles of co-constructions and co-working where mutual trust is paramount and permeates the entire research process (Vara and Patel, 2012).

Traditional customs, beliefs, and religious norms made contact and collaboration with potential participants difficult. These issues played out in the recruitment of research participants or in how to access them. The use of gatekeepers was helpful here as they acted as go-betweens in recruiting participants and boosting community trust. The palpable lack of trust between the researcher and participants who live in rural communities can often cause tension. Overcoming the perception as an 'outsider', with no connection to the region, was formidable, hence the prodigious use of gatekeepers as 'middle-persons' or 'go-betweens' to facilitate contact and collaboration with participants. This tactic worked well, permitting access that enabled collection of rich data in an environment devoid of guilt, or fear of reprisals.

Perhaps one of the most ethically challenging aspects occurred with regards to recruiting women. Women, because of the widely held perception that they were better household and care economy managers, are often disproportionately represented in SP programmes. Thus, unsurprisingly, women were over-represented as research participants in the study.

The second challenge was managing participants' sensitivities. This usually occurs when participants are afraid to speak their minds, especially negatively, for fear of repercussions. This also relates to participants who have multiple disadvantages and are harder to reach because they lack the formal attributes of equality, agency, and voice presumed by standard research ethics. In the case of Islamic women, observance of Islamic injunctions is critical. Hence, recruiting them as research participants can be challenging.

This was more so in the northern part of Nigeria where women observe the religious practice of purdah as part of their marital injunctions. This involves women's segregation from men, and complete body covering to conceal form, skin, and face. Breaching those injunctions attracts severe and punitive sanctions. To manage these challenges, unorthodox steps were employed with regards to location/venue of interviews; strategies for interviewing participants (involving covert methods – discussed in detail later); confronting issues of power and embedded gender norms that limit and exclude women; adapting to religious and cultural issues; and working under the pervasive dread and fear of the destructive influence of Boko Haram.

I confronted the dilemma of ensuring participants' compliance with the Islamic injunctions and creative, covert, and unorthodox methods were applied. During the initial interviews some of the Islamic women could not open up as they were interviewed in the presence of their husbands or men in the family. Some of them were however prepared to open up about some personal issues and experiences but wanted to do it without fear and not in the presence of their men or husbands. I took the unprecedented decision to dress in purdah as a woman to gain unrestricted access to the women alongside the female gatekeeper in order to undertake additional interviews and obtain unmediated information/data about some of the restrictive, obstructive, domestic abuses experienced by women (Lee-Treweek and Linkogle, 2000; Calvey, 2008).

Additionally, the unpredictable and constantly changing nature of affairs in Nigeria, although expected, impacted the research process. This is due mainly to the reality of the widespread low capacities of government and non-governmental institutions permeating society that seriously restricted the flow of information and access to critical sources. Conducting research in a multicultural, multi-ethnic, culturally diverse setting like Nigeria implies that the application of Euro-Western ethical principles in research is problematic. This was accentuated by the pervasive nature of insecurity, distrust, corruption, and unethical practices within Nigeria that restricted the logistics, the flow of information, and the recruitment of participants. Generally, progress and planning of data collection in fragile settings can be very slow.

Finally, compensation of participants was constrained due to the risk of motivating participation. However, compensating research participants is acceptable under certain circumstances. The informed consent process driving the recruitment of participants ensured that information leaflets and consent forms were displayed in the local languages of Yoruba, Hausa/Fulani, Igbo, Pidgin English, and English, summarising the research, the purpose of the study, and the assurance of anonymity for participants. Also, participants were informed of the measures that would be taken to secure the interview through audio-recording, and that they had the choice to either stop the interview completely and opt out, or stop and re-start, or completely withdraw from the interview and focus group. Because participants travelled long distances to the interview venues, their transportation costs were reimbursed. This was not an inducement but intended to appreciate participants for travelling long distances and for committing time and effort to the research. Concerns about compensation are widespread (Killawi et al, 2014); however, this was reasonable in the situation given that participants were recruited from among the poor and the disadvantaged and could not possibly be expected to pay for their participation in the project. Compensation raises ethical questions, and can be controversially perceived as coercion; conversely, non-compensation could create exclusion and bias participation in the research towards those who have free time and more money (Wilkerson and Moore, 1997). However, if research is conducted in a manner that does not override the principles of freely expressed, freely given, and fully informed consent, compensation is fine (Dickert et al, 2002; Jones and Liddell, 2009). Reimbursement can also spur participants' enthusiasm and interests (Kara, 2018).

Lessons and tips for managing ethical tensions appropriately

The golden rule for managing unpredictability in conducting research in fragile contexts is to appropriately evaluate the research contexts. As the saying goes, context matters. Researchers must familiarise themselves with the local laws, regulations, and guidelines for conducting research in the location. In Nigeria, the *National Research Guidelines of Nigeria* regulates ethical codes for research undertaken with research participants. As stipulated in the *Guidelines*, researchers are required to incorporate cultural considerations for participants in all research undertaken in Nigeria (Fadare and Porteri, 2010).

Understanding cultural belief systems, norms, traditional practices, and customs, often called 'cultural competence' (Kara, 2018: 29), and how these might affect the research, is crucial. The areas of particular concern are the process of informed consent, maintaining confidentiality and protecting participants from harm. There is no rule of thumb. As long as reasonable and rational safeguarding measures and precautions are taken, and the risks are properly evaluated, the researcher should be fine. Ethical tensions are considerably minimised when there is an understanding of the peculiar complexities of the research context which helps in confronting realities while managing uncertainties in the field by applying appropriate ethical standards that fit with the specific context. However, a culturally appropriate and informed research strategy must be anchored on an epistemological and ideological commitment to empowering the disadvantaged and vulnerable populations so as to uncover real truths. This is what informed the use of covert and unorthodox methods in interviewing women to obtain hard-to-get data.

Researchers do not only have a duty of care to participants but also have to amplify their voices as a way of contributing to positive changes in their lives. For example, the cases of HIV patients and commercial sex workers and child-brides in Nigeria, some of whom were research participants, provided ample opportunities to understand real issues in the community including risks of harm, the potential for social marginalisation, stigma, and discrimination.

Adopting a culturally informed research strategy that allows for greater flexibility in informed consent protocols is crucial. Whereas Western researchers participating in international projects are bound to Western regulations, researchers in tune with local conditions can re-adjust the standards to fit with cultural settings. Pressuring people to participate should never be done. If there are language and literacy barriers to written informed consent, verbal consent should be used. Assuring confidentiality is tricky but this is connected to trust. Once participants trust the researcher, many barriers are scaled and the research process can be augmented with a communal decision-making process, often a critical ingredient in such contexts. Participation in research requires more than one level of consent; for instance, married women will require permission of husbands to participate in research.

An adapted ethical standard is a necessity as this is helpful for recruiting and obtaining informed consent from participants and for dealing with compensations. For instance, hiring Nigerian police and private security companies (as gatekeepers and providers of security) in my case was extreme, but the practice is not uncommon in Nigeria given the level of insecurity and rampant kidnappings of foreigners or *diasporan* returnees (Killawi et al, 2014). Similarly, as this was self-funded research, no justification or approval was required from an approving authority. Besides, the police understood the threats to life and the importance of security, and their role in planning travel to locations and arranging security logistics was critical to my safety and security and that of the participants.

Researchers have a duty to protect the rights, privacy, and confidentiality of participants, and to guarantee optimal benefits by not causing harm, which is about ensuring fair and equal distribution of both benefits and risks of participation. This is crucial as the overarching objective of every research is protection of research participants.

Conclusion

Being accountable to research participants in a fragile and conflict-affected setting, especially one that is culturally diverse and multi-ethnic like Nigeria, is an ethical responsibility that should stem from an understanding that lives are intertwined. This calls for a deeper consideration of what we are doing in relation to others; sensitivities to participants' concerns and issues are paramount (Park et al, 2016). As highlighted in this chapter, I treated my participants and other stakeholders (gatekeepers, the police, and so on) with a great deal of respect, which constituted an ethical stance in the research process and also emphasised the spirit of co-working and inclusivity. In the end, participants in the research were made to feel that the research was being done *with* them rather than *on* them (Roth, 2005).

Ethical guidelines, predicated on Western research traditions that are approved for research in fragile contexts, will never be able to contemplate or envision or address the 'everyday ethical issues that arise in the doing of research' (Guillemin and Gillam, 2004: 263; Tomkinson, 2014) as it is impossible to follow a predetermined ethics protocol in fragile contexts due to extreme uncertainties. Therefore, to carry out effective research in such countries, researchers must work reflexively to produce research outputs that are highly contextualised, innovative (making use of non-traditional means of designing and implementing research and collecting data), and employing flexible approaches that are adaptive to the respective countries. Above all, researchers must strive to make their research culturally relevant. Ultimately, for SP to be effective and contextually sensitive, the research protocol must be fully adapted to understanding conditions in complex and fragile contexts.

References

Acemoglu, D. and Robinson, J. (2012) *Why Nations Fail: The Origins of Power, Prosperity, and Poverty*, London: Profile Currency.

Achebe, C. (1984) *The Trouble with Nigeria*, London: Heinemann.

Adewale, A. (2011) *The Political, Economic and Social Dynamics of Nigeria: A Synopsis*, Africa Institute of South Africa, AISA Policy Briefing No 39, February.

Akinsanya, A. and Ayoade, J. (eds) (2013) *An Introduction to Political Science in Nigeria*, New York: University Press of America.

Berg, B. (2009) *Qualitative Research Methods for the Social Sciences* (7th edn), Boston, MA: Allyn & Bacon.

Biros, M., Hauswald, M., and Baren, J. (2010) 'Procedural versus practical ethics', *Academic Emergency Medicine*, 17(9): 989–90.

Bushby, K., Chan, J., Druif, S., Ho, K., and Kinsella, E. (2015) 'Ethical tensions in occupational therapy practice: a scoping review', *British Journal of Occupational Therapy*, 78(4): 212–21.

Calvey, D. (2008) 'The art and politics of covert research: doing "situated ethics" in the field', *Sociology*, 42(5): 905–18.

Chilisa, B. (2012) *Indigenous Research Methodologies*, Thousand Oaks, CA: Sage.

Chiumento, A., Rahman, A., and Frith, L. (2020) 'Writing to template: researchers' negotiation of procedural research ethics', *Social Science and Medicine*, 112980.

Churchill, W. (1996) *From a Native Son: Selected Essays in Indigenism, 1985–1995*, Boston, MA: South End Press.

Denzin, N. and Lincoln, Y. (2005) 'Introduction: the discipline and practice of qualitative research', in N. Denzin and Y. Lincoln (eds) *Handbook of Qualitative Research* (3rd edn), Thousand Oaks, CA: Sage.

Dickert, N., Emanuel, E., and Grady, C. (2002) 'Paying research subjects: an analysis of current policies', *Annals of Internal Medicine*, 136: 368–73.

Edwards, R. (1998) 'A critical examination of the use of interpreters in the qualitative research process', *Journal of Ethnic and Migration Studies*, 24: 197–208.

Fadare, J. and Porteri, C. (2010) 'Informed consent in human subject research: a comparison of current international and Nigerian guidelines', *Journal of Empirical Research on Human Research Ethics*, 5(1): 67–73.

Gboyega, A., Søreide, T., Mihn-Le, T., and Shukla, G. (2011) *Political Economy of the Petroleum Sector in Nigeria*, Policy Research Working Paper 5779, Africa Region, Washington: The World Bank.

Gone, J. (2019) 'Considering indigenous research methodologies: critical reflections by an indigenous knower', *Qualitative Inquiry*, 25(1): 45–56.

Guillemin, M. and Gillam, L. (2004) 'Ethics, reflexivity, and "ethically important moments" in research', *Qualitative Inquiry*, 10(2): 261–80.

Ifejika, N. (2006) 'What does Ubuntu really mean?', *The Guardian*, 29 September, available at: https://www.theguardian.com/theguardian/2006/sep/29/features11.g2?CMP=Share_iOSApp_Other

Jones, E. and Liddell, K. (2009) 'Should healthy volunteers in clinical trials be paid according to risk? Yes', *BMJ*, 339: b4142.

Joseph, R. (1987) *Democracy and Prebendal Politics in Nigeria: The Rise and Fall of the Second Republic*, Cambridge: Cambridge University Press.

Joseph, R. (1996) 'Nigeria: inside the dismal tunnel', *Current History*, 95(601): 193–200.

Kara, H. (2018) *Research Ethics in the Real World: Euro-Western and Indigenous Perspectives*, Bristol: Policy Press.

Khan Mohmand, S. et al (2017) *Innovative Methods for Research on Social and Political Action in Fragile and Conflict-Affected Settings*, IDS Working Paper 487, Brighton: IDS.

Killawi, A. et al (2014) 'Procedures of recruiting, obtaining informed consent, and compensating research participants in Qatar: findings from a qualitative investigation', *BMC Medical Ethics*, 15(1): 9.

Kovach, M. (2009) *Indigenous Methodologies: Characteristics, Conversations, and Contexts*, Toronto: University of Toronto Press.

Lee-Treweek, G. and Linkogle, S. (eds) (2000) *Danger in the Field: Risk and Ethics in Social Research*, London: Routledge.

Mamdani, M. (2012) *Define and Rule: Native as Political Identity*, Boston, MA: Harvard University Press.

Mamdani, M. (2020) *Neither Settler nor Native: The Making and Unmaking of Permanent Minorities*, Boston, MA: Harvard University Press.

Mugumbate, J. and Chereni, A. (2019) Using African Ubuntu theory in social work with children in Zimbabwe', *African Journal of Social Work*, 9(1).

North, D., Wallis, J., Webb, S., and Weingast, B. (eds) (2013) *In the Shadow of Violence: Politics, Economics, and the Problems of Development*, Cambridge: Cambridge University Press.

OECD (2018) *States of Fragility*, Paris: OECD Publishing.

Paden, J. (2008) *Faith and Politics in Nigeria: Nigeria as a Pivotal State in the Muslim World*, Washington DC: United States Institute of Peace Press, p 141.

Park, E., Caine, V., McConnell, D., and Minaker, J. (2016) 'Ethical tensions as educative spaces in narrative inquiry', in *Forum Qualitative Sozialforschung/ Forum: Qualitative Social Research*, 17(2).

Pollock, K. (2012) 'Procedure versus process: ethical paradigms and the conduct of qualitative research', *BMC Medical Ethics*, 13(1): 25.

Poupart, J., Baker, L., and Horse, J. (2009) 'Research with American Indian communities: the value of authentic partnerships', *Children and Youth Services Review*, 31(11): 1180–6.

Roth, W. (2005) *Doing Qualitative Research: Praxis of Method*, Leiden, The Netherlands: Brill Sense Publishers.

Shadare, G. (2019) 'Transformation of social transfer programmes in Nigeria – a political settlement explanation', [online], available at: https://www.socialprotection.org/discover/publications/nigerias-social-protection-cusp-transformation

Shadare, G. (2020) *Conditional Cash Transfers in Nigeria – An Exploratory Study*, [Unpublished PhD thesis], Sheffield: The University of Sheffield.

Sinclair, R. (2003) *Indigenous Research in Social Work: The Challenge of Operationalizing Worldview*, [Discussion paper], Calgary: Faculty of Social Work University of Calgary.

Tomkinson, S. (2014) 'Doing fieldwork on state organizations in democratic settings: ethical issues of research in refugee decision making', in *Forum Qualitative Sozialforschung/Forum: Qualitative Social Research*, 16(1).

Vara, R. and Patel, N. (2012) 'Working with interpreters in qualitative psychological research: methodological and ethical issues', *Qualitative Research in Psychology*, 9(1): 75–87.

Wilkinson, M. and Moore, A. (1997) 'Inducement in research', *Bioethics*, 11: 373–89.

World Bank (2020) *Poverty and Shared Prosperity 2020: Reversals of Fortune*, Washington, DC: The World Bank.

15

Beyond extraction: co-creating a decolonial and feminist research practice in post-conflict Guatemala

Aisling Walsh

Narrations of extraction between North and South are permeated with necessarily troubling metaphors of predatory, life-sucking, monstrosities of ethnographic infestations and extraction from populations in crises. Thinking with such monstrous figures, this chapter explores the potential of research to contribute to or diverge from the continuum of (neo)colonial dispossession, expropriation, and extraction of land, resources, bodies, and knowledges. Reflecting on previous 'field experience' and centring the ethical concerns of undertaking ethnography in Guatemala as part of a PhD programme funded from Ireland, I seek to problematise the ways of doing research in the Global South while positioned at a university in the Global North. Specifically, I explore the ethics of embarking on research in the post-colonial, post-conflict context of Guatemala. I question how the neoliberal dynamics embedded in universities of the Global North privilege the metrics of production and publication, fostering a culture where data harvesting/mining, and knowledge extraction from the Global South to the Global North not only persists, but is encouraged (Connell, 2014; Burman, 2018; Cruz and Luke, 2020).

I am particularly attentive to the ethical and methodological challenges of conducting research on sexual and racial violence in contexts where data extraction from victim/survivors of genocide and conflict-related sexual violence (CRSV) has, to a large extent, characterised the relationship between the researcher and the researched. Understanding research as another form of intervention that has the potential, not only to do harm, but also to perpetuate the dynamics of exploitation in the Global South, critical post/de/anti-colonial scholars are increasingly insisting on a reflexive ethics which probes the (neo)colonial dynamics of knowledge extraction and production (Cruz and Luke, 2020; Bilgen, Nasir, and Schöneberg, 2021). Their ethical concerns around North–South research dynamics go much further than the bureaucratic form of ethics approval required by Institutional Review

Boards (IRBs) or Research Ethics Committees (RECs) (Detamore, 2010; Lai, 2020; Millora, Maimunah, and Still, 2020).

Finally, I problematise the imaginary of the field, as 'elsewhere' and 'other', and the potential for fieldwork in contexts of crises or sustained and persistent conflict to reproduce a (neo)colonial othering. Centring researcher positionality and reflexivity through a politically engaged and relationally entangled (auto)ethnography, I seek to ground my research in decolonial and feminist ethics. I explore the possibilities of meeting this challenge by using methodologies which privilege dialogue, friendship, affect, and the co-creation of situated knowledges. I consider whether these are enough to justify further research within this context, mitigate the possibilities for causing harm, and offer expanded possibilities for a plurality of knowledges?

Mining bodies for knowledge: research extractivism within colonial landscapes

Extraction implies flows of natural and corporeal resources, sustenance, and knowledge from the Global South to the Global North. Connell (2014: 211) argues how the 'role of the periphery is to supply data, and later to apply knowledge in the form of technology and method. The role of the metropole, as well as producing data, is to collate and process data, producing theory (including methodology) and developing applications which are later exported to the periphery.' According to Smith (2012: 64 and 70), research has historically served imperialism as a form of 'culture collection': to see, name, and know those to be colonised, through processes involving violent appropriation, extraction, erasure and dispossession, with anthropology and ethnography, in particular, long being regarded by indigenous peoples as the 'epitome of all that is bad about academia'.

Guatemala's 500-year legacy of (neo)colonial intervention is characterised by repeating cycles of dispossession through extraction and accumulation, resulting in social and geographical reconfigurations of the body–territory that continue to the present day. These reconfigurations have included mass dispossessions of peoples from their territories, the extraction of labour from peoples through enslavement, and feudal master–serf relations where the 'nexus territory-body (…) corresponds to a multiplicity of ways of producing death and life simultaneously' (Chivalán Carrillo and Posocco, 2020: 524). The authors characterise extractive process in Guatemala as vampiric – sucking life and bestowing death. The anomalous, disposable, and racialised bodies/territories of the colonised become sites of expropriation, experimentation, and knowledge creation for the benefit of the sovereign, white, and able bodies/territories of the colonisers (Chivalán Carrillo and Posocco, 2020; Chivalán Carrillo, 2020).

Chivilán Carrillo (2020) describes how, between 1946 and 1948, US doctors, with the approval of the Guatemalan government of the time, carried out a series of medical trials on incarcerated men and the patients of a local psychiatric institute. 638 individuals were inoculated with syphilis without knowledge or consent to test the effects of penicillin on the virus; 44 of them received no treatment and 71 died from the experiment. The author situates such experiments within a historical continuum of the dispossession and extraction of the body-territory, from the indigenous wet nurses captured to feed the offspring of Spanish Criollo families in the 16th century to the contemporary extraction of human egg cells from Guatemala to feed the fertility deficit in the Global North. The expropriation of anomalous and disposable bodies for the production of scientific knowledge is understood as 'vampiric' extraction (Chivalán Carrillo and Posocco, 2020).

Burman (2018), exploring the dynamics of academic extraction in Bolivia, explains how the fat-suctioning mythological creature of the *Kharisiri* is used as a metaphor to characterise the harm that outsiders have, perpetuated against the Aymaran and Quechua peoples (Burman, 2018). Within this imaginary anthropologists and other social scientists are most often associated with the *Kharisiri*, sharing the characteristics of strange, life-sucking, and exploitative creatures who prey on vulnerable populations. Disembedded from the local context, anthropologists who use their power to engage in exploitative infiltration of communities and extract knowledge for their own benefit appear as monstrous beings. The predominance of researchers parachuting into the field for ever briefer stays, the knowledge flows from South to North, the lack of feedback or any other kind of 'giving back' to the communities under study, the imperatives of publications and metrics, the Anglo-centrism of academic publishing, the maintenance of geographical and 'objective' distance, and the fictitious separation of theory from practice are all features of extractive or *Kharisiri* ethnography (Burman, 2018; Cruz and Luke, 2020). Nevertheless, it is this extractive 'monstrosity', rather than more critically and ethically engaged practices, which is rewarded within Western academia (Burman, 2018; Cruz and Luke, 2020).

Contemporary crises and researcher infestations

From every rock and cranny in the East they emerge, as if responding to some primeval fertility rite, and flock to the reservations. 'They' are the anthropologists. Social anthropologists, historical anthropologists, political anthropologists, economic anthropologists, all brands of the species (...) the most prominent members of the scholarly community that infests the land of the free, and in the summer time, the homes of the braves. (Vine Deloria Jr from *Custer Died for Your Sins*, cited in Sukarieh and Tannock, 2012: 500)

The types of places and communities which tend to produce such research 'infestations' share a number of characteristics, including: poverty; crises of war or natural disasters; the existence of historically marginalised communities, particularly indigenous peoples; communities engaged in active social struggle or resistance to inequality or marginalisation; and their relative accessibility to researchers from the Global North (Sukarieh and Tannock, 2012). Guatemala ticks many, if not all, of these boxes and might be said to have an infestation of many species of social, political, and natural scientists as well as a plague of national and international NGO staff, development professionals, and diplomats.

This infestation intensified following the signing of the Peace Accords in 1996, bringing the brutal 36-year internal armed conflict to an end. A UN mission (MINUGUA) was established to oversee the transition to peace and there was an avalanche of donor interest from a multitude of international multilateral and bilateral organisations keen to support national initiatives for peace, reconciliation, and post-conflict reconstruction and development. Two truth commissions were established which gathered testimonies from approximately 50,000 victims, survivors, and witnesses seeking to document the crimes committed during the war and led to the publication of two multi-volume reports: *Guatemala Nunca Más* (Never Again) and *Memory of Silence*. Multiple human rights NGOs began to gather further testimonies and collect evidence to support high-profile prosecutions of former military personnel for genocide and crimes against humanity. There was a surge in academic research as national and international social scientists sought to unveil and understand the mechanisms of genocidal violence and State repression, as well as NGOs and international bodies dedicated to documenting continued human rights abuses (Petersen, Samset, and Wang, 2009).

Within this context, research of all kinds takes place with varying degrees of ethical commitments and practices. To illustrate, let me reflect on one of the first tasks assigned to me when I started an internship with an international NGO in Guatemala in 2014. A recent graduate from an LLM in Economic, Social, and Cultural Rights with minimal research experience, I was asked to design and conduct research on the impact of rural social conflicts on indigenous and *campesino* women. The NGO had provided material aid to the communities proposed for the research as well as continued accompaniment in demanding the State and private companies respect their rights. One of the issues that my superior was most interested in 'uncovering' through the interviews and focus groups I had planned to conduct were denunciations of sexual violence which were suspected of having taken place during a series of violent evictions in 2011.

As an intern and inexperienced researcher I felt both uncomfortable and daunted by the task handed to me. I did not, however, have the experience to articulate my concerns nor argue for a more responsible research approach, and felt I had simply to go along with what I had been asked to do. I was left mostly alone to design, plan, and implement the research project. My discomfort at directly addressing the issues of sexual violence was sufficient for me to seek advice from more experienced researchers. One such researcher, deeply involved in advocacy around the UN Resolution 1325 on Women, Peace, Security in Guatemala, said it was suspected that violence had occurred during the evictions but it was unlikely that any of the women would openly reveal such information and cautioned against pushing for such a revelation. Indeed, Boesten and Henry (2018) caution that:

> researchers are not necessarily best placed to contribute to breaking silences and combating stigma in conflict-affected communities (…) the disclosure of experiences with sexual violence can have devastating effects in the everyday lives of survivors, in spaces where researchers may not enter, or after they have left.

Under this advice, I redirected the focus of the research to the economic, social, and cultural impact of the direct and structural violence experienced by the women, and tried to centre their voices and experiences throughout the report and in any presentations following its publication.

To recount this makes me wince, not just at my own inexperience and arrogance in believing that such research might make a material difference to these women's lives, but also at the lack of institutional support and the irresponsibility of the NGO in sending someone as inexperienced and, frankly, clueless as me into the field under such conditions. Indeed, the participants were probably unaware of my lack of experience, because my whiteness, and the institutional backing of a white NGO, may have bestowed a presumption of expertise I certainly did not merit.

I cannot help but wonder was part of the motivation for this research driven by the upsurge of interest in 'breaking the silence' around sexual violence spurred on by high-profile transitional justice cases that had centred CRSV such as the Ríos Montt genocide trial in 2013 and the Sepur Zarco trial which had, by then, begun preliminary hearings? CRSV had become a hype issue in Guatemala, attracting donor and research interests, and too often NGOs fall into the trap of victim appropriation in their competition for funds or to be seen as pioneers in advancing women's rights and the struggle against impunity which has become synonymous with criminal accountability for CRSV (Boesten and Henry, 2018).

Furthermore, this research did not involve any ethical approval, nor a systematic and transparent process for selecting participants and seeking their consent. The communities researched, focus groups convened, and participants interviewed were determined by the local partner NGO. The assumption was that women would be open to participating in a process aimed at advancing their struggle and 'giving voice' to their concerns. The possibility that they might reasonably refuse was never discussed. Indeed, the only thing the women were asked to sign was the attendance list to set against the modest lunch we provided.

I have recounted this experience to illustrate that such practices are not exceptional, but characteristic of research carried out by international agencies and NGOs in Guatemala. Often, such projects are further conditioned by the hiring of external consultants, tight budgets, reduced time frames, and the aim to demonstrate the need for, or impact of, a specific humanitarian intervention. As such it is all too common to rely on the same people to provide the desired data, usually project 'beneficiaries', or in the case of CRSV, victims/survivors of wartime sexual violence who have pursued justice through criminal prosecutions with the support of local and national organisations. Principally, however, this reflection has served to draw a line under my own complicity in extractive research practices within this fragile and conflict-affected context. Recognising my deep discomfort, guilt even, with this process, I determined any further engagement would have to be grounded in genuine collaboration and guided by a more considered reflection on and commitment to feminist and decolonial ethics. What can an ethically oriented researcher do in the face of these many arguments against reproducing extraction? How do we avoid become vampires or *Kharisiris* of others' lives and others' knowledges, extracted, ingested, absorbed, and repackaged to satisfy the conventions of Northern academia?

Sowing seeds of a decolonial and feminist research practice

Q'anil, in Mayan cosmology, represents a breach in the earth where seeds can be sown, the seed of life leading to creation or reality, the material manifestation of everything which is has form, pulse, and life. Q'anil's symbolism is embodied in two life forms: the rabbit and the four maize seeds (red, black, white, and yellow). In the Mayan calendar Q'anil is a good day for expressing gratitude for life and reviving the land, plants, and animals (Barrios, 2015).

I first heard of the Centre for Training, Healing and Transpersonal Research – *Q'anil* – a couple of months after moving to Guatemala but was unable, due to time commitments, to sign up for one of their courses until June 2016, by which time I was actively searching for pathways out of the development cooperation dynamics discussed previously. I was hooked from the first module of their diploma in *Cuerpos, Erotismos y Sexualidades* (CES – Bodies, Eroticisms, and Sexualities) and Q'anil's community has been a part of my life in Guatemala ever since.

The organisation, founded by Yolanda Aguilar in 2009, is dedicated to addressing the colonial legacy of patriarchal and racial violence in Guatemala through training and healing processes that blend feminist and decolonial theory with experiential therapy and somatic bodywork. They are open to people from any territory and of any gender, with participants travelling to Guatemala specifically to engage in their processes from as far as Chile and Argentina. Over the last four years I have moved through this space as a student, participant, workshop facilitator and volunteer, and now as researcher. Conscious of the legacy of research extraction in Guatemala and my own lingering discomfort with the 'field' experience described previously, it was with some trepidation I first approached *Q'anil* about the idea of a possible long-term collaboration towards a PhD. I feared I would be dismissed as yet another academic tourist, however, Aguilar was keen to document the first ten years of their existence and possible impacts of their processes, and accepted with enthusiasm. As we began discussing the terms of the research, tensions between the expectations of the organisation and the bureaucratic exigencies of a Western university (funding applications, enrolment, ethical approval, and so on) began to emerge. These have concentrated in confusions around research positionality, relationality, and fieldwork. Rather than becoming obstacles, these tensions have pushed us into further dialogue around needs and expectations on both sides and, as a researcher, have steered me towards a more robust reflexivity about my position with the organisation and in the 'field'.

According to Bilgen, Nasir, and Schöneberg (2021: 11), 'the colonial gaze is implicated in the circumstances of "going to the field" and the way researchers are taught to extract knowledge'. As a researcher straddling two contexts which I have called home at different points in time, Ireland and Guatemala, I am deeply uncomfortable with how I am expected to understand and direct myself towards 'the field'. Preparing my research ethics committee application, I gave as much, if not more, space to arguing how I would be safe in a country I had lived and worked in for six years, where I had many affective relationships and a solid support network, than I did to explaining how I would ensure the well-being of my research participants. Such arguments were considered necessary because Guatemala, as a 'field' site, is perceived from the outside in stereotypes of a generically dangerous and politically unstable developing country.

More generally, when called on to discuss my research, I struggle with the terminology of fieldwork, and the image it evokes of the field as a site of othering. *Q'anil* as a space feels like a second home, one of the few places where, on stepping through the door, I feel completely welcome, at ease and able to be myself. Many of the staff and volunteers, including Aguilar, are close friends with whom I have gone through deep emotional processes both within and outside *Q'anil*. It feels almost disrespectful to our relationships and history to describe *Q'anil* as my 'field' of study and the people as my 'research subjects'. Such an understanding creates false divisions between the space for theorising (my Irish university) and the space for harvesting data (Guatemala), between the knower (the academic) and the known (the field) which reproduced the colonial us and them (Rooke, 2016). My engagement with the space and the people began long before initiating this PhD and will hopefully continue long after, thus there is no linear separation for me between 'entering' and 'leaving' the field.

Rooke (2016) describes as fiction the idea that the field is 'elsewhere' or a place/space that is physically and temporally bounded. Emotionally speaking, I am almost always present in the 'field', even as I write this from the university library. Indeed, home is not simply a location, or the four walls that house me, it can be an emotional and sensory place (Bhattacharya, 2018). Rooke (2016) invites the ethnographer to embrace the fluctuating emotional and spatial boundaries of research, to allow ourselves to become enmeshed in the context, embrace intimacy, an ethic of vulnerability, and be open to the erotics of knowledge production.

Reflexivity and the emotional entanglements of research

Finding the possibilities of returning to the 'field' delayed considerably by COVID-19, Aguilar suggested that rather than going forward with remote interviews I could use the opportunity offered by the pandemic to reflect on what attracted me to *Q'anil* in the first place. This reorientation towards a deeper reflexivity through an expanded autoethnographical component in my methodology has mitigated, to some degree, the 'uncertainty, the frustration of waiting, and wanting intensely to reconnect' (Shankar, 2020) with my home and my work in Guatemala, and the impacts of the pandemic in general.

Indigenous, feminist, decolonial scholars have long argued for a reflexive, situated, social enquiry that is built around longstanding relationships (Haraway, 1988; Harding, 2012; Hesse-Biber and Piatelli, 2012; Smith, 2012; Land, 2015). Bilgen, Nasir, and Schöneberg (2021) argue in favour of reflexivity as one possible avenue for dismantling the hierarchies embedded in research and academia and interrogating the white colonial gaze imprinted in both our discourses and bodies. They caution against reflections on positionality as a formality, or indeed form of academic posturing, advocating for reflexivity throughout all aspects and phases of our research enquiries, exploring how were are positioning power structures and how this impacts our perceptions, judgements, and the very questions we ask.

Queer scholars are inviting reflections on intimacy, emotionality, and eroticism in ethnography that seem particularly appropriate in the context of this research (Nash and Browne, 2016). Jones and Adams (2016: 207–8), in their exploration of autoethnography, argue for identity as a relational achievement, situated in processes and interactions which 'implies that selves emerge from situated, embodied practices (...) which fluctuate across time and space, thus requiring constant attention and negotiation'. Such an understanding of identity/positionality invites us to make visible the emotionality, intimacies, and erotics of research alongside an understanding of our political identities as shaping what we ask and how we interpret data. Shankar (2020) argues that 'emotions are productive for human understanding', but their absence from traditional scholarship is based on the assumption that they impede knowledge-creation. The emotions of fear, sadness, nostalgia, and need for human connection which have come to the fore throughout the pandemic, and which are arguably present in other crises, can be used 'in evidence and as evidence' (Shankar, 2020).

Autoethnography 'works against the canonical, methodological traditions and disciplining normalising, social forces' (Jones and Adams, 2016: 199). In centring the 'I' and making meaning from experience, the use of autoethnography opens other possibilities for witnessing and testifying than the reliance on spectacular victimhood mentioned previously and 'puts pleasure, difference and movement into productive conversation' (Jones and Adams, 2016: 199). I thus recognise the contingency of my identities within a space where these are under constant interrogation, where I am produced and also producing, that has multiple and connected locations, where I am observed but also observing, and where emotional response and the moments when we *darnos cuenta* (become conscious) are privileged sites of knowledge. I can interrogate how my position of racial privilege influences the discussions around racial discrimination in my research while also sketching a map of my emotional and corporeal responses throughout the research process: the comfort provided by friendships and affect shared between staff, participants, and I; the discomfort of confronting and having my white, outsider, academic identities confronted, repeatedly, by staff, facilitators, and participants; the gratitude in knowing my presence within intimate spaces is trusted and the pain on realising this trust may not be shared by all and may still have to be proven.

Rooke's (2016) invitation to an ontology of vulnerability that embraces intimacy, sensory involvement, embodied experience, and which takes emotions seriously pushes questions of the knower/known, and questions to what extent we are willing to be pulled apart or undone by our own research. Though I am the researcher, it is often Aguilar who continues to interrogate me and why four, nearly five, years later I am still hanging around '*como una necia*'.[1] In fact, I would venture to say that Aguilar knows far more about me, my struggles and traumas, my joys and transformations, than I will probably ever know about her, even by the time this research project comes to an end. As a teacher and facilitator she has heard me share some of the most intimate details and reflections about my life, truths I have shared with few others. She has read the short autoethnography I completed for the CES diploma, seen me laugh, dance, and create art. She has seen me at my most vulnerable and has accompanied and observed, offering advice only when requested. In transitioning from student to researcher, our roles now shift a little as Aguilar, and the organisation she has directed for more than ten years, come under my observation.

Research, however, cannot be delayed indefinitely, nor can an autoethnography substitute or supplant the collaborative ethnography with *Q'anil* which was central to the original proposal. Indeed, Land (2015: 22) cautions centring autoethnography in research which purports to challenge whiteness and racial privilege, where writing about our 'struggles with privilege, risks becoming confessional redemptive and self-serving'. To avoid falling into this trap the autoethnographer must 'find a voice that does progressive political work' (Land, 2015: 22). Shankar (2020) writes how 'putting research on hold [indefinitely] raises questions about responsibility to participants, time-sensitive data, and unfinished projects'. As I pivot towards the online observation of *Q'anil's* processes, which continue to be delivered exclusively through Zoom, and the reality of virtual interviewing, it seems an opportune moment to reaffirm the commitment against extractivism.

Conclusion

Against the figure of the vampire, Chivalán Carrillo and Posocco (2020: 516) evoke the image of the *t'ot*, *caracol*, or snail in the Mayan Q'eqchí language, as a symbol of non-linear thinking around the problems of (de)coloniality. The *t'ot* represents 'multiple forms of extractivism to account for cycles of life and death in Guatemala (...) it weaves together the cyclical resistance of human and non-human inhabitants of the region (...) echoes histories of resistance in indigenous communities in Zapatista territories'. The latter use the *caracol's* corporeality '*lento, pero avanzo*' (I'm slow but moving forwards) to capture the nature of their struggle. Here too are echoes of Hadfield and Haraway's Tree Snail Manifesto (2019) which explores the minute and entangled efforts of Hadfield, colleagues, and allies to save the Hawaiian tree snail from extinction from multiple threats, including predatory species and US military imperialism. It is a lesson in collaboration which show us 'how to do the world in sympoietic material-semiotic relationality, where love, knowledge, and rage rekindle possibilities' in multispecies landscapes (Hadfield and Haraway, 2019: 231).

Our research practice may forever be haunted by the spectres of the vampire and the *Kharisiri*. Indeed, we may never fully free ourselves from their thrall, and the rewards offered by academia from inhabiting these creatures and thinking from their mindsets of 'data mining', publication metrics, outputs, and products. Thinking with and inhabiting the qualities of entangled human and non-human webs of relationality – the potential of seeds for birthing new life and creativity, the curiosity of rabbits and the necessity of neither rushing nor forcing but moving with the pace and care of a snail – perhaps researchers can achieve 'the visibility and emergence of new, less hierarchical and more pluralistic capacities for affiliation' and the co-creation of plural knowledges (Khoo and Vered, 2020: 228).

Acknowledgements

The research conducted in this publication was funded by the Irish Research Council under the Andrew Grene Postgraduate Scholarship in Conflict Resolution [GOIPG/2019/4454].

Note

[1]   This is a Guatemalan way of saying someone who will not let go of something; like a dog with a bone.

References

Barrios, C. (2015) *Ch'umilal Wuj – Libro del Destino*, Guatemala: Editorial Maya Wuj.

Bhattacharya, K. (2018) 'Coloring memories and imaginations of "home": crafting a de/colonizing autoethnography', *Cultural Studies, Critical Methodologies*, 18(1): 9–15.

Bilgen, A. Nasir, A., and Schöneberg, J. (2021) 'Why positionalities matter: reflections on power, hierarchy, and knowledges in "development" research', *Canadian Journal of Development Studies / Revue canadienne d'études du développement*.

Boesten, J. and Henry, M. (2018) 'Between fatigue and silence: the challenges of conducting research on sexual violence in conflict', *Social Politics*, 25(4): 568–88.

Browne, K. and Nash, C. (2016) *Queer Methods and Methodologies: Intersecting Queer Theories and Social Science Research*, London: Routledge, Taylor & Francis Group.

Burman, A. (2018) 'Are anthropologists monsters? An Andean dystopian critique of extractivist ethnography and Anglophone-centric anthropology', *HAU Journal of Ethnographic Theory*, 8(1–2): 48–64.

Chivalán Carrillo, M. (2020) 'Cuerpos en experimentación. Sífilis y fármacopoder en la Ciudad de Guatemala (1946–1948)', *EntreDiversidades*, 7(2(15): 127–59.

Chivalán Carrillo, M. and Posocco, S. (2020) 'Against extraction in Guatemala: multispecies strategies in vampiric times', *Interventions: Decolonial Trajectories*, 22(4): 514–32.

Connell, R. (2014) 'Using southern theory', *Planning Theory*, 13(2): 210–23.

Cruz, M. and Luke, D. (2020) 'Methodology and academic extractivism: the neo-colonialism of the British university', *Third World Thematics: A TWQ Journal*, 5(1–2): 154–70.

Detamore, M. (2010) 'Queer(y)ing the ethics of research methods', in *Queer Methods and Methodologies*, Taylor & Francis: pp 167–82.

Hadfield, M. and Haraway, D. (2019) 'The tree snail manifesto', *Current Anthropology*, 60(S20): S209–35.

Haraway, D. (1988) 'Situated knowledges: the science question in feminism and the privilege of partial perspective', *Feminist Studies*, 14(3): 575–99.

Harding, S. (2012) 'Feminist Standpoints', in N. Hesse-Biber *Handbook of Feminist Research: Theory and Praxis* (2nd edn), Thousand Oaks, CA: Sage.

Hesse-Biber, N. and Piatelli D. (2012) 'The feminist practice of holistic reflexivity', in S. Nagy Hesse-Biber (ed) *Handbook of Feminist Research: Theory and Praxis* (2nd edn), Thousand Oaks, CA: Sage.

Jones, S. and Adams, T. (2016) 'Autoethnography is a queer method, in *Queer Methods and Methodologies*, Taylor & Francis, pp 195–214.

Khoo, S. and Vered, A. (2020) 'Including the "invisible middle" of decoloniality', *Journal of International Women's Studies*, 21(7): 225–42.

Lai, D. (2020) 'A different form of intervention? Revisiting the role of researchers in post-war contexts', in B. Bliesemann de Guevara and M. Bøås (eds) *Doing Fieldwork in Areas of International Intervention* (1st edn), Bristol: Bristol University Press.

Land, C. (2015) *Decolonising Solidarity Dilemmas and Directions for Supporters of Indigenous Struggles*, London: Zed Books.

Millora, C., Maimunah, S., and Still, E. (2020) 'Reflecting on the ethics of PhD research in the Global South: reciprocity, reflexivity and situatedness', *Acta Academica*, 52(1): 10–30.

Petersen, S., Samset, I., and Wang, V. (2009) 'Foreign aid to transitional justice: the cases of Rwanda and Guatemala, 1995–2005⋆', in K. Ambos, J. Large, and M. Wierda (eds) *Building a Future on Peace and Justice*, Berlin: Springer, pp 439–67.

Rooke, A. (2016) 'Queer in the field', in *Queer Methods and Methodologies*, Taylor & Francis, pp 25–40.

Shankar, S. (2020) 'Emotions as the new ethical turn in social research, items: insights from the social sciences', [online], available at: https://items.ssrc.org/covid-19-and-the-social-sciences/social-research-and-insecurity/emotions-as-the-new-ethical-turn-in-social-research/ (last accessed 28 March 2021).

Smith, L. (2012) *Decolonizing Methodologies: Research and Indigenous Peoples*, London, New York: Zed Books.

Sukarieh, M. and Tannock, S. (2012) 'On the problem of over-researched communities: the case of the Shatila Palestinian Refugee Camp in Lebanon', *Sociology*, 47(3): 494–508.

Conclusion

Helen Kara and Su-ming Khoo

In this conclusion, we summarise some lessons from the examples and experiences in the preceding chapters, and in the e-books we edited on 'Researching in the Age of COVID-19' (Kara and Khoo, 2020a,b,c). We remember that crisis has two meanings: a sudden occurrence, such as a ship running aground, or a turning point, marking either recovery or deterioration during an illness. We also note that crisis can be fast or slow, one-off or recurrent, and that all these aspects of crisis can interact in complex ways. We offer some recommendations for doing research in times of crisis, and suggest some future directions for the development of methods and ethics in this arena.

The first lesson is that ethics come into sharper focus in times of crisis. We see evidence of Whyte's (2020) 'epistemology of co-ordination' in action throughout the whole book, particularly in the form of an emphasis on prioritising relationships, including taking more care of individuals, communities, and ourselves. We see increased connectedness with and care for participants in Hien Thi Nguyen and her colleagues' work with older Vietnamese migrants, and increased care for communities in Aisling Walsh's work on the aftermath of colonialism and conflict and their intersection with patriarchy. There is concern for researchers' well-being in Gbenga Shadare's sobering reminder that in some crisis situations researchers' lives may be at risk, and so methods such as covert research, that may otherwise be questionable, become necessary. Bibek Dahal outlines the layers of complication that can arise when a researcher's topic is ethics and they find themselves caught up in a crisis that requires an ethical response. In Gretchen Stolte and Lisa Oliver's work, we see discovery in the making of connections between First Nations women, and opportunities for yarning, reweaving connections to land, community, and knowledge, and to share survivorship and healing. In sum, this book speaks to Van Brown's call to expand the ethical frame of concern in research through 'methics' (Browne and Peek, 2014).

The second lesson is that crises promote creativity, reflexivity, and relationality in research. As the proverb says, necessity is the mother of invention, and we see that in action here in response to the COVID-19 pandemic. Maria Grazia Imperiale, doing long-term research amid the protracted crisis in the Gaza Strip, developed participatory methods that work online. This contradicts the long-standing dictum that participatory methods can only be used in face-to-face settings (Chevalier and Buckles, 2013: 9). Richard McGrath and his colleagues in Australia combined existing research methods to create autonetography, a collaborative online method using personal data. Deborah Green and her colleagues combine arts-based research and arts therapy to help their faculty and students express, explore, and endure the uncertainties of the pandemic, which they do with care, verve, and joy. And Gemma Sou's participatory comic creation enables a complex, three-dimensional depiction of participants' experiences, which directly challenges the dehumanising representations in mainstream media and extends research impact by considering how audiences might receive and use research findings in education, professional practice, and policy making.

Ali FitzGibbon makes it clear from the start that extra reflexivity is essential for research in times of crisis. As well as finding the energy to innovate and the care to manage relationships, we also need to find time to pause for extra thought. Participants, too, may be asked to reflect; Richard McGrath and his colleagues gathered reflexive stories within their innovative autonetography method. Bibek Dahal used highly reflexive methods of gathering and interpreting data, and Aisling Walsh and Gbenga Shadare reflected carefully on the implications of their transnational research. These and other contributors show us what a vital tool reflexivity is for ensuring research is done ethically and well.

Little space is usually given to the richness of relationality in, for, and around research in the research methods and ethics literature. Relationality permeates the chapters in this book to an unusual degree. Much of the research reported here has an insider element: Zania Koppe in Ireland, Hien Nguyen in Australia, Bibek Dahal in Nepal, Gbenga Shadare in Nigeria, and Deborah Green and her colleagues in New Zealand. This promotes a rich affective relationality in research methods and ethics that should not be restricted to insider work. Indeed, we also see it in Aisling Walsh's work in Guatemala, Maria Grazia Imperiale's work in the Gaza Strip, and Aaron Teo's work in Australia.

The third lesson is that secondary data has a bigger contribution to make than is often thought. In Volume 1 of the e-books, Paramjeet Chawla focuses on quantitative data in her investigation of the capabilities of young people in New Delhi (Chawla, 2020). In this volume, Anna Tarrant and Kahryn Hughes extol the virtues of re-using qualitative data. In both cases, this is treated not as a shortcut but as a distinctive methodological approach. Using secondary data raises new ethical questions around consent, confidentiality, and representation. However, with a colossal amount of data freely available online, and qualitative data repositories worldwide, we would suggest this is an idea whose time has come.

The fourth lesson is that the digital world provides both opportunities and challenges for researchers working in times of crisis. For some researchers, working online provides opportunities beyond simply moving interviews or focus groups into a digital space, as we have seen for Maria Grazia Imperiale. Maged Zakher and Hoda Wassif invited participants to bring to their online interviews an object of personal value to help facilitate a discussion on 'happiness in lockdown'. Richard McGrath and his colleagues found postgraduate students in online writing groups suggested research in which they themselves would be participants, which made data gathering very straightforward. And the research of Natasha Dwyer and her colleagues, about trust in digital systems in general and a specific chatbot in particular, is entirely Internet-enabled.

However, several chapters in this book, and in each of the e-books too, show that the so-called 'digital divide' is much more complex and nuanced than the simple binary that term suggests. There are a range of barriers to Internet access including age and digital literacy, identified by Hien Thi Nguyen and her colleagues, and poor Internet connections and frequent power cuts, identified by Maria Grazia Imperiale. In the e-books, Etivina Lovo, working in Fiji and Tonga, and Natalia Chávez and her colleagues in Colombia, recount difficulties in working online with Indigenous elders and communities (Lovo, 2020; Chávez, Castro-Reyes, and Echeverry, 2020). And working online creates new ethical problems which are not always easy to solve, such as how to follow community protocols for meeting with elders when meeting online instead of in person (Lovo, 2020). Not all of the complexity is challenging: Hien Thi Nguyen and her colleagues use the concept of 'digital kinning' to illustrate how technology can support and enhance human relationships.

The fifth lesson is that power dynamics may change in times of crisis. Several methods used by contributors explicitly aim to transfer some power from researchers to participants. This is the case with Maged Zakher and Hoda Wassif's enhanced interviewing, Gemma Sou's participatory comic creation, and the collaborative autonetography of Richard McGrath and his colleagues. Others aim to redistribute power more equally, such as Gretchen Stolte and Lisa Oliver's work of learning how to weave baskets in museums research with First Nations women, and the work of Deborah Green and her colleagues who use visual, performative, and written arts in practice-based arts therapy research. In her work in post-conflict Guatemala, Aisling Walsh struggles with the broader problems of over-research, extractivism (research with marginalised people that only benefits the researcher), and epistemic violence (privileged people imposing their knowledge frameworks on marginalised people). Because of the deficit-based approach usually taken by research, most researchers are more privileged than most participants. The dangers of extractivism and epistemic violence are not as obvious to all of us as they are to Aisling Walsh, yet such stark examples help to remind us that they are present much more often than researchers may realise.

From these five lessons come five recommendations. We suggest that, in times of crisis, researchers need to:

1. Broaden our ethical frames of reference and pay closer attention to ethical issues throughout the research process (Kara, 2018; Pohl, 2021). Ali FitzGibbon explains that all researchers need to rethink our work when crisis hits. In crisis situations we need to take more care of each other, and of ourselves. As Zania Koppe says, a myriad of ethical considerations requires ongoing reflexive and responsive decision-making. And Aisling Walsh shows us a way to tackle the broader problems: make a deep commitment to decolonial, feminist, and/or other relevant anti-oppressive work, and prioritise the quality of relationships throughout research.

2. Be open to creativity. Crises, whether fast or slow, involve change and movement. This requires researchers to adapt existing qualitative and digital methods, and devise new ones, as we practise our craft. We have seen this in many of the book's chapters – from protocol writing to chatbots, basket weaving to digital kinning, visual and performative arts to autonetnography – researchers in crisis situations drawing on creativity to help them conduct useful and ethical research.

3. Use secondary data first, and whenever possible, as shown by Anna Tarrant and Kahryn Hughes in this volume, and Paramjeet Chawla in Volume 1 of the e-books. This reduces the burden on research participants and researchers.

4. Use digital methods when they are appropriate. Retain an awareness of who you exclude by working digitally. Also, embrace the potential for digital methods to give rise to new forms of relationality, creativity, and learning in and beyond research, as, again, we have seen in many of this book's chapters.

5. Maintain a consciousness of, and do what you can to rebalance, the power dynamics in your research. Aiming to 'do no harm' is not enough in crisis (and, we would argue, other) situations. Researchers should aim to create positive change, through the process of their research work and through their findings and dissemination.

These recommendations are drawn from the lessons our contributors have shared in this book. Their implementation will result in a more integrated approach to qualitative and digital methods and ethics, within an epistemology of coordination that works to support connections between individuals and with communities. This is 'methics' in action.

This book, like all such books, presents a partial picture. The e-books help to fill that picture out but still there are gaps: geographical gaps, gaps in methods, gaps in types of crisis, and gaps in ethics. Geographical gaps include the Arctic regions and Canada. Gaps in methods include the impact of crises on research design, data analysis, and writing. Gaps in types of crisis include many natural disasters such as wildfires, floods and earthquakes, national political crises, and individual personal crises. Gaps in ethics include a frequent lack of recognition of how structural inequalities interact with and can be buttressed by research, and the division between researcher and researched which many of the contributions to this book have tested and transcended. And this is not exhaustive. So while we are confident our books offer much that is of use, we are also aware that there is much more work to be done on qualitative and digital methods in times of crisis.

References

Browne, K. and Peek, L. (2014) 'Beyond the IRB: an ethical toolkit for long-term disaster research', *International Journal of Mass Emergencies and Disasters*, 32(1): 82–120.

Chávez, N., Castro-Reyes, S., and Echeverry, L. (2020) 'Challenges of a systematization of experiences study: learning from a displaced victim assistance program during COVID-19 emergency in ethnic territories in Colombia', in H. Kara and S. Khoo (eds) *Researching in the Age of COVID-19 Volume 1: Response and Reassessment* (e-book), Bristol: Policy Press.

Chawla, P. (2020) 'Research methods to understand the "Youth Capabilities & Conversions": the pros and cons of using secondary data analysis in a pandemic situation', in H. Kara and S. Khoo (eds) *Researching in the Age of COVID-19 Volume 1: Response and Reassessment* (e-book), Bristol: Policy Press.

Chevalier, J. and Buckles, D. (2013) *Participatory Action Research: Theory and Methods for Engaged Inquiry*, Abingdon: Routledge.

Kara, H. (2018) *Research Ethics in the Real World: Euro-Western and Indigenous Perspectives*, Bristol: Policy Press.

Kara, H. and Khoo, S. (eds) (2020a) *Researching in the Age of COVID-19 Volume 1: Response and Reassessment* (e-book), Bristol: Policy Press.

Kara, H. and Khoo, S. (eds) (2020b) *Researching in the Age of COVID-19 Volume 1: Care and Resilience* (e-book), Bristol: Policy Press.

Kara, H. and Khoo, S. (eds) (2020c) *Researching in the Age of COVID-19 Volume 3: Creativity and Ethics* (e-book), Bristol: Policy Press.

Lovo, E. (2020) 'COVID-19 research crisis management for a human research ethics project in Fiji and Tonga', in H. Kara and S. Khoo (eds) *Researching in the Age of COVID-19 Volume 3: Creativity and Ethics* (e-book), Bristol: Policy Press.

Pohl, C. (2021) *Little Quick Fix: Research Ethics*, London: SAGE.

Whyte, K. (2020) 'Against crisis epistemology', in B. Hokowhitu, A. Moreton-Robinson, L. Tuhiwai-Smith, C. Andersen, and S. Larkin (eds) *Routledge Handbook of Critical Indigenous Studies*, Abingdon: Routledge, pp 52–64.

Index

References to figures and photographs appear in *italic* type; those in **bold** type refer to tables.